Student Companion to

Herman
MELVILLE

Student Companion to

Herman
MELVILLE

Sharon Talley

Student Companions to Classic Writers

GREENWOOD PRESS
Westport, Connecticut • London

Library of Congress Cataloging-in-Publication Data

Talley, Sharon, 1952–
    Student companion to Herman Melville / Sharon Talley.
        p. cm.—(Student companions to classic writers, ISSN 1522–7979)
    Includes bibliographical references and index.
    ISBN 0–313–33499–4 (alk. paper)
    1. Melville, Herman, 1819–1891—Criticism and interpretation—Handbooks,
manuals, etc.   I. Title.
    PS2387.T36   2007
    813'.3—dc22   2006031866

British Library Cataloguing in Publication Data is available.

Library of Congress Catalog Card Number: 2006031866
ISBN: 0–313–33499–4
ISSN: 1522–7979

First published in 2007

Greenwood Press, 88 Post Road West, Westport, CT 06881
An imprint of Greenwood Publishing Group, Inc.
www.greenwood.com

Printed in the United States of America

The paper used in this book complies with the
Permanent Paper Standard issued by the National
Information Standards Organization (Z39.48–1984).

10 9 8 7 6 5 4 3 2 1

Contents

Series Foreword

This series has been designed to meet the needs of students and general readers for accessible literary criticism on the American and world writers most frequently studied and read in the secondary school, community college, and four-year college classrooms. Unlike other works of literary criticism that are written for the specialist and graduate student, or that feature a variety of reprinted scholarly essays on sometimes obscure aspects of the writer's work, the Student Companions to Classic Writers series is carefully crafted to examine each writer's major works fully and in a systematic way, at the level of the nonspecialist and general reader. The objective is to enable the reader to gain a deeper understanding of the work and to apply critical thinking skills to the act of reading. The proven format for the volumes in this series was developed by an advisory board of teachers and librarians for a successful series published by Greenwood Press, Critical Companions to Popular Contemporary Writers. Responding to their request for easy-to-use and yet challenging literary criticism for students and adult library patrons, Greenwood Press developed a systematic format that is not intimidating but helps the reader to develop the ability to analyze literature.

How does this work? Each volume in the Student Companions to Classic Writers series is written by a subject specialist, an academic who understands students' needs for basic and yet challenging examination of the writer's canon. Each volume begins with a biographical chapter, drawn from published sources, biographies, and autobiographies, that relates the writer's life to his or her work. The next chapter examines the writer's literary heritage, tracing the literary influences of other writers on that writer and explaining and discussing the literary genres into which the writer's work falls. Each of the following chapters examines a major work by the writer, those works most frequently read and studied by high school and college students. Depending on the writer's canon, generally between four and eight major works are examined, each in an individual chapter. The discussion of each work is organized into separate sections on plot development, character development, and major themes. Literary devices and style, narrative point of view, and historical setting are also discussed in turn if pertinent to the work. Each chapter concludes with an alternate critical perspective from which to read the work, such as a psychological or feminist criticism. The critical theory is defined briefly in easy, comprehensible language for the student. Looking at the literature from the point of view of a particular critical approach will help the reader to understand and apply critical theory to the act of reading and analyzing literature.

Of particular value in each volume is the bibliography, which includes a complete bibliography of the writer's works, a selected bibliography of biographical and critical works suitable for students, and lists of reviews of each work examined in the companion, both from the time the literature was originally published and from contemporary sources, all of which will be helpful to readers, teachers, and librarians who would like to consult additional sources.

As a source of literary criticism for the student or for the general reader, this series will help the reader to gain understanding of the writer's work and skill in critical reading.

Preface

Student Companion to Herman Melville provides a critical introduction to the life and literary works of Herman Melville, the nineteenth-century American author of *Moby-Dick,* as well as nine other novels and numerous short stories and poems. Although scholars and critics were slow to recognize the significance of Melville's literary contributions, his reputation is now secure, and his masterpiece *Moby-Dick* is often cited as the preeminent American novel. As John Bryant has observed, "There are many Melvilles, each weighty and elusive, like a whale.... Time and the very limits of our critical perspectives subvert our desire to illume and encompass that conglomerate of Unknowns, Herman Melville" (*Companion* xvii). Accordingly, the goal of this introductory book is to create a foundation from which readers will be supported, challenged, and intrigued to make their own discoveries about the author and his diverse works.

The book begins with a biographical sketch of Melville's life in relation to his works. The second chapter covers his contributions to U.S. American literature, tracing the growing appreciation for Melville that began in the 1920s. This chapter explains Melville's central concern with what he termed "the great Art of Telling the Truth"; his complex relationship to the marketplace; his contributions to the genres of the novel, short story, and poetry; and his influence on later writers. Melville's early development as a writer of sea adventures is discussed in Chapter 3, which examines his first five novels: *Typee, Omoo, Mardi, Redburn,* and *White-Jacket*. Other chapters individually treat the novels *Moby-Dick*, *Pierre*, *The Confidence-Man*, and *Billy Budd*. In addition, two chapters are devoted to the short fiction and serialized novel that Melville published between 1853 and 1856. Another chapter covers his poetry, with special emphasis on his collection of Civil War poems titled *Battle-Pieces* and the long narrative poem *Clarel*. Each of these chapters features close readings of the literary texts that include analysis of point of view, setting, plot, characters, symbolism, themes, and historical contexts where appropriate. The four chapters devoted to individual novels, as well as the chapter on Melville's poetry, also feature alternate readings that introduce the reader to postcolonial, feminist, genre, reader response, and deconstructionist approaches to literary criticism. The bibliography that concludes the book provides information on Melville's published works, as well as lists of biographies, contemporary reviews, and recent critical studies.

1

The Life of Herman Melville

Writing to his friend Nathaniel Hawthorne in the summer of 1851, Herman Melville claimed, "Until I was twenty-five, I had no development at all. From my twenty-fifth year, I date my life" (*Letters* 130). With this dramatic statement, Melville was alluding to his discharge from the Navy on October 14, 1844, an event that concluded a series of ocean voyages that in many ways served as a gestation period for his subsequent birth as a writer of sea adventures. Even before these preparatory journeys occurred, however, significant events and experiences of Melville's early years were at least subtly influenced and shaped by the ocean.

The third of eight children and the second of four sons, Melville was born in New York City on August 1, 1819, to Allan Melvill and Maria Gansevoort Melvill. (Maria added the final "e" to the family name after her husband's death.) In 1819, the growing family lived at the tip of Manhattan Island between Battery Park and the wharves of the South Street waterfront. As a result, Melville's "first horizon was the Atlantic Ocean with a foreground of masts and rigging, cargo and sailors" (Rosenberry, *Melville* 21). Both the Gansevoorts and the Melvills were financially secure and socially prominent in early America, and Melville's parents were especially proud of their fathers' distinguished service during the American Revolution. After the Revolution, General Gansevoort and his sons maintained and extended their economic position through shrewdly timed land speculation. Major Melvill's sons, however, took reckless risks that steadily eroded the profits their father had made from mercantile trade during his appointment first as Inspector of Customs and then as Naval Officer of the Port of Boston (Parker, *Herman Melville* 1: 6–7).

Beginning in 1802, the major regularly financed Allan's voyages to France to purchase expensive dry goods for importation to the United States. After his 1814 marriage to Maria, Allan also borrowed heavily against his wife's inheritance to subsidize his business ventures. Allan's precarious credit structure collapsed in 1830, forcing him to move his family back to Maria's hometown of Albany. In a furtive step to avoid possible arrest for his unpaid debts, Allan kept his 11-year-old son Herman behind the rest of the family to help him pack the papers and personal belongings that the two of them could carry away with them. In the cover of night, they then boarded a steamboat for the journey upriver to Albany. Under such desperate circumstances, Melville made his last water crossing with his father (Parker, *Herman Melville* 1: 1–2). This trip undoubtedly made a deep impression on the boy, creating an ironic counterpoint to his father's earlier tales of aristocratic ocean crossings and experiences abroad. Although the Gansevoorts helped to reestablish Allan as a fur manufacturer in Albany, he died two years later, leaving his widow and children hopelessly mired in debt.

For some time before their father's death, the older children were certainly aware of his financial plight; however, to this point the family had maintained a façade of genteel comfort and privilege. Raised in the shadow of Gansevoort, his dynamic elder brother, the shyer and more stolid Herman suffered from the inevitable comparisons. He was slower to talk and to learn to read than Gansevoort, and his academic record was relatively undistinguished, at least from his parents' perspective. His mother observed that her second son did "not appear so fond of his Book as to injure his Health," while his father remarked that the child was "very backward in speech and somewhat slow in comprehension" (qtd. in Parker, *Herman Melville* 1: 28, 35). Maria raised her children by the strict tenets of Calvinism, and the family conformed to the Victorian indisposition to show affection openly. Melville's subsequent conflicted feelings toward his parents and his older brother were forged in such an environment. "He felt vaguely guilty toward his father and unloved by his mother," and his genuine admiration for Gansevoort was inevitably tainted by resentment (Robertson-Lorant 38).

After her husband's death in 1832, Maria was forced to ask for help from her brother, Peter Gansevoort Jr. Because of the debts he had already absorbed as a result of Allan Melvill's business failings, however, Peter was unwilling to assume all responsibility for the family's support. Demanding that the two eldest sons leave school, he set up 17-year-old Gansevoort as a fur manufacturer and put 13-year-old Herman to work as a bank clerk. After the failure of the fur business, Gansevoort eventually became a lawyer, but Herman managed only enough formal education and training to qualify him to teach elementary school. He did, however, supplement his interrupted schooling through his membership in literary and debating societies. He also began reading extensively from both his father's and his Uncle Peter's libraries, a pastime that stimulated a love of literature that continued throughout his life.

In 1837, Melville spent the summer running his uncle Thomas Melvill's farm in the Berkshire Mountains near Pittsfield, Massachusetts, where he had enjoyed summer visits as a child. He then taught for a term or so at a nearby rural school. Frustrated by the burdens of teaching 30 students of all ages and levels, he drifted back to Lansingburgh, New York, where Maria and the younger children had been forced to move to lower their cost of living. Although he completed a surveying course at the Lansingburgh Academy, Melville was unsuccessful in finding employment. To pass the time, he decided to try his hand at writing short fiction under the inexplicable pseudonym "L.A.V." The result was "Fragments from a Writing Desk," a humorous and possibly satiric piece that appeared in two installments of the *Democratic Press and Lansingburgh Advertiser* during May 1839. Seeing this piece in print may have whetted his literary aspirations, but he was in no position to indulge them. Unable to relieve his mother's financial anxieties and unsuccessful in courting at least two young women from the surrounding area, Melville satisfied his increasing restlessness by escaping to the sea. On June 4, 1839, at the age of 19, he signed on as a cabin boy on the *St. Lawrence,* a merchant ship bound for Liverpool. By this act, he finally stepped from the shadow of Gansevoort to follow in his father's wake. Taking with him the small green journal that Allan Melvill had kept under the ostentatious title "Recapitulations of Voyages and Travels from 1800 to 1822 both inclusive," Melville set out to become a world traveler himself.

During his first passage, Melville learned much about the hardships of life in the forecastle. He also spent six weeks roaming the docks and slums of Liverpool, which molded the social conscience that "informed every book he was to write with a passionate, sometimes embittered empathy for the poor and powerless" (Rosenberry, *Melville* 22). After arriving back in New York in the fall of 1839, Melville passed a winter teaching in Greenbush and then journeyed west to Galena, Illinois, in a failed attempt to find work where his Uncle Thomas had migrated. By early January 1841, however, he had returned to sea, this time set for the South Pacific aboard the whaler *Acushnet*. In those days, the crews of whaling ships were notoriously rough, and their living and working conditions were often squalid. Melville's willingness to commit himself to an undefined journey of three or more years under such conditions reflects not only his continued financial desperation but also his adventurous and restless spirit.

Weary after six months aboard the *Acushnet*, having sailed 3,000 miles west to the Marquesas Islands, Melville jumped ship with a friend called Toby and lived for a month among the Typees, an infamous tribe of cannibals. Separated from Toby, Melville became uneasy about his safety and managed to board an Australian whaler, the *Lucy Ann*, which unfortunately proved to have even worse conditions than the *Acushnet*. After a mutiny, he found himself under shore arrest on the island of Tahiti, where he nevertheless was relatively free to explore his surroundings, usually in the company of the ship's disreputable doctor. Two months later, Melville boarded another whaler, the *Charles and Henry*, which eventually transported him to Hawaii (then called the Sandwich Islands). In the summer of 1843, Melville worked briefly in Honolulu before being persuaded to sign on the Navy frigate *United States* as an ordinary seaman so that he could get back home. During the 14 months he served on the *United States*, Melville was forced to witness "over a hundred and fifty floggings, each done according to 'regulations'" (Parker, *Herman Melville* 1: 262). This experience soured Melville on the Navy, but he did in some ways find compensation through his association with John Chase, the captain of the maintop, whom he found to exemplify his ideal of human dignity and civilized behavior.

Curiously, Melville did not follow his father's example and keep a journal of any of these adventures at sea. Nevertheless, he amassed a stockpile of memories from which he began to draw literary inspiration almost directly after his discharge from the Navy in the fall of 1844. Melville found immediate success in his first attempt at storytelling, a romantic travel narrative based on his adventures in the Marquesas. Wiley and Putnam accepted the manuscript based on Washington Irving's recommendation, and they published it under the title *Typee: A Peep at Polynesian Life* (1846). However, the British publisher John Murray was unwilling to issue the book without the author's assurance that the experiences recounted in it were authentic. Living in London at the time, Gansevoort acted as his brother's agent to persuade Murray that the narrative was "the unvarnished truth" it claimed to be (*Typee* 10). To further strengthen Murray's confidence in his story, Melville made some rushed revisions and additions, which he developed from research rather than from his own limited knowledge of the Typees. Thus the text of the first British edition, published just before its American counterpart, differed in some ways from the domestic version and carried the more somber title *Narrative of a Four Months' Residence among the Natives of the Marquesas Islands.* Despite the immediate popular success of *Typee* on both sides of the Atlantic, however, Melville's problems with his publishers had only begun. Murray, as well as others, continued to voice suspicions about the book's factual basis even after Richard Tobias ("Toby") Greene came forward voluntarily to vouch for its veracity, prompting Melville to write "The Story of Toby" as a sequel for subsequent editions. Furthermore, concerns about Melville's sexual references and his unflattering portrayal of Christian missionaries in the South Pacific caused both publishers to expurgate the text before reprinting it.

Melville dedicated *Typee* to Lemuel Shaw, the Chief Justice of the Massachusetts Supreme Court. Shaw had been a close family friend and advisor for many years, and Melville was also courting his daughter Elizabeth at the time the book was published. Although Shaw admired the young author, he was leery of his ability to support a wife and family from his writings. Shaw's fears were reasonable since, to this point in time, James Fenimore Cooper and Washington Irving were the only American authors who had accomplished such a feat. Although the judge's concerns proved justified, he eventually gave his consent to the union, and Melville and Lizzie were married on August 4, 1847, at the Shaw family home in Boston. With the financial assistance of Shaw, the newlyweds bought a large house in New York, which they shared with Melville's mother, his younger brother Allan, and Allan's bride Sophia. Because Gansevoort had died suddenly in 1846, Melville was now considered the head of his family. Although Allan and Sophia subsequently moved into their own home, Maria Melville, who did not die until 1872, resided with her second son and daughter-in-law until 1855 and then visited frequently thereafter. Melville's unmarried sisters also lived with him and Lizzie for extended periods. In the early years of her marriage, the mild-mannered Lizzie often had to acquiesce to her mother-in-law's strong will, and Melville's rigid daily writing schedule increasingly came to dominate the household's routine.

In the same year of his marriage, Melville built on the success of *Typee* with *Omoo* (1847). This second book, a fictionalized account of his Tahitian adventures, extended his fame and provoked similar controversy among his publishers and readers. As a result, the young writer's popularity attracted the attention of Evert Duyckinck, and Melville was soon drawn into the New York literary circle that congregated around this well-known editor. Melville began to borrow books from Duyckinck's extensive library, which he supplemented with his own purchases. This practice established a lifelong pattern of voracious reading to stimulate his mind in preparation for writing.

The first result of this intellectual approach to his craft was *Mardi* (1849), which began as an account of his travels in the Pacific, but which grew into a complex allegory of the mind that alienated most of his reviewers and readers. Although he was frustrated by his inability to indulge his aesthetic desires and intellectual passions, the financial pressures of supporting a wife and extended family moved Melville to placate his audience by returning to the genre of the popular travel romance. There followed in quick succession, *Redburn* (1849), an account of Melville's first voyage to Liverpool, and *White-Jacket* (1850), a retelling of his experiences on the *United States* in which he condemned the disciplinary practice of flogging. Although both books were well received, Melville's bitterness at having to compromise his artistic principles in writing them surfaced clearly in a letter to his father-in-law in which he wrote: "no reputation that is gratifying to me, can possibly be achieved by either of these books. They are two *jobs*, which I have done for money—being forced to it, as other men are to sawing wood.... So far as I am individually concerned, and independent of my pocket, it is my earnest desire to write those sort of books which are said to 'fail'" (*Letters* 91–92).

Melville, who had now written five books in as many years, was not only bitter but also exhausted, causing his family to worry about his physical and emotional health. To give his son-in-law a break, Shaw agreed to pay for Melville to travel to England in October 1849 to negotiate a contract for *White-Jacket*. Because Lizzie had just given birth to Malcolm, their first of four children, she did not accompany him. As a result, Melville was soon homesick and so, after a brief excursion to the Continent, returned to New York in late January 1850. On arriving home, he immediately began a new writing project, a whaling novel that originally was to be based on his own experiences on the *Acushnet*. The family continued their practice of indulging him as he wrote almost continuously throughout the next several years. His routine was to write in privacy in his study each day until often late in the afternoon, but rarely later because he was troubled by weak eyesight. Apparently, no household duties were required of him, and one of his sisters regularly served as his copyist to relieve Lizzie, who was increasingly occupied with the care of children. A second son, Stanwix, was born in 1851, followed by daughters Elizabeth and Frances in 1853 and 1855.

During the summer of 1850, many of the family convened in the Berkshires at the Melvill farm, which had recently been sold but was not yet occupied by the new owners. Melville took a respite from drafting his whaling book, which by this time was nearly complete, to enjoy the company of many area notables, including doctor-poet Oliver Wendell Holmes, novelist Catharine Sedgwick, and especially the romanticist Nathaniel Hawthorne. Just before he met Hawthorne for the first time, one of his aunts gave him a copy of Hawthorne's *Mosses from an Old Manse*. Melville was so taken with the older man, who was 15 years his senior, that he dashed off a glowing review entitled "Hawthorne and His Mosses," which he sent back to New York with Duyckinck, who was visiting at the time. The review was immediately published in Duyckinck's *Literary World*, and although Melville attempted to disguise his identity as "A Virginian Spending July in Vermont," the secret of his authorship was soon out. The gushing praise that the emotionally wrought Melville bestowed on the always reserved Hawthorne set the tone for the intense personal relationship that the two were to establish, a relationship that has long intrigued biographers and that undoubtedly was more influential than any other in Melville's development as a literary artist. In the essay, which most believe says more about his own aspirations than the true accomplishments of Hawthorne, Melville first compares the tales in *Mosses from an Old Manse* to the depth and darkness of Shakespeare's plays. He then acknowledges their effect on himself: "Hawthorne," he exclaims, "has dropped germanous seeds into my soul" and "expands and deepens down, the more I contemplate him; and further, and further, shoots his strong New-England roots into the hot soil of my Southern soul" (1167). Drawn to his mentor's dark vision of human experience, Melville was inspired to rewrite his whaling manuscript and mold it into his critical masterpiece, *Moby-Dick* (1851), which he dedicated to Hawthorne.

Invigorated by his summer in the Berkshires, and perhaps seeking to remain close to Hawthorne, Melville persuaded Shaw to lend him more money so that he could buy 160 acres with a house near the Melvill farm. Relocating his surprised family there in October 1850, he named the place Arrowhead in token of the Indian relics he had found there. The New York house was slow to sell, and the new house required extensive renovations to make it habitable, which delayed the completion of *Moby-Dick*. As a result, he experienced increased financial stress that, in turn, reverberated throughout the family in related tensions. Driven finally to the reckless expedient of further mortgaging Arrowhead through a secret loan from Tertulus D. Stewart, an old friend, Melville apparently depended on the success of *Moby-Dick* to clear his debts. By this time, however, he also had serious doubts that the novel would sell. In June 1851, he wrote to Hawthorne, "What I feel moved to write, that is banned,—it will not pay. Yet, altogether, write the *other* way I cannot. So the product is a final hash, and all my books are botches" (*Letters* 128).

When disappointing reviews and sales followed the release of *Moby-Dick*, Melville wrote to Hawthorne's wife Sophia that his next novel, which he apparently had already started, would be just "a rural bowl of milk" (*Letters* 146). Evidently he again changed directions, however, as *Pierre* (1852) involves implications of incest and suicidal despair that could in no way be deemed either simple or uncontroversial. Because *Pierre* draws on some recognizably autobiographical elements, early biographers interpreted it as an ominous portrait of the ambivalent relationship between Melville and his mother. Recent scholarship has discounted many of these concerns, but *Pierre* can still be seen as a reflection of Melville's own loss of faith in himself as a writer. Perhaps Hawthorne's moving away from the Berkshires in late 1851 also contributed to this loss of confidence.

During the period that followed the publication of *Pierre*, his family tried unsuccessfully to secure a political appointment for Melville. A salaried consulship, they had hoped, would give him the opportunity to recover his emotional and physical health, which they saw as severely compromised by the extended strain of trying to support his family as a novelist. Instead, Melville turned to writing short fiction. Between 1853 and 1856, he wrote 16 stories; 14 appeared originally in either *Harper's New Monthly Magazine* or *Putnam's Monthly Magazine*. He subsequently collected five of these stories, "Bartleby, the Scrivener," "Benito Cereno," "The Lightning-Rod Man," "The Encantadas, or Enchanted Isles," and "The Bell-Tower," to publish in *The Piazza Tales* (1856), for which he also wrote "The Piazza" as an introductory piece. Another story, "The Two Temples," was rejected by *Putnam's* and never published during his lifetime (Newman ix, 341).

Melville was reasonably well paid for his short fiction, and during this period he also serialized a longer work, *Israel Potter* (1855), which was based on a pamphlet about an obscure Revolutionary War veteran. The last piece of prose fiction that he published during his lifetime was *The Confidence-Man* (1857), a book-length satire of gullibility and cynicism that failed to achieve the artistic balance of *Moby-Dick* (Howard 229). In fact, it was so "baffling to its few readers" that it was "generally received as proof of its author's final lapse into eccentricity or down-right madness" (Rosenberry, *Melville* 29). Reviewers had long made outrageous public accusations of Melville's possible insanity to explain the style and content of his novels, which served to intensify the concerns of Melville's family about his well-being (Parker, *Herman Melville* 2: 632). Pressed for funds, Melville sold half of his acreage in 1856, and with Shaw's assistance was finally able to clear the encumbrance to Stewart. Shaw then came forward at the family's urging to finance a six-month recuperative trip to Europe and the Holy Land. During his travels, Melville paid a last visit to Hawthorne, who had been appointed American consul at Liverpool in appreciation for his campaign biography of Franklin Pierce. Their reunion created a sadly tepid conclusion to what had once been a vital friendship, at least from Melville's perspective.

Upon returning from his last trip abroad in May 1857, Melville tried his luck lecturing, but with little critical or monetary success. Throughout the next years, tensions increased in the Melville home. Melville was undoubtedly depressed by the failure of his most ambitious novels to gain acceptance and embittered toward the publishing industry, which he thoroughly distrusted. In addition, even after the death of his father-in-law in 1861, when Lizzie's inheritance allowed them finally to live comfortably within their own means, he must have chafed from his financial dependence. Selling Arrowhead to Allan and Sophia for their use as a summer home, the family returned to New York in 1863. In 1866, Melville finally secured a position as an inspector in the New York Custom House, a "six-day-a-week, four-dollar-a-day job" of mostly mundane duties in which he was often surrounded by corruption (Parker, *Herman Melville* 2: 605). He scrupulously held this position for 19 years, even though it severely limited the time he could devote to intellectual and creative interests. A victim of erratic moods, Melville may have drunk too much on occasion, and he was sometimes at least verbally abusive to his family. Despite the rumors to the contrary, he was not mad, but even his wife by the mid-1860s had doubts about his sanity (Parker, *Herman Melville* 2: 585–86). Although evidence exists that she seriously considered leaving him, Lizzie remained devoted to her husband and to his memory after his death. Together they weathered the suicide of their oldest son Malcolm at the age of 16 in 1867, as well as the restless wanderings and lonely death of their other son Stanwix in San Francisco in 1886.

Melville's separation from the literary world during the final decades of his life, which popularly have been dubbed "The Silent Years," should not be exaggerated. Throughout this period, he remained quietly dedicated to writing, and he continued to see friends such as Duyckinck from time to time. Most of his late efforts were in verse, and although his poetry also failed to find an appreciative audience in his lifetime, he continued to produce it. In 1866, Harper and Brothers published his *Battle-Pieces*, a collection of poems about the Civil War. Ten years later, as a final gift to his nephew, Melville's Uncle Peter Gansevoort subsidized the publishing of *Clarel* (1876), an epic poem of more than 18,000 lines that was inspired by his travels in the Holy Land. Two other small volumes of poetry, *John Marr and Other Sailors* (1888) and *Timoleon* (1891), were published privately by Melville in editions of 25 copies for distribution to family and friends.

Seemingly content in writing for itself now, "[o]nly death prevented him from printing other such volumes" (Parker, *Herman Melville* 2: 879).

At the age of 72, Melville died in obscurity on September 28, 1891, and he was buried beside his son Malcolm in Woodlawn Cemetery in the Bronx. He left behind a manuscript of prose fiction that would take a new generation and a new century to appreciate and publish as *Billy Budd* (1924).

2

Melville's Contributions to American Literature

Melville's physical demise in 1891 caused little stir, as he had long been considered dead as far as his literary reputation was concerned. His early South Seas narratives had gained him recognition as a romantic travel writer, but the general public—and most critics—had been unable to comprehend and appreciate his later, more ambitious works. As a result, late nineteenth- and early twentieth-century critics relegated him to "minor status in American literary history... by means of two indices: his subject mater and his geographical location" (Dolan 33). Melville was deemed unimportant not only because he had written popular adventure books but also because he was a New Yorker rather than a member of the elite New England sphere of literary and intellectual influence.

Even in his obscurity, however, Melville had "a small but steadily growing cult of interest," especially in England and Ireland (Dolan 34). In 1921, 30 years after the writer's death, this contingent finally gained ascendance with the publication of Raymond Weaver's *Herman Melville: Mariner and Mystic*. In this first full-length biography, Weaver labored to rehabilitate his subject's reputation by stressing the authenticity of his writings of the South Seas and by recognizing *Moby-Dick* as a critical masterpiece. Although the former argument led to a subsequent overemphasis of the biographical component in Melville's writings, the latter argument formally launched the movement known as the Melville Revival, which redefined the way in which the author would be viewed from that time forward.

THE MELVILLE REVIVAL

Weaver's biography of Melville laid the groundwork for the 1924 publication of a collected edition of the author's works, which incorporated the previously unpublished manuscript *Billy Budd*. A burgeoning body of scholarship, both biographical and critical, soon followed. Writing about the changing perspective on Melville, one scholar from the 1920s observed, "Whenever a dead author is 'revived,' we must bear in mind that nothing of him has changed. It is we, his readers, who are changed, and for whom he has gained other values" (qtd. in Sealts Jr., "'Flower of Fame'" 103). As a result of the experience of World War I, a new generation of readers was now valuing the very qualities in Melville's writings that his contemporaries had condemned—his rebelliousness "against both human society and the cosmos itself" (Sealts Jr., "'Flower of Fame'" 105). Whereas nineteenth-century readers had been bewildered by what Hawthorne had called Melville's "freedom of view," modernist readers embraced his expansive metaphysical meditations and were not offended when his ideas could not be constrained by typical conventions of form and style.

This movement to reassess Melville's critical reputation culminated in 1941 with F. O. Matthiessen's extended treatment of the writer in his *American Renaissance: Art and Expression in the Age of Emerson and Whitman*. This landmark study "finally established [Melville] as a 'classic American author'" and gave him a "permanent place in the canon" of American literature (Dolan 40, 41). Describing Melville as "the American with the richest natural gifts as a writer," Matthiessen revised the previously accepted reading of Melville's literary career (371). "Rather than tracing a development from *Typee* to *Pierre*, Matthiessen showed one that instead moves from *Mardi* to *Billy Budd*." With this revision, which interpreted "Melville's life as a story of 'endurance' rather than as a 'tragedy,' Matthiessen spared Melville the fate of the one-hit wonder" and thus "guaranteed him literary immortality" (Dolan 46).

THE "NEW" MELVILLE

The Western canon is a loosely defined set of literary works and other art that over time have been deemed highly influential in shaping Western culture. Canonization—the method by which such a collection of "masterworks" is determined—is now viewed, and often condemned, as a much contested political process that serves to privilege the esoteric and the elite while marginalizing other voices and perspectives. Accordingly, recent Melville scholarship has again revised its opinion of Melville, viewing him now as representative, rather than "great," because of his diversity. Consistent with current values, the "new" Melville "is not so much great as he is full. He is not a cultural icon to worship or inflict upon the disempowered but a historical person and a body of texts—a person-text—whose fullness fills us. His diversity triggers in us a diversity of responses and, more, a deeper sense of cultural fluidity" (Bryant, "Persistence" 26). With this shift in perspective, Melville scholarship has moved from a preoccupation with the formal and aesthetic qualities of his texts in isolation to focus increasingly on the interconnections between his texts and their aesthetic, social, cultural, and political contexts.

As a result of events such as the Civil Rights movement, the women's liberation movement, the AIDS epidemic, and the Vietnam War, Melville's texts have been reread with new values and sensitivities, and previously ignored issues of race and ethnicity, nationality, class, sexuality, and gender have become central to their discussion. Current scholarship concerns itself with the Melville who sought to raise his contemporaries' consciousness by writing "impassioned indictments of American and European imperialism in *Typee* and *Omoo*, slavery in *Mardi*, pauperism and mistreatment of emigrants in *Redburn*, flogging and militarism in *White-Jacket*, the betrayal of the American Revolutionary ideals in *Israel Potter*, the complacency of the rich and the exploitation of the working class in 'Poor Man's Pudding and Rich Man's Crumbs,'" and gender determinism in "The Paradise of Bachelors and The Tartarus of Maids" (Karcher x). Further, Melville's attitudes toward male friendship, as a possible "alternative to the ideology of aggressive male domination," have also been probed by reconsidering his sea narratives to discern the link that they forge between sexuality and structures of power (Martin, *Hero* xi). Through his representation of many different marginalized social groups, Melville continually critiques the corrupting tendency of power and authority. In this process, he punctures many of the idealistic myths of the redemptive power of American society at the same time that he struggled to live within it. Unsurprisingly, perhaps, his life and his writings are not without contradictions, and he did not always find an audience ready or able to understand and appreciate either his ideology or its artistic expression.

MELVILLE AND THE MARKETPLACE

In looking at Melville as a man who wrote and published a large body of texts, his relationship with the literary marketplace demands consideration. Much has been written about the struggle that Melville waged to balance the private and public pressures of writing. Although often frustrated by the associated challenges and not always successful in meeting them, Melville was more attuned to the tastes and styles of nineteenth-century culture than many of his biographers have acknowledged. He succeeded in placing his novels and short stories with major presses and periodicals because he "planned his works and based them on existing popular narrative forms"; he "aimed specific works for particular readerships"; and he "considered his reliance on antebellum forms as fundamental both to his writing and to his creativity" (Post-Lauria xiii). Melville's early embrace of the travel narrative, his molding of *Pierre* along the lines of the popular domestic novel, his movement to the short-story form, his use of the character type of the confidence man, and his borrowings from previous biographical and historical treatments as the inspiration for some of his later narratives all support the argument that he continually worked to appeal to different audiences.

Melville's personal identity was tied to his vocation, and he was keenly sensitive to the response of his readers and critics. In attempting to reconcile himself to the failure of *Mardi* to achieve either critical or commercial success, Melville wrote in 1849 to Evert Duyckinck, "I am but a poor mortal, & I admit that I learn by experience & not by divine intuitions. Had I not written & printed 'Mardi,' in all likelihood, I would not be as wise as I am now, or may be. For that thing was stabbed *at* (I do not say *through*)—& therefore, I am the wiser for it" (*Letters* 96). After applying the lessons learned from *Mardi* to the writing of *Moby-Dick* and again failing to achieve recognition, however, Melville endeavored to convince himself that truth, rather than fame, should be his objective as a writer. In an 1851 letter to Hawthorne, he insists, "All Fame is patronage. Let me be infamous: there is no patronage in *that*.... I have come to regard this matter of Fame as the most transparent of all vanities" (*Letters* 129–30). Still, Melville continued to try to find an appreciative audience by repeatedly adapting his narrative form. Only in his movement from fiction to poetry after the failure of *The Confidence-Man* in 1857 does he seem truly to have reconciled himself to his avowed position on literary fame. "Led first to question and finally to abandon the conventions of fiction and the idea of a shared public world that those conventions imply," Melville turned "to poetry with the hope that its intricacies [would] allow him to speak truly" (Dryden, *Monumental* 13). Perhaps only as a result of surrendering his interest in the marketplace to his fundamental concern for truth was Melville able to return to writing fiction in *Billy Budd* and thereby effect a final and fitting reconciliation between form and content.

MELVILLE AND "THE GREAT ART OF TELLING THE TRUTH"

One cannot read Melville without noting his expansive power and ambitiousness. Consistent with his characterization as a romantic, he is always more concerned with ideas than with aesthetic control. Although fundamentally opposed to what he saw as shallow idealism in Ralph Waldo Emerson's transcendental philosophy, Melville enthusiastically responded to one of his lectures by exclaiming, "I love all men who *dive*" (*Letters* 79). Melville was just such a thought-diver, relentlessly "attentive, enquiring, and never willing to settle for less than a reckoning with First Causes, the absolute condition of things. He expresses the ambition ... of wanting to confront Truth whole, Truth a term he always capitalized and which appears and reappears in his writing like a beckoning obsession" (Lee, *Reassessments* 9). In his texts, Melville repeatedly charts, while simultaneously denying, the quest for totality in human experience. Unable to define absolute Truth because of its evasiveness and the inadequacy of language, Melville instead dramatizes different responses to the fundamental question of how to respond to evil. In the end, "Melville's concern with the priority of ideas and the imagination finally take him beyond the political and theological values of his era to depict the devaluation of value that occurs when persons surrender their intellectual independence, deny the possibility of change, or close off interpretation by labeling as 'apocryphal' any explanation that accounts for the nature of things" (Duban 253).

In his early writings, and most especially in *Mardi*, Melville's diving "rush of ambitiousness" sometimes outruns his "technical competence, overtaxing the natural sense of pace and proportion in narrative" (Berthoff 12). His development as a thinker and a writer, however, can be traced through his successive works. "Nothing tried is lost. Images, figures, strategies, tonalities, and structural principles get carried along, revised, commented on, combined, turned upside-down, elaborated, and reapplied in a process which often leaves them clotted with multiple layers of rhetorical significance" (Short, *Cast* 3–4). As a result, his texts are characterized by a gathering rhetorical and ideological complexity that work in concert with each other. A central example of this interwoven complexity can be seen in Melville's vision of life as a masquerade.

Melville believed, as he wrote in "Hawthorne and His Mosses," that "the great Art of Telling the Truth" required speaking "craftily," since "it were all but madness for any good man, in his own proper character, to utter, or even hint" of the things we feel "to be so terrifically true" (1160). In his writings, Melville gives structural expression to this "paradoxical problem of telling the truth that can't be told" through "his predilection for impostors as narrators and protagonists" (Renker xvi). The most obvious examples of this practice are the narrators in *Typee, Omoo, Mardi, White-Jacket,* and *Moby-Dick,* who all use assumed names. Some scholars interpret Melville's use of narrative masks as a way to allay his own psychological anxieties about the truths he discerned. Others suggest he is only exploring the human tendency to project a false innocence as a means to evade the necessity of dealing with evil in the world and in themselves.

"Melville's characters who wear masks are of two kinds: those who don the mask to conceal nefarious purposes and those who put on masks unconsciously and mistake them for their own true face." According to Melville, the greatest claim to innocence, ironically, is made by those rare individuals who do not hide behind its mask (Miller 5). As he explains in extolling Shakespeare's King Lear, the ideal tragic hero has the strength to stand naked before the world as he "tears off the mask, and speaks the sane madness of vital truth" ("Hawthorne and His Mosses" 1160). This lack of pretense that Lear projects in confronting both the self and the world suggests the loss of innocence that Melville associates with the essence of tragedy. From this perspective, Melville's Billy Budd wears the mask of innocence and Claggart the mask of deceit, whereas Starry Vere arguably represents the maskless individual who balances the dictates of heart and head, emotion and reason, as he comes to terms with evil and thereby fashions a vision of life, however tragic in its repercussions.

Tragic heroes such as Starry Vere apprehend what Melville described to Hawthorne in 1851 as "visible truth,... the apprehension of the absolute condition of present things as they strike the eye of the man who fears them not, though they do their worst to him—the man who... declares himself a sovereign nature (in himself) amid the powers of heaven, hell, and earth" (*Letters* 124). However, although tragedy was the dominant mode for Melville's expression, his early narratives were written in the comic spirit. And, although he praised the "power of blackness" ("Hawthorne and His Mosses" 1159), "beginning with *Mardi,* it was Melville's principal artistic struggle to achieve a synthesis of the two halves"—the tragic and the comic—"that should contain the whole truth of life" (Rosenberry, *Comic Spirit* 5). In his maturity, he sought to project a "reposeful moral sensibility—one resonant equally in mirth and insight—a voice that could sustain a tension between self-consciousness and transcendent joy." Interpreted in this light, the apparent failures of his works after *Moby-Dick* "are not due to problems inherent in language or being but are the natural fallout" of "healthy narrative experimentation" in which humor played a fundamental role in teasing the reader into deeper thought. Unable to speak for God to provide answers to the fundamental questions he posed, he voiced "the voicelessness of truth" by creating genial and increasingly distant narrators to force his "readers to enact for themselves the drama of doubt and belief" (Bryant, *Melville and Repose* 4, 5, 20).

Raised in the still-lingering shadow of Calvinism, Melville rejected its notion of God as a power that inspired fear rather than love. Although he resisted the determining dictates of early nineteenth-century American Protestantism, however, Melville's formative years were still colored by those religious values and influences. As Hawthorne observed, Melville could "neither believe, nor be comfortable in his unbelief" (433). His writings reflect his discontent by charting a continuing search to find a certainty to sustain him, a search that mirrors many of the strains and pressures that the country at large was experiencing as it gradually moved toward religious pluralism. Early in his career, he sought to appease his conservative readers by expurgating *Typee* when he was labeled a heretic for living with the cannibals and for criticizing the Christian missionary presence in the South Seas. With *Mardi*, Melville depicts a survey of mythologies and idols in an elusive "search for a truth behind and beyond them" (Franklin 17). In *Moby-Dick*, he not only dismantles the remnants of Calvinism, but he also uses Ishmael to critique certain transcendentalist beliefs. In *Pierre*, he parodies the piety of young female characters in the popular domestic fiction of the mid-nineteenth century. Nearly 20 years after his own failed journey to the Holy Land, he writes the epic poem *Clarel*, in which his pilgrim finds only suffering in his quest for spiritual truth. At the end of the poem, Melville refuses his readers closure, engaging them in the tense balancing act he has created between the two poles of belief and disbelief. That the search continues despite the absence of answers suggests his conviction that moral and spiritual values are necessary for democracy to survive (Robertson-Lorant 356).

MELVILLE'S CONTRIBUTIONS TO THE NOVEL

The novel emerged in England as an art form in the early years of the eighteenth century when writers fused adventure and romance with verisimilitude. Encouraged by British models and an increasingly stable economy, American writers in the nineteenth century also began to achieve success with their experiments in this new genre. In the first phase of his career, Melville gradually developed the technical abilities required to blend effectively the tensions inherent in the novel. He began his career by writing *Typee* and *Omoo*, both full-length travel narratives of adventure and romance that—in reality—blended fact and fiction but were purported by Melville to be "unvarnished truth" (*Typee* 10). After trying a more ambitious allegorical romance in *Mardi*, he returned to the original pattern with his next two books, *Redburn* and *White-Jacket*. Only with his sixth full-length effort, *Moby-Dick*, did he create what by today's standards is almost universally recognized as an exceptional, although highly unconventional, novel. In his own day, however, his readers and critics were as confused by *Moby-Dick* as they had been by *Mardi*. They "agreed that they were not novels, though they also agreed that it was hard to say what they were" (Baym 202).

Melville and Hawthorne both referred to their fiction as "romance," which reflects their primary concern with the art of creation itself (Dryden, *Thematics* 19). In "Hawthorne and His Mosses," which Melville wrote in 1850 on first meeting the older writer, Melville uses his review of Hawthorne's collection of short stories as a vehicle to communicate the assumptions that underlie his own theory of fiction. A novelist, he claims by implication, succeeds in "the great Art of Telling the Truth" through the use of indirection, through the ability to perceive the "axis of reality" and then move beyond it to create a fictional life in a symbolic literary landscape (1160, 1159).

In creating his fictional worlds and the characters that inhabit them, Melville wrote several different kinds of novels. Although some scholars have emphasized his belief in the "value of instinctive composition," more recent scholarship has argued instead that Melville purposefully "used the many forms of the novel, with their distinctive typologies of the hero" to explore his thematic concerns (Brodhead, *Hawthorne, Melville* 126; Sten 2). Within each of his novels, he also freely incorporated other genres. As a result, categorization becomes nearly impossible. Only in the last few decades, as attitudes toward genre have become dramatically more elastic, have scholars begun to recognize rather than apologize for Melville's eclectic approach to form.

MELVILLE'S CONTRIBUTIONS TO THE SHORT STORY

In what has been termed the second phase of his career, Melville wrote 16 short stories. Although commercially popular in their time, these tales, all written between 1853 and 1856, received little critical attention until the 1960s, in part because of a tendency to view this genre as less important or serious than the novel. In 1960, Richard Harter Fogle published the first full-length treatment of the short fiction, which judged the tales less successful than the longer fiction because of Melville's desire to say more than his scope would allow (12). Writing just two years after Fogle, however, Warner Berthoff turned the critical tide with his view that the shorter works "in variety of theme and invention and in technical control" are "distinctly superior" to what Melville had published before *Moby-Dick*, proving him to be "at least the equal of Poe and only a little less of a master than Hawthorne" (138). Critical opinion since this time has rarely disputed Berthoff's verdict.

Melville's body of short fiction is distinguished by its dualities. Like Poe and Hawthorne, Melville presents riddles of human existence, but unlike them he does not rely on the power of human intelligence to solve them. Consistent with his longer narratives, the shorter fiction creates a sense of ambiguity and poses contradictions that are as puzzling as they are fundamental to the human condition. Several critics have commented on the "art of concealment" that Melville uses to urge the reader to probe beneath the surface of the texts. In terms of narrative pace, this characteristic is supported by "a painstaking casualness of exposition." In all of the tales, "the rhythm of the recital alternates... between the quick pace of immediate happenings and the slower fluctuations of the teller's progress toward an understanding of them" (Berthoff 149). This technique creates a tense, off-balance effect for both narrator and reader. Of particular note is Melville's use of the diptych, a two-part tale designed for social contrast and criticism. Melville wrote three formal diptychs—"The Two Temples," "Poor Man's Pudding and Rich Man's Crumbs," and "The Paradise of Bachelors and the Tartarus of Maids." In addition, other stories also suggest possible pairings, such as "The Happy Failure" and "The Fiddler."

MELVILLE AS POET

Melville is often acknowledged as "nineteenth-century America's leading poet after [Walt] Whitman and [Emily] Dickinson, yet his poetry remains largely unread, even by many Melvillians" (Buell, "Melville the Poet" 135). The longstanding tendency has been to discount Melville's poetry as a "left-handed" pastime of his later years. This conclusion seems wrong-headed, however, given the perseverance with which he pursued his interest in this genre and the quantity of verse that he produced, proof above all that he never retreated into silence during the last three decades of his life. Rather than the frustrated, embittered choice of a man hardened by the public's disdain of his fiction, Melville's movement to poetry was a logical transition to a new art form that would enable him to continue his "quest for usable, tested Truth, and his continuing penchant for contraries and ambiguity" (Lee, "'Eminently Adapted'" 123). Nevertheless, Melville's poems remain the least studied of his works, and even today, edited collections of essays on Melville do not always address his poetry; however, the poetry is now considered seriously when it is considered, and meaningful connections between it and his fiction are becoming more commonplace.

Melville's poetry inevitably suffers by comparison to that of Whitman and Dickinson because of "the comparatively traditional character of its language and prosody; ... its severe emotional restraint; and the deliberate entanglement of the larger narrative continuities" (Buell, "Melville the Poet" 136). Studied on their own merits, however, the poems fare much better from a critical perspective. *Battle-Pieces*, Melville's 1866 collection of Civil War poems, has received the most scholarly attention to date. These poems, although tightly restrained, are emotionally moving and intellectually compelling meditations not just on the Civil War but on "human impotence in the face of the power of destructiveness and evil which at frequent intervals rises to take over the course of history and human events" (Shurr 356). *Clarel*, published 10 years after *Battle-Pieces*, has garnered recent attention as well. This epic poem of more than 18,000 lines challenges even the most dedicated reader's powers of concentration but provides a fitting closure to Melville's canon in the recognition of the importance of endurance.

MELVILLE'S INFLUENCE

Although springing from a kernel of truth, myths and legends move beyond the realm of reality to gain an exaggerated yet exalted status that make them impervious to factual probing. In the case of Melville, the establishment of such myths in the first place was facilitated by the fact that early biographers had few materials except his writings on which to base their suppositions about the man himself. Recent biographers, aided by the discovery of new documents, have sought to revise the portrait that was created as a result of the earlier generation's approach. Keeping in mind that the writer was human with human inconsistencies and failings, scholars have now discounted the more lurid claims that Melville was an insane alcoholic who beat his wife, drove his son Malcolm to commit suicide, and harbored homosexual desires for his mentor and friend Nathaniel Hawthorne. They also have argued that the tendency to read Mary Glendinning, the manipulative and controlling mother in *Pierre*, as a realistic representation of Melville's own mother has resulted in distorted extrapolations about Melville's childhood.

Other legends about Melville, although less sensational, have proven equally hard to displace in the public's memory. First and foremost among these is the myth that Melville's later works—those after *Moby-Dick*—are inferior creations that are as unreadable as they are undeserving of critical attention. Such a view has resulted in the neglect of those works that is only now beginning to be corrected. Although *Moby-Dick* remains central to and the vortex of Melville's body of texts, scholars are now wrestling with the creative outpourings that followed it. Rather than finding only the signs of failure, exhaustion, and isolation in *Pierre, The Confidence-Man,* and *Clarel,* scholars are now concluding that "the diversity and experimentation after *Moby-Dick* reveal an active, still searching, highly inventive artist" (Bryant, *Companion* xxii). As a result of this new scholarship, Melville is now appreciated "not simply as the author of a few famous prose fictions but as a writer whose lifelong engagement with language pushed him through generic boundaries in search of new ways of shaping and questioning the world" (Clark Davis ix).

The single greatest influence on Melville's own writing was by all accounts Nathaniel Hawthorne, to whom he linked his own aspirations as a writer in his essay "Hawthorne and His Mosses" and who then inspired him to rewrite his nearly completed whaling manuscript and turn it into *Moby-Dick.* The effects of the friendship between these two writers almost always has been credited to Melville's sole advantage, and Hawthorne's influence has especially been posited in Melville's discovery of the nature of evil. Evidence exists, however, that Hawthorne also benefited from the relationship, most noticeably in *The Blithedale Romance,* published in 1852, just a year after *Moby-Dick.* Adopting a first-person narrative style reminiscent of Ishmael's narration in *Moby-Dick,* Hawthorne creates the fictional commune of Blithedale by drawing from his own experiences living at Brook Farm, just as Melville's novel was inspired by his time on a whaler. In addition, at least one study suggests that the narrator Coverdale "is not Hawthorne's vision of what he could have become had he remained a bachelor, as has often been suggested, but Hawthorne's vision of what he in fact felt himself to be at forty-seven." Such a reading suggests Hawthorne, "feeling decidedly middle-aged and torpid," may have "mourned his lack of Melville's passion and creative energy" (Mitchell 68).

Melville apparently had little effect on other writers of his own day, in large part because the only literary success he enjoyed during his lifetime was in his twenties as a writer of sea adventures. In the disillusion and alienation that followed World War I, however, modernists found much to admire in what they read as his mythic vision, and through their embrace of the archetypal struggle of *Moby-Dick,* they fashioned Melville into an American cultural hero. Somewhat ironically, the British writer D. H. Lawrence, often harsh in his comments about America, was a fundamental voice in this movement to make an icon of Melville, whom he saw as a struggling victim of American duplicity. During this period, the poet Hart Crane wrote "At Melville's Tomb" (c. 1925), in which he draws on the ending of *Moby-Dick* to mourn the death of his predecessor, an event that he sees as symbolic of America's lost vision. Crane also quotes from *Battle-Pieces* in his epic poem *The Bridge* (1930), and many scholars have commented on the influence of Melville elsewhere in his poetry.

After World War II, as the Cold War brought conservatism to the forefront of American politics, the influence of Melville continued with a shift of focus to his softer, romantic elements. In addition to the continuing influence of *Moby-Dick, Billy Budd,* as a Christian allegory, had particular appeal to this generation. Robert Lowell's "The Quaker Graveyard in Nantucket" (1946) draws on *Moby-Dick,* and William Styron's *The Long March* (1953) has been linked to *Billy Budd,* while the poetry of W. H. Auden reflects the influence of both texts. In his treatment of Nantucket, John Steinbeck also nods to Melville in his *East of Eden* (1952). Nor was Melville's influence during this period limited to American writers. French philosophers Albert Camus and Jean-Paul Sartre, for instance, also acknowledge their debt to Melville in their essays.

Despite the current critical disinclination to speak in terms of cultural icons, Melville retains a certain mythic status in the public consciousness. Even the many who have never read his works understand the symbolic implications of the related allusions; in fact, the "unreadability" of Melville has itself become part of the myth. Woody Allen acknowledges this vogue in his movie *Zelig* (1983), when the narrator finally begins to read *Moby-Dick* only to die before finishing it. In this typically playful manner, contemporary writers, filmmakers, and songwriters continue to invoke *Moby-Dick.* For instance, Kurt Vonnegut Jr. jokingly mimics Ishmael by opening *Cat's Cradle* (1963) with the words, "Call me Jonah," and Philip Roth opens *The Great American Novel* (1973) with the line, "Call Me Smitty." Continuing this tradition in *Ahab's Wife* (1999), Sena Jeter Naslund begins the spiritual journey of her first-person narrator with the words, "Captain Ahab was neither my first husband nor my last." Melville's works have been adapted in different mediums for all types of audiences, and a vast array of commercial products has drawn from his recognition value. There are Moby Dick comic books, toys, and T-shirts. Moby Dick restaurants flourish throughout the United States, and every child learns that "Moby Grape" is the answer to the question, "What's purple and lives at the bottom of the ocean?"

Although it is easy to argue that Melville and his Whale are now engrained in American folklore, the reason why is not as clear. Perhaps Charles Olson comes closest to explaining the attraction when he admits,

"I am willing to ride Melville's image of man, whale and ocean to find in him prophecies, lessons he himself would not have spelled out" (13). *Moby-Dick* will always be out of a reader's "grasp just as the whale forever escaped Ahab" (Weiner 87). Nonetheless, Melville still encourages his readers—even those who do not read him—to dive with him into the ambiguous quest of life.

3

Early Narratives of Adventure, Romance, and Rites of Passage: From *Typee* to *White-Jacket*

Inspired by his youthful adventures at sea, Melville began his literary career by writing and publishing *Typee, Omoo, Mardi, Redburn,* and *White-Jacket* in the five-year period between 1846 and 1850. Often dismissed as apprentice works, these books can be read profitably in terms of what they anticipate in *Moby-Dick,* the masterpiece that followed them. Although these narratives place *Moby-Dick* in critical perspective, however, they are also "finished works of art which would have assured Melville a considerable reputation even had he written nothing more" after them. Thus, "*Moby-Dick* is both the outgrowth of Melville's early work and a mirror of it" (Dillingham, *Artist* 2, 3). In addition to revealing much about Melville's development as a writer, these early texts reflect the major thematic concerns, ideological issues, and aesthetic choices that figure prominently in all of his writings.

From the beginning, these early works frustrated their critics by defying easy classification. Blending elements of the popular nineteenth-century genres of autobiography, travelogue, and romance, all five books feature first-person narrators who look back on their experiences at sea as a way to give meaning to the past. For Melville's narrators, "memory is an imaginative act which makes the present a moment of creative understanding of a past adventure that was experienced initially as an unintelligible and frightening chaos of sensations" (Dryden, *Thematics* 35). Although much effort has been spent trying to separate Melville's facts from his fictions, his aim in the end was always the truth that could be found only through an amalgamation of the two modes. Only by achieving a distance from the original experience and fictionalizing it in "a literary landscape" could he define its truth or meaning for himself and his reader (Dryden, *Thematics* 35).

TYPEE (1846)

Although questions about the veracity of *Typee* even predated its publication, it was not until Charles Anderson published *Melville in the South Seas* (1939) that definitive proof was offered to substantiate the longstanding charges that Melville had deliberately augmented and fictionalized his own experiences in the South Seas that form the basis of this narrative. Largely as a result of Anderson's work, Melville studies were released from the biographical straightjacket that had limited appreciation of the literary aspects not only of *Typee* but of Melville's later works as well. Basically episodic in nature, *Typee* nevertheless maintains narrative interest and is consistently readable. Further, the book "is a symbolically created thematic construct rather than a haphazard piece of reporting or a tale which is merely picaresque adventure" (Stern, *Fine* 34). As a result, it can be read as the genesis of Melville's continuing concern with identity as formulated through questions about nature and society, good and evil, innocence and experience.

Point of View

Recent scholarship differentiates between Melville and his fictionalized first-person narrators; however, in *Typee*, the link between Melville and the narrating Tommo remains clear, as does the writer's concern for how this voice will be received. "The narrator-hero of *Typee* ... seems anxious not to shock or to offend" (Abrams 42). Even when criticizing the Christian missionary movement, Tommo remains genteel and polite, even conciliatory. "Let the savages be civilized," he comments, "but civilize them with benefits, and not with evils; and let heathenism be destroyed, but not by destroying the heathen" (Melville 230). This "intensely audience-conscious" voice is "Melville edited," although essentially self-edited. At this stage, the point of view is probably not "a radical departure from Melville's own personality and voice" (Abrams 42).

Setting and Plot

In addition to creating a fictionalized narrative voice as his alter-ego, Melville expands his own 1842 stay in the Marquesan Islands from four weeks to four months in creating the South Pacific setting for *Typee*. Arriving at Nukuheva Bay after six monotonous months at sea, the narrator Tommo and his shipmate Toby jump ship to journey into the interior. Descending from the mountain, they are received amicably by the natives of the Typee valley. The Typees offer them food and shelter, as well as a servant for Tommo, whose leg has been injured during the escape. When Toby fails to return after leaving to find medicine for his friend, Tommo becomes increasingly lonely and fearful for his safety despite his attraction to the innocence of life in the valley. Eventually, he flees the valley and is picked up by another brig in the bay. Toby's disappearance is explained in a sequel appended to the original edition of the narrative.

Characters

Although Tommo is the most fully developed character, he never achieves the status of central consciousness in the narrative (Lee, "'Varnishing'" 209). Tommo's perceptions vacillate throughout the narrative from one extreme to another, and although he comes to understand something of Typee life, he ultimately is unable to overcome his own human limitations and cultural biases. Tommo's companion Toby serves principally as a foil or counterpoint to the narrator. Because he remains skeptical about the Typees, he is more aligned with the values of Western civilization than the narrator. Mehevi, the chief of the Typees, gains Tommo's respect through his many kindnesses to him, as well as through his nobility in governing his people. He can be seen as the "noble savage" that the romantic philosopher Rousseau believed represented the virtues of living close to nature as opposed to the corrupting influence of civilization. Continuing this romantic perspective, Fayaway, the beautiful native maiden to whom Tommo is attracted, represents innocence and the purity of sexuality that is untainted by sin.

Allegory and Symbolism

In creating an allegory, a writer tries to create a story that is not only interesting in itself but that also suggests a meaning beyond the literal. Such a reading, however, is usually clear-cut in its implications. By contrast, when a writer uses symbols in creating a text, the possible meanings become more complex and open to interpretation. Considering *Typee* only for its allegorical implications, the innocence of the Typees contrasts with the corruption of society, as represented by the life on the whaler, the *Dolly*, from which Tommo and Toby escape at the beginning of the narrative. At this level, Melville shows the superiority of Typee to "civilized society" by repeatedly describing it as an Eden before the Fall. Observing that "[t]he penalty of the Fall presses very lightly upon the valley of Typee," Tommo shudders to think of the changes that the French will bring to this "paradisaical abode" (*Typee* 229–30). Such a reading would see Tommo as "Adam" to Fayaway's "Eve."

However, Melville disrupts the reader's ability to accept such a simplistic duality between nature and society, good and evil, innocence and experience, by using repeated symbolic references to create ambiguity and ambivalence in the narrator's perceptions of Typee. Tommo's injured leg, which swells and pains him only when he is conflicted about the Typees, represents his feelings of powerlessness in the face of his fears about this alien culture. The dark side of this Edenic paradise is symbolized by its practice of cannibalism, a mysterious religious rite that both intrigues and repulses Tommo. Cannibalism appears early in the text "as a literal point of reference, but increasingly comes to express a whole range of threats which Tommo fears can endanger, and likely consume, his inner being" (Lee, "'Varnishing'" 208).

Tattooing is developed similarly as a threat to Tommo's identity both as an individual and as a member of Western society. He expresses the dual fear represented by this custom when he explains, "I now felt convinced that in some luckless hour I should be disfigured in such a manner as never more to have the *face* to return to my countrymen, even should an opportunity offer" (*Typee* 255). More than fearing that the Typees will devour his body, Tommo fears they will devour his identity by *defacing* him. Unable to resolve the complex tensions he has discovered, Tommo flees the valley, choosing to return to the civilization he just as emphatically abandoned at the opening of the narrative.

Themes

Although the central theme in *Typee* is anticolonialism, the way in which this theme is read has evolved as political sensitivities have sharpened in the latter half of the twentieth century. During the Melville revival, critics such as Anderson generally interpreted *Typee* as a "brief against civilization" that presents "a whole-hearted defense of the Noble Savage and a eulogy of his happy life, his external beauty, and his inward purity of heart" (Anderson, *Melville* 177, 178). Recent scholarship, however, argues that *Typee* "fails to value Typee culture for its own sake, but rather values it because it is not capitalism, not civilization, not America." Because the text represents the Typees as living only in the present moment, it negates their history, as well as "the validity of Typee society as human" (Ivison 125). In particular, these critics point to the book's conclusion to support a more complex reading of the text. In the end, Melville's narrator "although highly critical of colonialism, nonetheless affirms his position as colonist in order to maintain the separation on which his racial and cultural identity depends" (Schueller 3).

Typee also uses "the story of a journey as a way of exploring the part that male friendship may play in the life of a man, if only he could be transported from the world of his own Western culture" (Martin, "'Enviable Isles'" 69). Just as he will revisit the theme of anticolonialism in his later writings, Melville will also address male friendship in many of his subsequent works.

Historical Context

American writers such as Melville "had ample reason to be interested in the ideology, practice, and effects of colonialism, given the discourses of colonialism and imperialism in circulation in mid-nineteenth century America" (Schueller 3). Even after the abolition of slavery in the United States, Americans continued to justify the territorial conquest of non-Western peoples "by an assumed Euro-American cultural primacy, America's divine mission, and the need to 'civilize' the savages" (Schueller 4). When Melville published *Typee* in 1846, the Marquesan Islands had endured a long history of colonization that began in 1774 with British explorer James Cook's discovery. The French claimed the Marquesas in 1791, and the islands briefly became the first colony of the United States when Captain David Porter took possession of them during the British-American War of 1812. After further disputes with the British, France annexed the Marquesas shortly before Melville's arrival in 1842. In short, "the discovery, exploration, and exploitation of the Marquesas by various European powers and the United States was a microcosm of modern imperialism at its worst" (Rowe 259). During the nineteenth century, the population of the islands declined from an estimated 100,000 to less than 5,000. This "destruction of the Marquesan way of life," which Melville's *Typee* anticipates, has been called "one of the principal horrors of Pacific history" (Herbert, *Marquesan Encounters* 19).

OMOO (1847)

Responding to the popular success of his first book, Melville shaped *Omoo* as a sequel to *Typee*. Most consider the result less successful overall than the original work, although Melville demonstrates a greater command of form, genre, and characterization. "While the sentimental and sensational style of *Typee* generates romantic description, the conventions of the nautical reminiscence shape the author's method in *Omoo*" (Post-Lauria 53). The word "Omoo" is Tahitian for wanderer, and as Melville explains in the preface, one of his objectives in writing this sequel is to describe the life of "a roving sailor" in the South Seas "by means of a circumstantial history of adventures befalling the author." In addition, he wishes "to give a *familiar* account of the present condition of the converted Polynesians, as affected by their promiscuous intercourse with foreigners, and the teachings of the missionaries, combined" (*Omoo* 325). As a result, the structure is looser and more episodic than in the earlier narrative, which results in less dramatic tension and thematic coherence. The predominant tone in *Typee* is romantic, whereas *Omoo* projects more realism and humor.

Point of View

The point of view in *Omoo* is again that of the retrospective, first-person narrator, but the perspective remains more constant than in *Typee*, without radical shifts in position. "Melville's second fictional 'I' evolves" from the cautious voice of the socially circumspect Tommo to that of Omoo, "an emancipated vagabond strolling down an open road into an indeterminate future" (Abrams 49). The difference in voice reflects not only the narrator's growing confidence and experience but also the writer's.

Setting and Plot

Whereas the setting in *Typee* depicts the Marquesas before the natives' conversion to Christianity, *Omoo* shows the aftereffects of the colonizing impulse in Tahiti. The story opens as the narrator escapes from the Typees by boarding the *Julia*, an Australian whaler. Tommo—now Omoo—looks back nostalgically on his days in the Typee Valley and soon has misgivings about the state of "civilization" in which he finds himself. The *Julia's* crew consists of "wild, haggard-looking fellows," the captain is sick and ineffectual, and the first mate is often drunk (*Omoo* 329). When they arrive at the Tahitian harbor of Papette, 10 of the crew—including Omoo and the ship's surgeon Long Ghost—are charged with mutiny when they refuse duty, and they are imprisoned onshore in the "Calabooza Beretanee," the British jail. Eventually allowed to "escape" after the *Julia* departs, Omoo and Long Ghost wander from island to island, surviving by their wits and the goodwill of others. After experiencing the positive and negative aspects of life in all of these locales, however, Omoo eventually departs from Tahiti by boarding another whaler, the *Leviathan*, which for this wanderer promises to be just another temporary home.

Characters

Melville presents the narrating Omoo as an unassuming man who is essentially honest, open, and compassionate in his dealings with others. Because Omoo is more important as an observer than as a character in his own right, he represents Melville's first use of what is known as a "dissolving narrator." Although Omoo and Long Ghost are both rogues— or *picaros*—who enjoy each other's company, the two men have almost no qualities or values in common. The American Omoo reveals conventional ties to home and family; the British Long Ghost brags of an exaggerated and shady past. "His early history," Omoo reports, "was enveloped in the profoundest obscurity; though he threw out hints of a patrimonial estate, a nabob uncle, and an unfortunate affair which sent him a-roving.... [F]rom whatever high estate Doctor Long Ghost might have fallen, he had certainly at some time or other spent money, drunk Burgundy, and associated with gentlemen" (*Omoo* 336). "By personifying the characteristics of a gentleman-adventurer and rake, Doctor Long Ghost counterpoints the identity of the honest, simple sailor-narrator." It is Long Ghost rather than Omoo who serves the role of hero in the story; "thus the demands of disparate readers for simple narrators and romantic heroes are equally met" (Post-Lauria 57). Throughout the narrative, Long Ghost usually initiates the adventures that Omoo records. Omoo's yearning for "home," however, moves him finally to return to sea, whereas Long Ghost, ever the romantic scamp, stays behind to continue his Tahitian escapades.

As a further mark of Melville's growing artistic abilities, he also populates *Omoo* with detailed comic portraits of secondary characters that add richness and depth to the reader's enjoyment of the narrative. In particular, "*Omoo* marks the first appearance in Melville's fiction of the black man in the figure of the Negro cook Baltimore, and the first appearance of a savagely vindictive nonwhite who seems to embrace evil for itself alone, the Mowree harpooner from New Zealand, Bembo." Melville's portrait of Baltimore reflects nineteenth-century racial stereotypes: He "is a good-natured, comic character, the butt of practical jokes." In contrast to Baltimore's docile subservience, however, Bembo reacts savagely to mistreatment and "brooks no insult from whites." Both of these characters "offer insights into Melville's growing racial consciousness" (Grejda 30). Although he does not condone Bembo's viciousness, Melville does show justification for it in the humiliation he is forced to suffer at the hands of the other sailors. Bembo's pride, "though savage, is also courageously human," and in Bembo's rebellion, the reader views "a terrifying assertion of his manhood and of his self-respect" (Grejda 37).

Themes

Extending the theme of anticolonialism that he began in *Typee*, Melville uses his second book to present a sharp critique of European imperialism and especially of the Christian missionary movement. The narrator is horrified by the degeneracy of the Tahitians, which he expresses in both physical and moral terms. "I was painfully struck," Omoo explains, "by the considerable number of sickly or deformed persons; undoubtedly made so by a virulent complaint, which, under native treatment, almost invariably affects, in the end, the muscles and bones of the body. In particular, there is a distortion of the back, most unsightly to behold, originating in a horrible form of the malady" (*Omoo* 455). "Unknown before the discovery of the islands by the whites," this disease, Omoo advises, now "taints the blood of at least two-thirds of the common people of the island," threatening extinction of the native population (455, 518). The longstanding Polynesian custom of "making bosom friends at the shortest possible notice" has mostly "degenerated into a mere mercenary relation" (480). In contrast to the harmonious social order that the narrator found in Typee, the Tahitians are beginning to divide themselves between "better and wealthier orders" and the "common people" (496). In general, "Melville depicts the Tahitian Polynesians as people mired in indolence, fickleness, and licentiousness—a society stripped of social harmony and individual goodness" (Grejda 32). He also makes clear where the responsibility lies for the decimation of this culture: "These evils," he writes, "are solely of foreign origin" (*Omoo* 518). Quoting the verdict of an early voyager, Wheeler, he concludes, "'How dreadful and appalling...the consideration that the intercourse of distant nations should have entailed upon these poor, untutored islanders a curse unprecedented, and unheard of, in the annals of history'" (518–19).

In addition, *Omoo* continues Melville's thematic concern with male friendship. "Omoo and the Doctor come together not out of any weakness but out of strength; they have no neurotic need for one another, nothing beyond the natural desire for good fellowship." Although they play tricks on each other, they remain essentially loyal, forming a healthy bond of companionship that never "constrains either man's natural identity or forces him to compromise his personal integrity" (Sten 51).

Consistent with the *picaresque* tradition, the theme of disorder also appears prominently in the narrative. In the first section of the book this theme is presented through the hapless and chaotic state of the *Julia*, mirrored in both its debilitated physical condition and that of the crew, which suffers from a lack or discipline and the effects of rampant alcoholism and disease. In the section of the narrative that is set on land, this theme continues, most obviously through the depiction of the deterioration of Tahitian life under European occupation.

Allegory and Symbolism

Melville's use of symbolism at this stage of his career is still mostly static rather than dynamic. Polynesia continues to represent the extremes of good and evil, signifying both the state of innocence in nature and the loss of that innocence. Since 26 of the 81 chapters of *Omoo* take place onboard ship, the symbolic implications of the sea are also developed more fully than in *Typee,* where only the opening pages are set in that realm. The ship continues to function as a microcosm of the failures of "civilization," but the sea, both at the beginning and end of the narrative, provides a means of transition from one state to another—an escape that offers uncharted possibilities for redemption.

Historical Context

Because Melville focuses on the results of colonization in *Omoo,* it sparked considerable controversy when first published, which in turn caused some critics and readers to reevaluate *Typee* as well. In addition to the old charges that Melville's writing lacked authenticity and offended common decency in its overt depiction of sexuality, new complaints were lodged concerning his irreverent tone and his defense of paganism. A minority of reviewers attacked "him roundly on three scores: dishonesty, unfounded abuse of the missionaries, and personal immorality" (Anderson, "Contemporary American Opinions" 18). In most circles, however, the book was enthusiastically received and defended, and its sales increased Melville's already immense popularity with the general readership.

MARDI (1849)

Mardi is far from a flawless book. "It is the loosest and baggiest of prose monsters, a book that changes direction freely on its way it knows not where, its ramblings held together only by the flimsy framework of a quest for an insubstantial maiden." In addition, Melville's style is often bombastic with "mechanical poetic effects," and his philosophical insights are sometimes embarrassingly obvious and simplistic. However, "the important thing is not that *Mardi* has flaws but that it has ones of such an order" (Brodhead, "*Mardi*" 27). Many of the themes, ideas, characters, images, forms, and stylistic features of Melville's later writings can be traced back to *Mardi*. As a result, "the true significance of *Mardi* is that it is the first draft of all his subsequent works" (Brodhead, "*Mardi*" 39). As an artistic achievement, the book has serious shortcomings, but it nevertheless substantiates Melville's continued growth and future promise as a writer of imaginative power.

Mardi, at least from Melville's perspective, was his first work of fiction. Frustrated by the concerns that his first two books raised on the issue of their factual basis, Melville declares in the preface of his third book that he has determined this time to write "a romance of Polynesian adventure … to see whether, the fiction might not, possibly, be received for a verity: in some degree the reverse of my previous experience" (*Mardi* 661). Although the narrative begins in the realistic mode of *Typee* and *Omoo*, its eventual focus becomes the metaphysical rather than the physical. A sprawling book of 195 chapters of visions, fantasies, and dreams, *Mardi* fulfills Nathaniel Hawthorne's idea of the realm of romance as "'the world of the mind,' … a meeting place of the 'Actual and Imaginary,' a place where each may 'imbue itself with the nature of the other.'" As the narrator "Taji's experiences suggest, however, Melville regards this union as momentary and destructive" (Dryden, *Thematics* 52).

Point of View

Melville continues his use of first-person retrospective narration in *Mardi*. This time, however, his decision regarding point of view raises obvious questions, as the narrator is presumably recollecting a series of adventures that ended in his death. In addition, during much of the second half of the narrative, Taji is largely absent from the scene of action, and on the infrequent occasions when he speaks, he often refers to himself in third person ("Taji") rather than first person ("I"). Because Taji is not developed fully as either a narrative voice or a character, the reader struggles to engage with and find coherence in his tale.

Setting and Plot

The initial setting, like that of *Typee* and *Omoo*, is in the South Seas, this time aboard the whaler the *Arcturion*, from which the as yet unnamed narrator escapes with a companion named Jarl. After 16 days in an open boat, they meet the *Parki*, a brigantine with only a couple remaining on board, Samoa and Annatoo. After a storm in which Annatoo is drowned and the *Parki* sinks, Samoa, Jarl, and the narrator return to the open boat, heading west until they come upon a large double canoe that holds a native priest called Aleema, his three sons, and the mysterious white maiden Yillah, whom they intend to sacrifice as part of a religious ritual. To save Yillah, the narrator kills Aleema, and he and his companions then flee with Yillah to escape the vengeance of Aleema's sons. Once they reach the Mardian islands, they become guests of King Media on the island of Odo, and the narrator enjoys being called Taji by the natives, who mistakenly believe he is a demigod who has arrived from heaven with his bride. A few days later, Yillah mysteriously disappears, possibly spirited away by Queen Hautia from the neighboring island of Flozella.

Taji initiates a protracted quest throughout the Mardian Islands to find Yillah, and he is accompanied in his search not only by Samoa and Jarl, but also by King Media and three of his noblemen: the philosopher Babbalanja, the historian Mohi, and the poet Yoomi. Eventually Samoa and Jarl are left at the island of Mondoldo, and Taji learns later that his two friends have been killed by Aleema's sons. After circling the islands and finding no trace of Yillah, the remaining five travelers reach Serenia, where all but Taji believe the search should end. Babbalanja's vision of heaven convinces him to remain at Serenia, but Media returns to Odo. Finally, after meeting with Hautia, Taji resists the temptation to remain with her, as well as Mohi and Yoomi's entreaties to abandon his senseless quest and return to the "haven" of Serenia. Instead, Taji bids Mardi farewell, renames himself "the unreturning wanderer," and sets out alone "over an endless sea," pursuing Yillah even in death (*Mardi* 1316).

Characters

Like Melville's earlier narrators, Taji is young and idealistic. He fails to recognize his complicity in the loss of Yillah, which comes from his unacknowledged guilt in killing the priest Aleema and which ultimately results in the deaths of Samoa and Jarl. Taji ultimately destroys himself because he is unable to accept the impossibility of his ideals and fashion a more realistic understanding of himself and of humanity in general. He remains bound to his romanticized conception of the past, which prevents him from living in the present. All of the travelers search for Yillah; however, all but Taji grow through their travels and are able to recognize the futility of the search and abandon it before it can destroy them. The four

Mardians—king, historian, philosopher, and poet—are essentially what is called "'humor' characters who, with only a few individualizing manner-isms, represent the type or profession of their stated calling in the Mardian world and in what they say reveal their special interests and the underly-ing bias of their minds" (Merrell Davis 160). Babbalanja, the most fully developed of the four, serves as a counterpoint to Taji, and he is the voice for much of Melville's speculative thinking. As Babbalanja explains, "'I am intent upon the essence of things, the mystery that lieth beyond...that which is beneath the seeming'" (*Mardi* 1008). "With him the emphasis is on mind, with Taji it is on will. The two supplement each other, yet there is a structural and philosophical antithesis between them" (William Ellery Sedgwick 41–42).

Allegory and Symbolism

Part of the difficulty in reading and understanding *Mardi* has been explained by its division between symbolism and allegory. Successful allegories depend on authorial certainty that results in clarity of vision and expression. As a result, allegorists typically work "backwards from settled abstract principles" to make "flesh and blood of spiritual and divine attributes." Melville instead works "forward into unknown territories of speculation from the bases of real and solid fact which he knew as the chief and abiding experiences of his life" (Mason 51). The complex and shapeless allegory of the journey through Mardi, although pointed and penetrating, "fails on the whole to reflect either an ordered attitude to existence or a solution to the complexities it records." Similarly, "its symbolism, even at its most powerful, is encumbered with a set of images and personifications too derivative and decadent to illuminate their material counterparts with any conviction" (Mason 64). The book is technically flawed by an agenda that is overly ambitious for Melville's still developing expertise to manage effectively; however, it embodies qualities of beauty, spirit, and urgency that anticipate the maturity of Melville's creative powers in *Moby-Dick*.

The central symbol in *Mardi* is that of the voyage, which begins liter-ally but then evolves into the realm of the allegorical and symbolic; the individual adventurers become representative of humanity, and the islands they sail among become the whole world (Mason 49). Taji, Yillah, and Hautia are the only three characters that function allegorically in the text. The idealistic and willful Taji, in searching to find the lost Yillah, seeks to find a lost innocence that cannot be regained. Ultimately, she represents a state of perfection, goodness, and total happiness that is inconsistent with human life. "Taji's Yillah cannot be found wherever evil exists; and since evil is universal, a condition of existence, Yillah can never be discovered—indeed, does not exist. As the more philosophical Babbalanja finally tells Taji, 'She is a phantom that but mocks thee'" (James E. Miller Jr. 47). The converse of Yillah, Hautia beckons Taji by calling, "'Come! Let us sin, and be merry'" (*Mardi* 1312). She signifies the converse of Yillah, the world of the flesh and the spiritual death that results from excessive sensuality and pride.

During their search for Yillah, the travelers visit 16 islands and pass by others, discussing the characteristics of each in a satirical style that is reminiscent of Jonathan Swift's *Gulliver's Travels*. A satire is a literary work that exposes human folly and vice through sarcasm, irony, or wit. In particular through his use of irony—a literary style in which the intended meaning is opposite from the literal meaning—Melville offers wide-ranging social criticism on contemporary issues of religious, political, economic, sexual, literary, and philosophical import. Even today's readers can easily identify the major countries and institutions that are being critiqued. Dominora, for instance, is Great Britain, Franko is France, and Vivenza is the United States. Similarly, Maramma stands for Roman Catholicism, and Serenia represents a spiritual realm of Christianity that is free of dogma and institutional dictates. Topical satire is only of secondary interest to Melville, however; his primary concern is with the universal. As a result, the sea comes most fully to represent the mythical timelessness of truth and the ideal fullness and unity of human consciousness.

Themes

Developing further his interest in the conflict between innocence and experience, Melville's central theme in *Mardi* is the human mind's quest for truth. Melville directs the search "outwardly at the objective truth about creation and inwardly at the realities of being," identifying Babbalanja "with its outward and Taji with its inward action" (William Ellery Sedgwick 40, 42). In so doing, Melville emphasizes the "continual interaction between objective truth and inward reality, between knowledge and being" (William Ellery Sedgwick 42). Because human life is unable to achieve the unity it seeks, however, *Mardi* presents a tragic vision that would become central in all of his works from this point forward. In the end, the book represents the circularity of such a quest, as well as the questioning of it. "Taji simply refuses to accept the implications of his own experience. His dream of attaining oneness with the universe is so intense that it blinds him to the facts of the world's recalcitrance." Melville wants the reader "to see these dreams both as irresistible and impossible; thus defined, Taji's quest is as hopeless as it is necessary to his self-definition" (Grenberg 47).

Another theme that Melville develops for the first time in *Mardi* is monomania, the pathological obsession with one idea or subject. Although Taji is totally committed to finding the lost Yillah, through most of the narrative he remains capable of philosophically discussing other subjects. "Not until near the end of *Mardi* does the narrator's madness become more recognizable" (McCarthy, *"Twisted Mind"* 29). In the final chapter, one of his companions even calls him a "madman" for refusing to return to Serenia (*Mardi* 1316). Taji "is defiant, rebellious, and ultimately suicidal. In romantic terms, he is insane, separated from society by reason of his madness" (McCarthy, *"Twisted Mind"* 30). Melville will continue his interest in insanity with increased focus in *Redburn,* and his concern with monomania will also resurface in *Moby-Dick* and *Pierre.*

REDBURN (1849)

When *Mardi* failed to receive favor with readers or critics, Melville grudgingly turned back to his original formula for success to shape his next two books around his own experiences at sea. In a letter to his publisher, Melville described *Redburn* as "a plain, straightforward, amusing narrative of personal experience—the son of a gentleman on his first voyage to sea as a sailor—no metaphysics, no conic-sections, nothing but cakes & ale" (*Letters* 86). Although his description is not entirely accurate, as *Redburn* has little if any humor, Melville does chart a more conventional narrative course in both this book and in *White-Jacket,* which follows it. These two books also taught Melville, "even as he railed at them, the disciplines he needed to control his expanding conceptions" (Rosenberry, *Comic Spirit* 93).

Aptly subtitled "His First Voyage," *Redburn* is most often described as a bildungsroman, which in German means "formation novel." This genre or type of novel, which traces the moral, psychological, and intellectual development of a usually male youth from childhood or adolescence to adulthood, was extremely popular with nineteenth-century American and British readers. By choosing this genre, Melville was consciously shaping *Redburn* to appeal to a wide audience. Although *Redburn* is the closest Melville would ever come to obeying the formal literary conventions of his day, he still manages to challenge "basic assumptions, both modern and those specific to the 1840s, about the process through which a boy is supposed, by progressive stages to become a 'mature' man, and about the way in which a 'mature' man looks back on the events of his childhood and adolescence" (Hall 259). As a result, popular and critical opinion is divided as to whether the protagonist defines a fully mature sense of self and completes his initiation into adult knowledge.

Point of View

Because Wellingborough Redburn, the protagonist, is both a character and a narrative voice in *Redburn*, point of view is again problematic. Although Redburn's presence remains central throughout the novel, the reader must periodically shift between a sense of the present tense in terms of characterization and narrative action and the retrospective narrator's recollection of himself and his actions as happening in an ambiguously defined past. In Chapter 14, for instance, the speaker's voice is that of a naive youth who is clearly uneducated in shipboard hierarchy. As he explains, "When two or three days had passed without the captain's speaking to me in any way, . . . I began to think whether I should not make the first advances, and whether indeed he did not expect it of me" (*Redburn* 80). Conversely, in Chapter 41, the narrative voice, clearly older and looking backwards, describes himself as "[b]eing so young and inexperienced then" (222). On the surface, the young Redburn's qualities are most apparent, but Melville uses the "older narrator as his mouthpiece to provide social commentary on Liverpool and reflections on universal themes quite foreign to the younger Redburn" (Press 172).

Setting and Plot

Melville uses clear autobiographical elements in drawing his protagonist's background. Redburn is the "Son-of-a-Gentleman," an importer who has died in bankruptcy, leaving his family in financial ruin. Remembering his father's romantic tales of his own voyages to Europe, Redburn, who is about 15 years old, leaves his home on the upper Hudson River to sign on as a green hand on a trade ship, the *Highlander*. During the six weeks that follow, Redburn is indoctrinated into the life of a sailor, and when the ship reaches England, he is also introduced to the harsh realities of life around the docks of Liverpool. During his six weeks there, Redburn tries in vain to assist a destitute woman and her two children, who are dying of hunger on a street called Launcelott's-Hey. He also meets Harry Bolton, who—like Redburn—is "forever striving to proclaim to himself and the world an identity as a gentleman that is not his—or is no longer his, if it ever was" (Sten 108). The two visit London briefly, and on their return, Harry—who also unconvincingly claims to be an experienced sailor—joins the crew of the *Highlander* for its return voyage to America. The *Highlander*'s voyage back to America is a four-month crossing that is marked by violent storms, disease, and death. When he reaches New York, Redburn is refused pay by Riga, the ship's captain, who charges Redburn for lost gear and missing duty. Unable to find employment as he had promised for Harry, Redburn leaves him in New York to return home. Years later, serving as a whalesman in the Pacific Ocean, he learns that Harry was crushed to death when he fell overboard from a whaler off the coast of Brazil.

Characters

Redburn, like Melville's other narrators, reflects an essentially open, honest, and compassionate nature. Although he feels the pain and misfortune of others, however, he remains essentially separate from them, suggesting a certain air of superiority. Aligning himself initially with the captain rather than the crew, Redburn comes even to hold himself aloof from that representative of leadership and authority when he determines that the captain acts as one man on the ship and another in port. As Redburn remarks, "I put him down as a sort of imposter; and while ashore, a gentleman on false pretenses; for no gentleman would have treated another gentleman as he did me" (84). The sailor Jackson, who bullies the crew and especially resents Redburn for his youth and vitality, is Melville's "first character of outstanding dramatic quality.... Jackson is not just another shipmate of Redburn's; he is personified iniquity" (Mason 71). In the dissolute young figure of Harry Bolton, Melville creates a contrast to Redburn. Although the young American matures by his experiences at sea and learns to accept the reality of his circumstances and station in life, the "jaunty self-confidence" of his British counterpart is "stripped off him" by the same experiences, and he eventually "yields himself, completely broken in spirit, to the luxury of passive misery" (Mason 71).

Symbolism

Rites of passages—the rituals that define transitions between life stages—are central both to the process of self-identification and socialization. By embarking on "His First Voyage," Redburn initially seeks to regain the security and lost innocence of his childhood rather than to achieve and celebrate his independent manhood. Thus the romantic "Old World" of England, with all of its ties to father and fatherland, is a fitting destination, as is the circular nature of the journey that ends up back where it began in the dynamic "New World" of America. Before he leaves home, Redburn contemplates the old glass ship that his father brought home to America from Europe. Refusing to repair the broken spars and ropes or the fallen figurehead within the glass, Redburn feels a "secret sympathy" with the fallen sailor, and makes of this figure a model of his own romantic expectations of how he will set his life right again at sea (14). In sending Redburn off, his older brother gives him a hand-me-down shooting jacket, which has numerous symbolic implications. Not only does the secondhand nature of this gift reflect the family's poverty, but it also suggests his family's fall from the world of affluence and leisure, where such garments are worn. Further, as such a jacket is designed to be worn on land, not at sea, it is wholly inappropriate to his new environment and so represents his lack of experience and knowledge of the world he is entering.

Melville continues the motif of family in Redburn's search for a reliable guide. The youth begins his new life by turning first of all to the captain, who quickly fails as a surrogate father. Redburn's father's outdated guide book to Liverpool proves equally ineffective, causing Redburn finally to realize that "the thing that had guided the father could not guide the son" (*Redburn* 171). His symbolic encounter with the starving family of Launcelott's-Hey and the visit he and Harry make to London also reveal to Redburn the corruption of England. As a result of these experiences, his misguided search to reconnect with his father's memory and recover his innocence in the Old World ends, and Redburn turns back toward America, which represents his independent identity, both individually and nationally. Redburn's fate is contrasted ultimately with that of both Harry Bolton and Jackson. By rejecting the genteel weakness of Harry and the evil hardness of Jackson, Redburn finds a healthy balance and independent identity for himself.

Themes

On the surface, *Redburn* presents a deceptively simple and traditional story of innocence and experience, but recent scholarship has suggested that the theme of identity formation is actually more central in the novel. Redburn fails to extend brotherly love to Harry, his fellow sufferer, which seems inconsistent with what he has supposedly learned in his experiences at sea and in England; however, Redburn does ultimately gain self-knowledge, but Harry does not. Arguably, he must leave Harry, his alter-ego, behind to claim his future and release himself from the negative influence of the false guides that have misled him in the past. Thus, rather than reading his parting with Harry as a betrayal of his friend that suggests his fall from innocence into the world of evil, it is possible to view this act as a necessary step in Redburn's development. At the end of the novel,

Redburn still has no money and no prospects of employment, but he has gained the maturity needed to enter the next phase of his life journey with a realistic understanding of himself.

Through his depiction of the starving mother and children in the slums of Liverpool, Melville indicts society's indifference to the poor and shows the dark side of mid-nineteenth-century urban life and industrialization. He also continues his interest in madness through his depiction of Jackson, who has been driven to insanity and ultimately to death through his experiences with "inhumanity, poverty, and evil" (Dryden, *Thematics* 66). As Redburn observes, "there seemed to be more woe than wickedness about the man; and his wickedness seemed to spring from his woe; and for all his hideousness, there was that in his eye at times, that was ineffably pitiable and touching" (118).

WHITE-JACKET (1850)

Many readers consider *White-Jacket* a fitting conclusion to the narrative that Melville began in *Redburn*. Inspired by Melville's own service aboard a man-of-war, *White-Jacket* was for many years accepted as straight autobiography, in part because of the misleading "Note" that he appended to the first American edition: "In the year 1843 I shipped as 'ordinary seaman' on board of a United States frigate, then lying in a harbor of the Pacific Ocean…. My man-of-war experiences and observations are incorporated in the present volume" (*White-Jacket* 343). Although it has been substantiated now that Melville fictionalized his own experiences and supplemented them with other source material, *White-Jacket* nonetheless lacks the complexities of plot and character development that distinguish most novels. As his subtitle announces, Melville's focus instead is on documenting "The World in a Man-of-War." Because of its hybrid nature, *White-Jacket* anticipates the form of *Moby-Dick* by combining elements of autobiography, fiction, exposition, and propaganda.

Point of View

White Jacket, the first-person retrospective narrator of the book, is named for the makeshift garment that he fashions for himself when no regulation jacket is available. Although he is older than his predecessor Redburn and lacks his foolish naiveté, his perspective is still that of an unsophisticated young man who is isolated from society with others by his class consciousness. The point of view is more consistent in *White-Jacket* than in the book that preceded it, but because White Jacket is not as fully developed for the reader as Redburn was, he seems more like an aloof voice than an alienated or lost individual. Until the end of the book, the narrator is so identified with his jacket, that he is only minimally humanized for the reader. Although he does show emotional and mental qualities, "he is not so much an individual personally involved in various incidents and situations on the *Neversink* as he is an observer" (McCarthy, "Symbolic" 312). This distinction between character and narrator is by now common in Melville. White Jacket, however, lacks the story-telling ability that characterizes most of Melville's narrators; he "is also more critic than philosopher" (McCarthy, "Symbolic" 312).

Setting and Plot

White-Jacket opens at Callao, on the coast of Peru, with the narrator's retrospective description of the "strange-looking coat" he improvised to protect himself from the winter storms that his ship, the *Neversink*, would encounter in rounding Cape Horn on its return to the United States (*White-Jacket* 351). As all hands are called on deck to raise the anchor, White Jacket loosens the main-royal from his perch high aloft the ship. White Jacket provides the reader with a detailed description of the crew's divisions and hierarchy, recalling how difficult it originally was for him to learn the shipboard routine and his responsibilities. The narrator then describes his few friends on board and especially the noble Jack Chase, the first captain of the maintop. On its return to home port, the crew suffers from a shortage of supplies, leaky life buoys, dangerous maneuvers in stormy weather, and the needless cruelty of some of the officers in asserting their authority over the men below them in rank. Because there is no grog for the men, Captain Claret permits the staging of a Fourth of July theatrical, starring Jack Chase as Percy Royal-Mast. A storm causes the presentation to be cut short, however, and the crew is soon at odds with each other again. All hands are called on deck to witness the flogging of four seamen for fighting, and the inhumane cruelty of this practice is discussed at length.

Finally the *Neversink* enters balmy seas and arrives at Rio de Janeiro. While the ship is in harbor, Bland, the sergeant-at-arms, smuggles liquor onboard and sells it to the crew at outrageous prices and then flogs them when the sailors are caught inebriated by the officers. Eventually the captain learns of Bland's scheme and temporarily demotes him; however, because he behaves courageously, he is not harmed by the crew and is eventually reinstated as sergeant-at-arms. Various other incidents are recounted, including an account of Dr. Cadwallader Cuticle, the surgeon of the *Neversink*, who amputates a seaman's leg after he is shot while trying to swim ashore when he is denied liberty. The surgery, although successful from the perspective of Cuticle, who enjoys showing off his surgical skills, results in the death of the seaman. After the ship leaves Rio, Captain Claret accuses White Jacket of being absent from his assigned post, arraigns him at the masthead, and is about to order him flogged, when Jack Chase and Corporal Colbrook successfully defend him from this fate. A lengthy critique of the Articles of War follows this incident. When the ship nears home, the captain orders all beards shaved off, which results in a near mutiny, as well as the flogging of the captain of the forecastle, who successfully resists the order. As the *Neversink* approaches the coast of Virginia, White Jacket falls into the sea when he is ordered aloft at midnight; however, he manages to save himself from drowning by cutting himself out of his oppressive jacket, which he has been unable to rid himself of or replace throughout the voyage. He kisses Jack Chase's hand at Norfolk, and the crew soon disburses ashore.

Characters

Because "Melville reserves his most vivid personifications for [the] inanimate features" of the ship and the jacket, most of the "characters appear and disappear according to their use in clarifying the dynamics of shipboard life" (Otter 52). "*White-Jacket* has neither a strong central hero around whom a continuous and developing action is built, nor consequently any similar sort of villain. It has, rather, a set of people known from a voyage, not from a plot" (Vincent, *Tailoring* 33). The narrator and Jack Chase are the most fully developed characters in *White-Jacket*, but even they lack roundness. In describing Chase, the narrator presents an idealized portrait of the Handsome Sailor of tradition, without providing insight into the man's thoughts and feelings. As a result, Chase lacks the depths and conflicts of a fully human figure and instead comes across as a one-dimensional hero and role model, not unlike the character he plays in the shipboard theatrical.

Symbols

Whereas *Redburn* examines "the spiritual and imaginative growth of a single man, … *White-Jacket* shows the scope of Melville's study immeasurably widened." He is here primarily interested in "The World in a Man-of-War," rather than in the narrator-sailor. As a result, the ship serves as the central symbol in *White-Jacket*. In his descriptions of both the ship and its crew, Melville depicts a highly organized and rigidly structured society that is efficient, rational, and brutally inhumane. Although the *Neversink* exists in the realm of sea, not land, Melville draws analogies between the two realms so that his portrait of the ship becomes a critique of antebellum American society. In particular, Melville uses the repeated motif or image of flogging to force his mid-nineteenth-century readers to draw an analogy between sailors and slaves (Otter 55–58).

The other key symbol in *White-Jacket* is the garment the narrator makes for himself and introduces to the reader in the first chapter. The ambiguities inherent in the jacket are obvious from the beginning. Because he devised the jacket to protect himself from inclement weather, it can be deemed a "life jacket." From the beginning, however, the narrator also identifies the jacket with death. Anticipating the emphasis on the color white in *Moby-Dick*, the narrator calls the jacket "white as a shroud" (351). The jacket separates the narrator from the rest of the crew, and it increasingly becomes a burden to its wearer. The "jacket also has a more corporeal dimension. It is padded, porous," and again it is white. "The jacket is skin" (Otter 87). Although originally meant to protect the narrator, this skin becomes degraded because of its association with slavery through flogging. Ultimately, White Jacket cuts himself free of this skin and is miraculously reborn. However, "White Jacket's removal of his skin is a procedure, like the surgeon of the fleet's, directed at the cuticle and not at the quick. It offers a fantasy cure for the social and somatic diagnoses of *White-Jacket*," and the final chapter "suggests that the narrator's corporeal escape is illusory" (Otter 95–96). As White Jacket observes, "There are no mysteries out of ourselves" (768).

Themes

To illustrate the general theme of evil and injustice in *White-Jacket*, Melville emphasizes the disjunction between the ideal and the actual, between appearance and reality. This theme surfaces most obviously in the satiric description of Cuticle and his operation, where the procedure is a success but the patient dies; however, it also exists throughout the book as abuses of authority and human frailties undermine the carefully structured and regulated naval setting. "The *Neversink* would be ideal without flogging, without stealing, without injustice. But there are flogging, stealing and injustice; role and position are seldom congruent as men are determined by their positions. The ideal cannot be ignored; it forms the basis for the actual: but the two cannot be reconciled by

White Jacket" (Albrecht 19–20). In such a world, only those of superior strength—men like Bland and Chase—can succeed "without such defensive protection as a white jacket. They are the exceptions that White Jacket wants to emulate: to be free and to be a member of the community" (Albrecht 20).

The narrator, however, does not seek to be one of the common "mob"; he holds himself aloft—both literally and figuratively—seeking to be a citizen of the maintop and to pattern himself after the example of Chase, the "gentleman," whom he describes as "better than a hundred common mortals" (361). Chase himself points out and fosters this duality of attitude toward humanity by exclaiming, "'The public and the people! Ay, ay, my lads, let us hate the one and cleave to the other'" (549). As one critic claims, "he is the ideal uncommon man" (Reynolds 16). Thus, through their class consciousness, even Chase and White Jacket demonstrate the difference between the appearance of democratic sentiments and the reality of elitist, aristocratic superiority. Although some see such elitist elements as mere pretensions that are undermined in the narrative's conclusion, such a reading seems too simplistic. White Jacket does experience a symbolic fall from his lofty perch and manage to rid himself of his burdensome jacket, which some view as proof of his new democratic fellowship with all. The reality is, however, that White Jacket's attitude remains unchanged. Since the arrival of the *Neversink* into port marks the end of the narrator's service in the Navy, "White Jacket is initiated not into the man-of-war society but *out* of it" (Seelye 46). Thus, considered in full, "*White-Jacket* reflects the divided nature of its creator.... White Jacket, like Melville, is both a democratic idealist at times and an antidemocratic realist at others" (Reynolds 27). Although the tendency in Melville scholarship is to stress the democratic aspects of his art, this tension in his writings can be traced back to *Typee*, and it will continue through *Billy Budd*.

Historical Context

Although Melville ostensibly sought to influence public opinion and Congress with *White-Jacket*, some have suggested he was consciously playing it safe with his audience by waiting to write and publish his expose until such abuses as it condemns had been thoroughly aired and public sentiment, as well as a corrective course of action, largely had been determined. "*White-Jacket* was published less [than] a year before the Congressional vote to prohibit flogging in the American navy, following two years of legislative debate on the issue and more than a decade of public agitation on the part of seamen and naval reformers" (Otter 78). In *White-Jacket*,

Melville notably was also careful to balance the pious, Christian rhetoric of his narrator's "defense of natural rights with descriptions of the disorder resulting from too much liberty, . . . inviting readers to consider the slim line separating abstract egalitarianism from social chaos" (Duban 76). Through this strategy, he avoided causing unnecessary offense to either side of the debate, but he also arguably displayed his own divided sensibilities.

4

"The Great Art of Telling the Truth" in *Moby-Dick*

Fortified by the confidence and experience gained from writing his first five books and inspired by his subsequent introduction to Nathaniel Hawthorne in the summer of 1850, Melville revealed his own literary aspirations in the essay "Hawthorne and His Mosses" (1850), which he ostensibly wrote to praise his new friend's artistry. With *Moby-Dick* (1851), he arguably achieved his objectives by mastering "the great Art of Telling the Truth" ("Hawthorne and His Mosses" 1160). Taking up again the experimental and metaphysical ambitions of *Mardi* (1849), *Moby-Dick* "prob[es] at the very axis of reality" to present a tragic vision of "the sane madness of vital truth," a vision that, although steeped in the tradition of Shakespeare, is peculiarly American in both design and sensibility ("Hawthorne and His Mosses" 1159, 1160).

Moby-Dick, like the five books that preceded it, defies genre classification. Within the book, Melville incorporates short story, drama, travelogue, romance, quest, adventure, sermon, tall tale, folklore, and myth, as well as economic, historical, and other expository information about the American industry of whaling and biological data about the cellular structure or cetology of whales. By moving "from form to form, never remaining long within a single genre," he creates a final shape "that encompasses forms, a 'symphony' or 'marriage' that brings together all opposites" (Martin, *Hero* 67). Further, these "[c]hanges in narrative form exemplify the philosophy of a necessary multiplicity of perspective" that is consistent with Melville's thematic purposes. In *Moby-Dick*, "comprehension and insight occur through considering existence 'in every light,' seeking truth through empirical, metaphysical, theological, and economic approaches" (Post-Lauria 117, 113–14). Through this complementary process of mixing genres and perspectives, Melville creates what many describe as the first American epic. Although it is not a narrative poem, *Moby-Dick* nevertheless accomplishes the work of epic by conveying a heroic story that incorporates myth, legend, and history to reflect the past accomplishments and future aspirations of a people or a nation.

Taking as its ostensible subject the recounting of a whaling voyage in which the pursuit of a white whale results in the death of all of the ship's crew except the narrator, *Moby-Dick* ultimately concerns itself not only with key issues at stake in mid-nineteenth-century America but with questions that modern readers still have about American life and the nature of reality itself. Considered for what it has to say about American culture, the book examines and critiques the American Dream and the sometimes interrelated elements of democracy, expansionism, industrial capitalism, Christianity, and slavery. Considered in more universal terms, however, *Moby-Dick* can also be interpreted as an inquiry into good and evil, power and authority, alienation and friendship, the limits of human knowledge, fate, and the relationship between the individual and nature.

POINT OF VIEW

With the directive, "Call me Ishmael," *Moby-Dick*'s first-person narrator introduces himself, drawing the reader into his story. In what by this point has become a commonplace practice for him, Melville obscures Ishmael's real name and background. Like Tommo, Omoo, Taji, Redburn, and White Jacket before him, Ishmael narrates a past adventure at sea that he undertook as a result of his dissatisfaction with life in conventional society. Ishmael has other qualities that recall previous Melville narrators. Open-minded and capable of personal growth and development, he is essentially a loner. Sometimes—especially during the first 21 chapters of the novel—the narrative voice reflects the experiencing character, the younger Ishmael; at other times, it reflects the retrospective storyteller, the older Ishmael. One of the most distinctive features of Ishmael's voice is its range of narrative tone. Ishmael moves from brooding meditation to bawdy humor, from scholarly authority to comical parody, from suicidal despair to jolly buffoonery. This range of emotional tone both mirrors and supports the breadth of his experiences and observations at sea and the dichotomous nature of land and sea, life and death, appearance and reality that he seeks to comprehend and communicate.

The journey to self-knowledge that Ishmael travels as a result of his decision to go to sea forms one strand of the novel, but his narrative also charts the journeys of other characters, virtually all of whom are more central to the external action than he is. He narrates his tale in a rambling fashion that is characterized by much digression. At times, especially during the middle section of the narrative, he disappears entirely from view, seemingly leaving the characters to speak for themselves, sometimes in dramatic monologues that reveal events and insights of which Ishmael could have had no knowledge. As a result, many critics have faulted Melville's handling of the novel's point of view as carelessly inconsistent. Others, however, argue convincingly that Melville intentionally "breaks the linear flow of the first-person narrative to open the text to different voices" for much the same reason that he incorporates multiple genres (Fredricks 43). This practice deepens and enriches the symbolic life portrait that *Moby-Dick* creates.

SETTING, PLOT, AND STRUCTURE

Moby-Dick begins in New Bedford and Nantucket Island, Massachusetts, which were then the centers of the American whaling industry. From there, the novel's setting shifts to the *Pequod*, a whaling ship under the command of Captain Ahab that Ishmael joins to travel the Atlantic and Pacific Oceans. Significantly, the novel charts a circular journey that ultimately returns Ishmael, the narrator, to his point of departure to reflect on what he has learned.

Although early critics were dismayed by *Moby-Dick*'s jumble of genres and seeming lack of organizational structure, the novel rather is patterned after the nineteenth-century romantic belief that organic unity results when form responds to and flows out of content. It is just this sensibility that Ishmael upholds when he declares that "[t]here are some enterprises," such as his own narration, "in which a careful disorderliness is the true method" (*Moby-Dick* 1180). Despite its formal discontinuities, *Moby-Dick* can be divided into three main narrative sections. Throughout these three sections, Melville charts two central stories: Ishmael's internal, lyric meditation and Ahab's external, tragic drama. In alternating between these two stories, Melville contrasts "Ishmael's quest to represent the whale and Ahab's quest to destroy it" (Fredricks 30). In the end, the whale eludes both representation and destruction.

The prevoyage section of the novel (Chapters 1–21) centers on Ishmael and the friendship that develops between him and Queequeg, a Polynesian harpooner, when they are forced to share a bed because the whalers' inn is full. They both secure berths on the *Pequod*, negotiating their salary with the ship's surly Quaker owners, who explain that the mysteriously missing Captain Ahab is still recovering from losing one of his legs in a battle with a whale during his last voyage. As they prepare to board the ship, Ishmael and Queequeg meet a wild, haggard man who calls himself "Elijah" and who warns them against sailing on the *Pequod* with Ahab. Dismissing this prophetic warning, they set sail with the *Pequod* on Christmas Day.

In the middle section of the novel (Chapters 22–105) the reader's attention moves from Ishmael and Queequeg to the *Pequod* and its crew, which is made up of men of various races and nationalities. Although the ship's captain remains below deck in his cabin, Ishmael carefully explains the hierarchy that governs the ship's operations and introduces the crew to the reader in rank order, beginning with Starbuck, the first mate, and ending with Pip, the cabin boy. When Captain Ahab finally appears on deck in Chapter 28, his commanding presence establishes him as the focus of most of the subsequent narrative action. Nailing a gold doubloon to the mast, he declares that it will be awarded to the first man who sights Moby Dick, the white whale that caused the loss of his leg. Through his persuasive and passionate rhetoric, Ahab moves the crew to join him in what becomes a single-minded, ceaseless, and vengeful search for Moby Dick. During the search, the *Pequod* meets various ships, whose men tell stories about the White Whale, and Ishmael also repeatedly breaks the narrative action to digress about whales and the whaling industry. In these interwoven expository chapters, which form what is called the cetological center of the novel, Ishmael explains the process of hunting and killing a whale and processing it for oil, and he describes whales from a variety of perspectives—mythological, historical, literary, scientific, and physical.

The final section of the novel (Chapters 106–135) recounts the sighting and three-day chase for Moby Dick. Ahab himself sights the whale on the first day and is almost killed when it sinks his whaling boat. During the second day of the chase, Moby Dick breaks Ahab's ivory leg, and Starbuck urges him to suspend his mad pursuit of the whale, arguing that it would be "'[i]mpiety and blasphemy to hunt him more'" (*Moby-Dick* 1394). Although oddly moved by his first mate's counsel, which he has previously rejected out of hand, Ahab nevertheless refuses to suspend the hunt, explaining, "'Ahab is for ever Ahab, man. This whole act's immutably decreed'" (1394). The pursuit ends on the third day when the whale drags

Ahab to his death and sinks the ship, killing the entire crew of the *Pequod* except Ishmael, who alone survives to tell the tale.

CHARACTERS

Although controversy still exists as to which of the major characters—Ishmael, Ahab, or the Whale—is most central to *Moby-Dick*, "in the final analysis the book is not the story of any one or even two of its characters. The only feasible way *to* Ahab and at last to the White Whale is *through* Ishmael, Melville's necessary surrogate and the reader's veritable guide, philosopher, and friend; and *all three figures* are equally indispensable to the author, to his book, and to its readers" (Sealts Jr., "Whose Book" 69–70). The experience of individual readers of *Moby-Dick* will ultimately vary depending on their response to these three figures.

By his choice of name, Ishmael aligns himself with his biblical counterpart as an outcast and wanderer. Because this name also translates as "God hears," however, it suggests a sensibility well suited for its bearer's role of observing and perceiving the world and its inhabitants. In the opening chapter, he speaks of his own spiritual malaise and views his decision to become a seaman aboard a whaler as a type of suicide because he considers such men as lost to the world. His tone is often comical, however, and his potential for fellowship with others is established through his relationship with Queequeg. Marked by his language and his research as intelligent and well educated, he reflects that the *Pequod* was his "Yale College and [his] Harvard" (*Moby-Dick* 912). Ishmael's openness to change and personal growth is also suggested by his evolving attitude toward the "savage" Queequeg, of whom he is terrified initially but quickly grows to appreciate and love for his compassion, generosity, loyalty, courage, and wisdom. The relationship that develops between Ishmael and Queequeg returns Melville again to the subject of male friendship that he first treated in *Typee* (1846) and *Omoo* (1847).

Although drawn also to Ahab and his heroic quest to find the white whale, Ishmael often disengages from his active role in the narrative, giving Ahab center stage for long stretches of time. As a result, Ahab and Ishmael can be seen in juxtaposition to each other. Whereas the storytelling Ishmael is essentially an "everyman" with qualities that connect him to his readers, the older and more powerfully commanding Ahab is a majestic figure who is first described by one of the owners of the *Pequod* as "a grand, ungodly, god-like man" (878). When he enters the action of the narrative, he is first described from the exterior. "He looked," Ishmael recollects, "like a man cut away from the stake," and in his countenance,

Ishmael observes "an infinity of firmest fortitude, a determinate, unsurren-derable willfulness" (924, 925). Gradually, the reader also comes to know something of Ahab's inner torment through the dramatic soliloquies—or speeches to himself—in which he reflects, for instance, on why "'smoking no longer soothes'" him (930). At other times, such as in Chapter 41 ("Moby Dick") and Chapter 44 ("The Chart"), an omniscient—or all-knowing—third-person perspective also supplements Ishmael's own narrative to deepen the psychological portrait of Ahab as a tragic hero whose inflexibility and willful pride—or hubris—bring his downfall. Ahab, who describes himself as "madness maddened," is destroyed by monoma-niac conceptions of self and power (*Moby-Dick* 971). Through his dramatic depiction of Ahab, Melville thus returns to the subject of insanity in the form of monomania that he first probed in *Mardi* and *Redburn* (1849), cre-ating "a credible sense of the ineluctable mysteries and complexities of the deeply troubled mind" (McCarthy, "*Twisted Mind*" 73). In the process, he contrasts Ahab's delusions with Ishmael's lucidity.

In particular, this contrast between Ishmael and Ahab surfaces in their views of the white whale. Ishmael views the whale in its relation-ship to other whales, studying them from multiple perspectives in an effort to abstract their true nature, the mysterious, sublime essence that lies behind their physical aspects. "The fixed definitions of his whales are balanced by an open-ended fluidity: '... I now leave my cetological System standing thus unfinished,'" he writes in Chapter 32 (Hartstein 37). Conversely, Ahab sees Moby Dick as fixed and entirely evil. In first questioning Ahab's motives for seeking vengeance on the white whale, Starbuck observes, "'To be enraged with a dumb thing, Captain Ahab, seems blasphemous.'" In response, Ahab curses Moby Dick by exclaim-ing, "'He tasks me; he heaps me; I see in him outrageous strength, with an inscrutable malice sinewing it. That inscrutable thing is chiefly what I hate; and be the white whale agent, or be the white whale principal, I will wreck that hate upon him. Talk not to me of blasphemy, man; I'd strike the sun if it insulted me'" (*Moby-Dick* 967). Outraged by what he considers the injustice and implacable mystery of reality, he seeks through the force of his will to "'strike through the mask'" and destroy the evil behind it (967). Whereas Ahab sees the whale only as a symbol, however, Ishmael comes to see it as a vital force in the universe. Signifi-cantly, Moby Dick can be viewed by the other characters and the reader only from the outside. No one has access to his thoughts or feelings. He exists, in the end, as an impersonal force that cannot be represented or defeated.

ROLE OF MINOR CHARACTERS

To support his narrative and thematic purposes, Melville populates *Moby-Dick* with many colorful secondary characters. One vivid example who appears only briefly, but who sets the tone for much of what follows, is Father Mapple, who preaches a sermon at the Whaleman's Chapel that Ishmael and Queequeg attend before leaving New Bedford. Mapple, who was a harpooner in his youth, refers to the members of his congregation as his "shipmates" and peppers his sermon with sea imagery. Taking as his text the story of Jonah and the whale, Mapple foreshadows Ahab's struggle with Moby Dick. The message that Mapple relays "arises directly from that orthodox piety which liberals considered an insult to human dignity" in Melville's time (Herbert, *Calvinism* 109). According to this view, as formulated by John Calvin, worldly suffering is justified because all humans are depraved as a result of the original sin that resulted in Adam and Eve's expulsion from the Garden of Eden. Redemption, thus, can be achieved only by God's grace and requires submission to God's wrath. The lesson that Mapple preaches—and that Ahab struggles against—is that "'if we obey God, we must disobey ourselves; and it is in this disobeying ourselves, wherein the hardness of obeying God consists'" (*Moby-Dick* 838). Melville, however, contrasts Mapple's orthodox Calvinism and the example of Jonah not only with the conflicted figure of Ahab but also with the noble example of the much-beloved sailor Bulkington, who dies in a heroic battle with the forces of nature at the helm of the *Pequod* when a storm strikes the ship as it leaves shore. "Against the background of Father Mapple's sermon, Bulkington's struggle is thrown into relief as an effort to maintain his masculine self-sufficiency in the face of a God who raises storms in order to humiliate his creatures" (Herbert, *Calvinism* 115). Ishmael memorializes Bulkington in a "six-inch chapter," for his strength, courage and equanimity in facing his fate (*Moby-Dick* 906).

Onboard the *Pequod*, the crew is led by the three mates, all of whom are rational men who function from a materialistic perspective as operatives of the whaling industry. Providing philosophical contrasts with Ahab, the three range beneath him along a spectrum of intellectual and spiritual capabilities. Starbuck, the first mate, is an eminently reasonable and prudent man who relies on his Christian faith for guidance. Whaling, for Starbuck, is purely a business that he approaches in terms of dollars and cents. As he tells Ahab, "'I came here to hunt whales, not my commander's vengeance. How many barrels will thy vengeance yield thee even if thou gettest it, Captain Ahab? It will not fetch thee much in our Nantucket market'" (*Moby-Dick* 966). Although Starbuck is the only one openly to oppose

Ahab, the first mate ultimately fails to take any action to stop the captain when he becomes convinced that Ahab has crossed the line from sanity to madness. As a result, Starbuck proves himself to be morally weak and totally lacking Ahab's powerful spirit and strength of character. Stubb, the jovial second mate, is "an easy-going, unfearing man" who presides over his whale boat "as if the most deadly encounter were but a dinner, and his crew all invited guests" (*Moby-Dick* 918). Cool in moments of crisis, his principal function in the novel is to provide comic relief, as when he urges Fleece the cook to preach to the sharks in Chapter 64 ("Stubb's Supper"). Although he is not as speculative as Starbuck, he still has "some capacity to be moved by what is outside of himself," and since he has the ability to dream—as he demonstrates in Chapter 31 ("Queen Mab")—"he can in his way respond imaginatively to events. He is also responsive enough to admire Ahab," who in turns sees his second mate as brave but merely mechanical in nature (McSweeney 85). Demonstrating his fatalistic and sensual nature, Stubb dies yearning for the body of a young woman. Falling at the end of the spectrum, the third mate Flask demonstrates no reflective, intellectual, or spiritual powers. Even in his own death, he finds only monetary significance as he ponders the "few coppers" that his mother will receive as a result of the voyage being cut short (*Moby-Dick* 1405).

Of the four harpooners, Queequeg and Fedallah in particular offer comparative qualities. Queequeg, who projects natural innocence and goodness "presents less the primitivistic escape from the confining limits of cultural existence than the freedom of imagination to look on culture with a renewed eye" (Cowan 87). In contrast to the positive human compassion and spirituality of Queequeg, who is aligned with Ishmael and renews his faith, the Asian harpooner Fedallah is a shadowy figure who, in his infrequent appearances, functions to reflect and intensify Ahab's darkness of spirit. Reputed to be a Parsee, a member of a religious sect descended from the ancient Persians, Fedallah counsels Ahab by offering ambiguous prophesy that proves true even as it misleads the captain into his death.

Deemed "the most insignificant of the *Pequod*'s crew," and scorned by many of them for his cowardice in the face of danger, Pip is a playful and "tender-hearted" black child originally from Connecticut but identified with Alabama by both Ishmael and Starbuck (*Moby-Dick* 1233). "Pip appears in *Moby-Dick* just as infrequently as Fedallah, but he is a more interesting character and plays a richer and more suggestive role" (McSweeney 79). Unnerved by the "panic-striking business" around him, he twice leaps into the ocean during a whale chase and is the second time left behind, a "lonely castaway" in mid-ocean (*Moby-Dick* 1233, 1236). Rescued by "the merest chance," Pip returns to the deck an "idiot" as a result of seeing

"God's foot upon the treadle of the loom" (1236). However, as Ishmael observes, "man's insanity is heaven's sense, and wandering from all mortal reason, man comes at last to that celestial thought, which, to reason, is absurd and frantic; and weal or woe, feels then uncompromised, indifferent as his God" (1236–37). Pip, thus, from this point conveys the mysterious wonder and wisdom of "heaven's sense" in his observations of the world around him. Reflecting on all the different responses of the crew to the doubloon that Ahab nails to the mast, Pip comments, "'I look, you look, he looks; we look, ye look, they look'" (1258). With these words, he acknowledges the multiple perspectives possible in observing any material object, but also the fact that "looking" at an object does not mean the same thing as "seeing" or "perceiving" its true reality. Pip forms a particularly close bond with Ahab, becoming his almost constant companion during the final leg of the voyage before Moby Dick is sighted. Through Ahab's interactions with Pip and Starbuck, Melville reveals the human possibilities that still lurk within the captain's soul. In separating himself from them, Ahab cuts his last connections with humanity, ensuring his fate.

ALLEGORY AND SYMBOLISM

On the surface, *Moby-Dick* is just an adventure story about a whale. Because it presents abstract ideas about good and evil and the nature of reality through representational forms such as the whale, however, it is also an allegory. Further, Melville complicates these representational forms to create complex symbols that defy simplistic explanation. In *Moby-Dick*, the allegorical and symbolic elements work together to represent "the complex relation between two dimensions of existence," the temporal and the timeless. The novel essentially "presents a drama of exile—from being, from tradition, and from community" (Cowan 6). On the level of allegory, Melville presents the two realms of heaven and earth on separate levels, whereas his use of symbolism serves to interblend them. From this perspective, "[h]istory is composed of fragments, but in the allegory of history nothing remains that is not finally gathered into the [symbolic] weaving of the text" (Cowan 181). In weaving together his allegorical text, the major symbols that Melville develops are the white whale, the ocean, the *Pequod*, and Queequeg's coffin.

Moby Dick, the great white whale, is an open-ended symbol that represents "the central mystery of this mystery-wrapped world" (Grenberg 106). Like the doubloon, the whale is seen differently by different characters. For Ahab, Moby Dick is wholly evil; for Starbuck, he is merely a "dumb brute" that struck Ahab from instinct (*Moby-Dick* 967); for Stubb, he is a commodity to hunt, process, and exploit for profit and physical nourishment. Ishmael ponders these definitions and many others. In "The Whiteness of the Whale" (Chapter 42), he contemplates both the physical and supernatural qualities of the white whale's hue, asking finally, "Is it that by its indefiniteness it shadows forth the heartless voids and immensities of the universe...? Or is it, that as in essence whiteness is not so much a color as the visible absence of color, and at the same time the concrete of all colors; is it for these reasons that there is such a dumb blankness, full of meaning...?" (1001). In the end, the whale remains an enigma that eludes definition. The majority of the whale will always remain hidden beneath the ocean and, thus, evade human perception.

The ocean in *Moby-Dick*, the source of both life and death, is a place of transition between these two states. After Pip jumps into the ocean and is saved only by chance, he behaves as if he had "drowned the infinite of his soul" (*Moby-Dick* 1236). Melville explores this idea also in his presentation of Ishmael's suicidal despair as the motivation for his taking to sea, as well as in his depiction of the other sailors on the *Pequod*, many of whom escape to the sea because they are lost to the trappings of "civilized" life on land.

Traveling across this domain of life and death, the *Pequod* can be seen from one perspective as a living community—a nation or world of its own and a microcosm of capitalistic enterprise; however, its physical appearance and eventual doom suggest not only the approaching demise of the whaling industry but also broader implications about the possibility of fulfilling the dreams on which the "New World" of American democracy had been founded. In addition to these historical, cultural, and political implications, the *Pequod* from a universal perspective points again to the same dimensions of existence that the ocean represents. In his first inspection of the *Pequod*, Ishmael describes it as a "most noble craft, but somehow a most melancholy!" (*Moby-Dick* 868). Dark and weathered, the ship is a "cannibal of a craft," decorated in the "chased bones" and teeth of "her hereditary foe," the whale. In deciding that the *Pequod* is "the very ship" for himself and his companion, Ishmael recognizes it as embodying the same dualities represented by the despairing Ishmael and the uplifting Queequeg (867).

Through the symbol of Queequeg's coffin, which also represents both life and death, Melville enriches and complicates his depiction of the relationship between the two dimensions of existence. Queequeg has the carpenter build his coffin when he becomes ill with a fever and anticipates dying. Recovering, however, he keeps it as a sea chest, carving it with the tattoos on his body, which in accordance with the beliefs of his land represent "a complete theory of the heavens and the earth, and a mystical treatise of the art of attaining truth" (*Moby-Dick* 1307). Through the repeated image of the coffin, *Moby-Dick* forms a complete circle. "[I]n the beginning of the book Ishmael confesses that he sets out to sea to pacify his impulse to stop in front of the coffin warehouse. And ironically, at the end of the book, it is a coffin that rescues him and brings him back to the land of the living" (Chang Young-hee 952). Queequeg's coffin becomes the buoy that saves Ishmael from drowning, ensuring that he will remain in the temporal world to pass on the knowledge he has gained about the nature of truth.

THEMES

As Ishmael advises the reader, "To produce a mighty book, you must choose a mighty theme. No great and enduring volume can ever be written on the flea, though many there be who have tried it" (*Moby-Dick* 1280). Melville takes no less than the nature of reality as the central theme of his mighty book. The events that take place on the *Pequod* "present man at odds with nature and determined by the gods but not in touch with them" (Cowan 163). Although Ishmael survives, he is again alone among men— an orphan and an outcast—which seems to compromise any reading of his rescue as representing "salvation." Ishmael, however, has learned "that community exists most permanently in remembrance. It has no charter for establishment on earth and can only be re-created by those who recall it and reclaim it out of the past, seeing those saving moments in the past as models and as promises" (Cowan 180). Thus, as a result of his reading of the past, he is able—through his storytelling—to give witness to things that he swears are truth. In presenting the truth he has learned about the nature of reality, Ishmael touches on many issues: the individual versus nature, the limits of human knowledge, good and evil, and fate.

The themes of the individual versus nature and the limits of human knowledge are played out in Ahab's pursuit of Moby Dick. Through this struggle, which Ahab inevitably loses, Melville explores the attributes of natural forces. "The whale that Ahab would destroy Ishmael would understand, yet these impulses are not contradictory, but complementary. Although Ahab can and does act against Moby Dick, he 'comprehends' neither his adversary nor himself" and instead destroys himself by seeking to "'strike through the mask,'" the "wall" that suggests the boundaries of human knowledge (Grenberg 110; *Moby-Dick* 967). Ahab is destroyed by his failure to accept human limitations, but Ishmael comes to a serene acceptance of these same limits.

Moby-Dick teaches that the world is a complex web of good and evil because of the limitations of human knowledge and the abuses that can result from free will. As a result, people are often alienated from each other and from a sense of any divine guidance in the world. Human fate at such times seems directed by a force that, like the whale, appears wholly indifferent or even satanic. The world Ishmael returns to after his voyage remains unchanged. "It can still be wolfish, mysterious, and primarily dark. But he has learned to see beyond his own horizon, and thus experience the world in a wider perspective. The solid demarcation between oppositions in the world has dissolved, enabling Ishmael to have the vision of 'one seamless whole'" (Chang Young-hee 952). Unable to determine the reason why he lived while others perished, Ishmael gains no final answers or proof of God's existence or nature. Like Melville, however, he becomes a diver for truth who, through his writing, continues to explore the multiple faces of reality. What Hawthorne wrote about Melville applies equally to Ishmael: "He can neither believe, nor be comfortable in his unbelief; and he is too honest and courageous not to try to do one or the other. If he were a religious man, he would be one of the most truly religious and reverential; he has a very high and noble nature, and better worth immortality than most of us" (433).

HISTORICAL CONTEXT

During the first half of the nineteenth century, "the Christian community in America was the scene of a proliferating debate" (Herbert, *Calvinism* 5). At the conservative end of a growing spectrum of views, the Calvinists interpreted the relation between God and humans from an orthodox and fundamentally Old Testament perspective that stressed humanity's innate depravity and the resulting inevitability of human suffering on earth. On the other end of the debate were the Unitarians, who interpreted this same relationship from a New Testament orientation that emphasized human dignity and possibility as inherent and inviolable gifts from God. In his religious upbringing, Melville was exposed to both of these versions of Christian doctrine. "His saturation in these hostile traditions occurred under conditions that made it impossible for him to accept either, and gave him instead a deeply rooted preoccupation with the problems posed by their incompatible interpretations of existence." In many ways, his personal "quest for a Truth that would harmonize the conflicts within himself was equally an effort to come to terms with his cultural heritage" (Herbert, *Calvinism* 6, 88). Similarly, his own experience reflects the cultural upheaval that was occurring during this period as America moved forward toward religious pluralism and a more secular orientation. In *Moby-Dick*, he takes up this religious crisis and reframes it through his depiction of Ishmael's spiritual voyage and meditation on how humans are to conceive of themselves and the world.

ALTERNATE READING: POSTCOLONIAL CRITICISM

Postcolonialism, "an elusive and contested term…designates at one and the same time a chronological moment, a political movement, and an intellectual activity, and it is this multiple status that makes exact definition difficult" (Moore-Gilbert, Stanton, and Maley 1). The overriding objective of postcolonial studies is to rewrite history to correct its erasure of non-Western or "Other" voices and its erroneous representation of non-Western peoples. To accomplish this goal, the intellectual activity of postcolonialism, which is principally cultural and literary in focus, studies all types of texts to discern their theoretical relation to imperialism or nation-building. As a strategy of reading, postcolonialism specifically seeks to point out what was missing in previous readings of race, class, and nation as markers of difference that facilitate and undergird repression. The focus of such a rereading and rewriting of literary history typically emphasizes the political and ideological rather than the aesthetic. Although the posture of postcolonial studies is often described as global, the intent is not to eradicate difference between and among cultures but rather to locate and celebrate it in its actual fullness and to recognize not only the wrongs of the past but the need for continuing social change. The "post" in postcolonialism frequently is misconstrued as implying an end or renunciation of colonization; however, decolonization is a slow and uneven process that continues to the present day.

Although antecedents exist in both the classical and enlightenment eras, much postcolonial criticism addresses the nineteenth century, which is often termed the age of Euro-American imperialism. As a writer of this time period, Melville was in some ways unusually sensitive to the atrocities committed by both America and Europe in their colonizing enterprises, as both *Typee* and *Omoo*, in particular, bear witness. In other ways, however, he was—as these books also reveal—unconsciously immured in the imperialist perspective of his own cultural environment. Melville composed *Moby-Dick* when tensions were mounting in America about both slavery and industrialization and when the country was in a mode of rapid expansionism. In particular, the novel can be read from a postcolonial context to reveal his conscious and unconscious perspectives on race and the racial implications that facilitated American industrialization and continental expansion.

When writing from a self-conscious perspective, Melville recognizes that humanity is not circumscribed by race. In his depiction of Queequeg, his satirical thrust functions to reveal his belief that human dignity should not be awarded on the basis of skin color. His representation of Queequeg's religious rituals, for instance, can be read as an "oblique criticism of Christian worship," and ironically, it is through this idealized character that Ishmael is restored to the world and learns the meaning of Christian brotherhood (Grejda 96). Melville also pointedly indicts his country's internal colonizing and western expansion practices by naming the doomed *Pequod* after a Native American tribe in Massachusetts that did not survive the arrival of the Puritan settlers to New England. The *Pequod*, on its surface, is "a World's Fair of nationality and habit, a deliberate representation of racial accord and divergence" (Mason 138), but in his representation of what D. H. Lawrence calls, "the ship of the white American soul"—"American industry!," Melville acknowledges the unjust practice of creating and using an ethnic and racial underclass to support capitalistic enterprise (160, 151). The captain and his three white mates, who all hail originally from New England, are served in the *Pequod*'s hierarchical structure by harpooners who represent the three races upon which America, "it might be said, had built its prosperity in the early nineteenth century": Native American, African, and Asian (Heimert 501–502).

Nevertheless, Melville unconsciously compromises his intended satire by acquiescing to conventional metaphors and imagery that privilege white over black and that reveal his own ethnic and racial anxieties and biases through a mask of comic patronizing. Melville sometimes uses language and racialized imagery that do not carry ironic tones in linking blackness with primitivism, madness, and evil. For instance, he reverts to the racial stereotype of the carefree and playful "darky" in his depiction of Pip, as when he condescendingly observes that the child has "that pleasant, genial, jolly brightness peculiar to his tribe" (*Moby-Dick* 1233). The novel continually associates Ahab's madness with darkness and blackness. With the exception of Queequeg, Melville equates the nonwhite pagan characters with diabolic and Satanic rituals that he links to Ahab. In "The Try-Works" (Chapter 96), he uses striking Satanic imagery to describe the harpooners. As they tell stories of their "unholy adventures" around the fire, "their uncivilized laughter forked upwards out of them, like the flames from the furnace; … and the sea leaped, and the ship groaned and dived, and yet steadfastly shot her red hell further and further into the blackness of the sea and the night." This passage culminates with the image of the "rushing Pequod," which "freighted with savages, and laden with fire, and burning a corpse, and plunging into the blackness of darkness, seemed the material counterpart of her monomaniac commander's soul" (1246). Passages such as this reveal Melville's unconscious anxieties by reflecting Christianity as their basis and moral foundation at the same time they ostensibly work to question its doctrines.

From a postcolonial perspective, then, *Moby-Dick* is not an uncompromised text; however, it does reveal much about nineteenth-century ideologies and politics in its representation of the hypocrisy of American culture. Although sometimes flawed by its unrecognized complicity with the very falseness it outwardly deplores, it nevertheless represents a noble attempt by Melville to uncover hard truths about his day that still have relevance in ours.

5

The Ambiguities of *Pierre*

With *Pierre*, Melville turns inland from the sea to write a novel that has long perplexed, shocked, and astonished its readers. Far from the "rural bowl of milk" that he promised Nathaniel Hawthorne's wife Sophia, *Pierre* is also not the "regular romance" he described to his British publisher Richard Bentley. Although Melville advised Bentley that his new book was "very much more calculated for popularity than anything you have yet published of mine," he was either disingenuous or deluded in this estimation (*Letters* 146, 150). Alternatively, as some have surmised, Melville may have revised his plan for *Pierre* in the midst of the writing process as he became increasingly disillusioned and embittered by the negative reviews and poor sales of *Moby-Dick*.

Pierre does contain many of the stylistic and narrative elements common in the domestic novel that was immensely popular at the time: artificial and elevated language, class consciousness, familial settings, interest in the emotions, and concern for Christian virtue. However, it also parodies and subverts the literary and social conventions associated with this genre, which traditionally has been associated with women writers and castigated for its sentimentality and social conservatism. In addition, Melville's subtle and complex characterization of his protagonist in *Pierre* anticipates the psychological realism that came into vogue in the late nineteenth century with the novels of Henry James. Written thus at cross-purposes, "*Pierre* has not been well received because it is a novel . . . deeply at odds with itself. As its subtitle ['The Ambiguities'] more than hints at, it is a novel that takes division—conflict, irresolution, ambiguity—as its subject" (Sten 216). *Pierre* almost universally is recognized as a flawed text, but despite the disparity of critical opinions and even outright disdain that the novel has provoked, it is now recognized as one of Melville's most important works, closest to *Moby-Dick* not only in time but also in the ambitiousness of its aims and in the power of at least some of its passages (Higgins and Parker, *Critical Essays* 1). No student of Melville can seriously attempt to understand the author or his works without wrestling with its ambiguities.

POINT OF VIEW

One of the most "far-reaching innovation[s] in *Pierre* is Melville's abandonment of the first-person protagonist-narrator for a third-person voice that is at once omniscient and personal...—sympathetic, yet critical, worldly wise, yet powerless to affect the world he describes" (Grenberg 123). Although disembodied, this voice both dominates and confuses the reader's responses to the novel. Early on, the narrator's comments warn the reader not to take Pierre Glendinning, the protagonist, at face value, and this superior perspective is necessary because Pierre is too naïve to analyze his own experiences or emotions fully. The narrator, however, often seems inconsistent in his knowledge of and attitude toward the protagonist, perhaps in an intentional effort to create ambivalence in tone and perspective. In his earliest description of Pierre, for instance, the narrator "asserts his omniscience, in reproducing Pierre's thoughts, and hints at a lack of omniscience, in his questions" about him: "Why now this impassioned, youthful pause? Why this enkindled cheek and eye?" the narrator asks (Bellis 159; *Pierre* 7). Further, at times the reader is uncertain when the narrative voice is merely replicating Pierre's emotional responses and when he is mocking them. In the end, the instability of the narrator's commentary supports the novel's thematic concern with the vagaries of truth and the impossibility of representing the inner life of a human being. In this conclusion, he mirrors both Pierre's and Melville's frustrated efforts at authorship.

SETTING, PLOT, AND STRUCTURE

To reflect the divided nature of his protagonist and his textual concerns, Melville splits *Pierre* into two sections. The first 13 chapters are set in or near Saddle Meadows, the ancestral country estate of the Glendinning family, which is described as a seemingly idyllic "green and golden world" (7).

This part of the narrative takes place over five days during an unspecified summer in the early nineteenth century. Melville uses this setting as a background for introducing the four major characters and for describing the familial conflict that arises between them and the protagonist's subsequent decision to act. Chapter 14 forms the pivot of the novel, during the course of which the narrative action moves to the tenements of New York City, where the tragic consequences of the protagonist's choice occur. Transpiring over a number of months, the main events in this section of the novel take place in winter.

Melville begins the novel by introducing Pierre, an aristocratic and high-minded young man of 19, and Mary Glendinning, his mother. Mrs. Glendinning rules the family estate in the absence of her husband, who died when Pierre was 12 years old. As the story opens, Pierre is engaged to marry Lucy Tartan, with whom he has grown up in Saddle Meadows and of whom his mother approves as a suitable mate for her son. Shortly before the wedding, however, he meets the dark and mysterious Isabel Banford, who tells him that she is the illegitimate daughter of his father's affair with a beautiful French woman. Despite his shock at Isabel's revelations, Pierre determines to acknowledge and care for Isabel to redress his father's failure to do so. At the same time, however, he seeks to protect both his father's reputation and his mother's exalted memories of her husband. As a result, he decides to pretend to marry Isabel, keeping her true identity a secret. Pierre's mother, however, disowns him when he tells her he has broken his engagement to Lucy and plans instead to marry Isabel, a servant woman of unknown origins. Pierre and Isabel move to New York City, taking with them Delly Ulver, another young woman who has become a social outcast after giving birth to an illegitimate child, now dead. Once they reach New York, Pierre's affluent cousin Glendinning Stanly refuses his previously promised assistance, and they are forced to take lodgings in the Church of the Apostles. Pierre learns that his mother has died from the shock of losing her son and that she has changed her will to leave her inheritance to Glen Stanly. Although Glen courts Lucy, she rejects him and instead comes to New York to join Pierre's unconventional household. Pierre attempts to make a living by writing a novel, but the publisher rejects his manuscript and begins legal proceedings to recover its cash advances to him. Driven to despair by the unraveling of his life, Pierre kills Glen, who has continued to harass him for alienating Lucy's affections. When he is arrested and incarcerated, Isabel and Lucy visit him that night. During this visit, Lucy falls dead from a broken heart, and Pierre and Isabel commit suicide by drinking poison.

As this synopsis reveals, the plot is decidedly melodramatic in its reliance on contrived and sensational situations and acts. In both sections of the novel, "dramatic scenes in which Pierre gains insight are frequently alternated with solitary episodes in which he attempts to understand the insights or related matters" through highly stylized soliloquies (McCarthy, "Twisted Mind" 79–80). For example, as he struggles to decide how to tell his mother about Isabel, he thinks to himself: "My mother!—dearest mother!—God hath given me a sister, and unto thee a daughter, and covered her with the world's extremest infamy and scorn, that so I and thou—*thou*, my mother, mightest gloriously own her, and acknowledge her, and,—Nay, nay, groaned Pierre, never, never, could such syllabus be one instant tolerated by her" (*Pierre* 108). Significantly, although melodrama parodies tragedy, it also provides a forum for exploring "the interests of those traditionally excluded from the center of the tragic stage—the working and servant classes. Melodrama adopts the device of stylized speech to heighten the drama of the lives of the lower classes" (Fredricks 100). Thus, although some argue that Melville merely mocks the popular literary tastes of the day in *Pierre*, others claim that he also uses this conventional form subversively to expose social injustices from the perspective of the oppressed and marginalized.

CHARACTERS

Consistent with much of the melodramatic and sentimental literature of the nineteenth century, the characters in *Pierre* are basically stereotypical in their representation and most often have been interpreted in moral terms. The idealistic and high-minded Pierre is "not only the solitary head of his family, but the only surnamed male Glendinning extant" (*Pierre* 12). Standing on the "noble pedestal" of his family's aristocratic heritage, he carries the name of both his father and grandfather and aspires in his naïve innocence to emulate the example of his dead father, whom he has been raised to believe was nothing short of godlike perfection in human form (17). Throughout the novel, he strives to follow "the true path" of virtue but is continuously confounded in his efforts because he has not been raised to make the kind of moral decisions that are increasingly forced upon him (108).

Absent the influence of a father's embodied presence, Pierre's character and values have been molded by his mother. A beautiful and "haughty widow," Mary Glendinning is "certain of her family's prominence and superiority and her own singular position in the family" (*Pierre* 8; McCarthy, "Twisted Mind" 81). She is continually characterized in terms of her inflexibility and pride, and the trait she most admires in her son is his "sweet docility," which enables her to keep him under her control (*Pierre* 27). Throughout his childhood and youth, Pierre "has been kept within his mother's world of selfish exclusiveness where conventions and what is pleasant to believe are substituted for the truth about life" (William Ellery Sedgwick 139). In his innocence, Pierre fails to realize that his mother stands in the way of his achieving manhood, a state that he can reach only by confronting the realities of life outside the artificial environs of Saddle Meadows. As the narrator explains in giving the background of the Glendinning family, "So perfect to Pierre had long seemed the illuminated scroll of his life so far, that only one hiatus was discoverable by him in that sweetly-writ manuscript. A sister had been omitted from the text" (11). In a misguided attempt to fill this absence in her son's life, Pierre's mother has usurped the role of sister, which has further destabilized their relationship. Perhaps surprisingly, Mrs. Glendinning supports Pierre in his decision to marry Lucy Tartan, but Lucy offers no threat to the mother's influence. Raised in the same environment as Pierre, she too is docile in nature, and Mrs. Glendinning shrewdly surmises that Lucy will never estrange Pierre from her. With Pierre's introduction to the influence of Isabel Banford, however, Mrs. Glendinning's worst fears are realized. Her intense anger, her impulsive and inflexible response to her son's decision, and the "final insanity" that leads to her death suggest not only the extent of her own emotional instability but also the debilitating effects that she has had on her son's psyche and the insupportability of the lifestyle she created for him (*Pierre* 334).

Lucy and Isabel are most often seen in opposition to each other. Some go so far as to align Lucy with the forces of light and goodness and Isabel with the forces of darkness and evil. Such a reading, however, oversimplifies their natures and is inconsistent with Melville's thematic intent. Rather than using *Pierre* to posit merely the duality of life, Melville speculates about the complex uncertainties of life. Accordingly, a more nuanced interpretation of these two characters seems appropriate, one that views the darkly mystifying, impoverished, but hard-working Isabel—a musician—as a marginalized figure of experience and human suffering who "paradoxically represents that which is excluded from representation" (Fredricks 91). Similarly, the sweet, blond, and aristocratic Lucy, who is a painter, can be linked with the world of appearances. Through losing Pierre, Lucy comes to discern the shallowness of the worldview in which she has been raised, but because of her sheltered upbringing, she—like Pierre—is unable to temper her engrained idealism with a more reasoned and realistic view of humanity. Unable to reconcile their conflicting natures and perspectives into a unity of outlook that will sustain them amidst the complex ambiguities of life, all of the major characters are ultimately doomed.

Many critics have pointed to undeniably autobiographical elements in the drawing of these characters. For instance, Melville's father died when Melville was 12 and may have fathered an illegitimate child, his mother was a proud and class-conscious woman, and his literary frustrations are given voice in Pierre's failed attempt to write and publish "a deep book" to expose the problems of existence (*Pierre* 341). Such elements, however, should not mislead readers into viewing *Pierre* as factual in its depiction of its more sensational aspects of family relationships. Melville was writing fiction, not fact.

ROLE OF MINOR CHARACTERS

Several minor characters play important roles in the novel, both in serving as points of comparison to major characters and in supporting Melville's thematic concerns. The first of these characters to be introduced is Reverend Falsgrave, who is described as he sits at the Glendinning breakfast table as "so mild and meek; such an image of white-browed and white-handed, and napkined immaculateness" (*Pierre* 120). Nevertheless, "his Christian faith is pompous, platitudinous, and superficial" (Grenberg 130). When Pierre goes to his house late at night for counsel in his distress, Falsgrave rebukes him, failing the youth not only as his surrogate father but also in his ministerial role as a man of God.

The character of Delly Ulver also functions as a vehicle for Melville's criticism of institutional religion and for his depiction of social oppression. Her tale counterpoints the story of Isabel's life and starkly exposes the hypocrisy of the upright Christian society of Saddle Meadows, which has settled her "wretched affair" by turning their backs on her (*Pierre* 117). Like Pierre in his act to protect Isabel, the only protection that Isabel can offer Delly consists of "isolation, seclusion, and withdrawal from the world" (Stern, *Fine* 187).

Representing the unconscious and negative aspects of human nature, Glendinning Stanly, Pierre's cousin, functions as the novel's villain and perhaps Melville's most stereotypical and melodramatic character. A successful young man of society with worldly experience that Pierre lacks, he serves as a foil to Pierre, enhancing the distinctive characteristics of the hero-protagonist through contrast with his own. Pierre sees magnified in Glen the same false values and destructive attitudes that lie below the surface of Saddle Meadows: selfish greed, pride, passion, and a callous disregard for those marginalized and oppressed by the class structure that protects his own position in society. Through his deadly assault on his cousin, whose name mirrors his own, Pierre makes a last desperate and confused attempt to resolve the ambiguities of his own divided nature.

Charlie Millthorpe, a boyhood friend of Pierre's, appears only in the New York City section of the novel, but the narrator provides details about his earlier relationship with the protagonist. The son of a farmer whose family had worked the Glendinning lands for several generations, Charlie was originally befriended by Pierre because of "[t]he hereditary beauty and youthful bloom of this boy; his sweetness of temper, and something of natural refinement" which "contrasted with the unrelieved rudeness, and oftentimes sordidness, of his neighbors" (*Pierre* 321–22). In Pierre's childhood attitude toward Charlie, an unconscious condescension seems present. As the narrator explains, "even in boyhood, Pierre possessed a sterling charity, which could cheerfully overlook all minor blemishes in his inferiors, whether in fortune or mind" (*Pierre* 322). Through the information that the narrator provides about the Millthorpe family's struggles, Melville bolsters his critique of the economic and social structure that supports the Glendinning estate and that prevents boys like Charlie from achieving their aspirations. Further, when he solicits Charlie's assistance in the city, it is clear that Pierre's old prejudices remain. Charlie's earnest kindness in finding lodgings for Pierre counterpoints Glen's "heartless neglect" (*Pierre* 326). Eventually, Charlie even pays the rent for Pierre, who mutters condescendingly behind his back, "'Plus heart, minus mind'" (*Pierre* 372). Although recognizing the superiority of the heart to the intellect, Pierre nevertheless snubs Charlie for not possessing the keenness of mind that would keep his faculties in balance. Significantly, "Pierre addresses Charlie only once directly in the several times they meet. That one time is after the porter bringing Lucy's belongings is dismissed: 'The porter is gone then?... Well, Mr. Millthorpe, you will have the goodness to follow him'" (Canaday, "*Pierre*" 400). Because of his inability to embrace the well-intentioned Charlie as an equal, Pierre reveals again his own lack of self-awareness and isolates himself further from the human society that might have saved him.

ALLEGORY AND SYMBOLISM

On one level, *Pierre* can be read as a moral allegory that reworks the myth of the Fall of Man in the story of the title character's loss of innocence. Although critics are divided as to whether Melville's intentions were wholly satirical in creating the pattern of imagery that sustains this reading, this design does in some ways serve to unify the novel in spite of the many ambiguities that threaten to dissolve its coherence. Saddle Meadows is consistently, although often ironically, described as a green Eden that exists beyond the limits of time, frozen in a "trance-like aspect" (*Pierre* 7). Meanwhile, Pierre is clearly Adamic in his youthful innocence and naivety, qualities that his fiancée Lucy matches as Eve. Saddle Meadows "is essentially feudal in its life and government, and Pierre, like many of Melville's heroes, is cut off from the world by his feeling of innate superiority.... Thus, as an aristocrat..., Pierre is sole heir to a way of life which cannot long survive in the midst of democratic America, 'a vulgar caldron of an everlasting uncrystalizing [*sic*] Present.'" Although Melville takes care "to qualify this American Eden by undermining its social structure and the heritage with which it protects its heir," Pierre himself is "unfallen, even though his innocence ... is not wholly perfect" (Moorman 18, 19). Isabel's entrance marks the disruption of Eden, but although she is shadowy and mysterious, Melville does not link her directly with evil. "The serpent imagery in *Pierre* clusters about the Fall situation rather than about any single character" (Moorman 21). Isabel's tale incorporates serpent imagery, but Pierre, too, is called "'reptile! reptile! that could sting so sweet a breast'" by Lucy's maid, and Mrs. Glendinning's beauty is also associated with "venom" in the same passage (*Pierre* 236). Melville's intent is that the situation be observed as evil rather than any specific character. In the second half of the novel, the imagery is correspondingly dark and cold, in keeping with the fallen condition of Pierre, who has gained knowledge of good and evil through his embrace of Isabel.

As the subtitle of his novel warns, however, Melville is not interested merely in the straightforward level of allegory. He also uses images in a recurring pattern to frustrate any simplistic interpretation of characters, settings, and events. In particular, Melville "consistently counterpoises the green fertility of vegetation with the arid intractability of stone" (Strickland 303). Pierre's name itself means "stone" in French, which links him to two of the most "dominant images of *Pierre*: "the Memnon Stone, with its threat of crushing weight, and the Enceladus Rock, trapped by the earth in a gesture of futile defiance and aspiration" (Grenberg 122). Symbolic of God, the inscrutable and silent Memnon Stone, which Pierre also calls the "Terror Stone," offers the protagonist no solace or guidance when he turns to it for a sign of what he should do in the moral dilemma that Isabel's story raises (*Pierre* 161). Near the end of the novel, Pierre dreams about the earthbound Titan Enceladus and the symbolic rock he bears, suggesting his own feelings of hopelessness in struggling against the forces that thwart him.

Imagery of marble also links many of the novel's seeming oppositions, oppositions that appear most strikingly in Melville's depiction of Lucy and Isabel: light and dark, good and evil, heart and head (Strickland 303). Similarly, Pierre's father is described in terms of stone and marble, consistent with both his manufactured sainthood and his lifelessness. In his heart, the reader is told, Pierre has enshrined "the perfect marble form of his departed father; without blemish, unclouded, snow-white, and serene; Pierre's fond personification of perfect human goodness and virtue." Having lost his father's living presence, he has "marbleized" his memory into an idealized vision to guide and sustain him (*Pierre* 83).

As part of this effort, the son has also built an actual shrine to his father, a closet in which hangs one of two portraits of the dead man. These portraits serve as the central symbols in *Pierre*. Pierre's mother cherishes the official portrait, which hangs in the drawing room of Saddle Meadows, because it represents her husband as a "middle-aged, married man" who "seemed to possess all the nameless and slightly portly tranquilities, incident to that condition when a felicitous one" (*Pierre* 88). In contrast, the smaller "chair-portrait" in Pierre's closet reflects the father as a "brisk, unentangled, young bachelor, gaily ranging up and down in the world, light-hearted, and a very little bladish perhaps; and charged to the lips with the first uncloying morning fullness and freshness of life" (90, 88). Mrs. Glendinning has always found this older portrait, "namelessly unpleasant and repelling," claiming that it "did signally belie her husband" (88). Drawn to the smaller painting, perhaps for its lifelike qualities, Pierre has long sought unsuccessfully to reconcile it with the later, more dignified and formal representation of his father. After Isabel's story destroys his unrealistic memories of his father as wholly virtuous, the son burns the chair portrait, scorching and blackening his hand in the process. When he inadvertently transfers this mark to Isabel, both of them are symbolically blackened by the sins of the father.

As the three outcasts—Pierre, Isabel, and Delly—make their way to the city by coach, Pierre finds and reads a torn fragment of a pamphlet by Plotinus Plinlimmon entitled "Chronometricals and Horologicals." Although there is general consensus that the pamphlet, which is reproduced in Chapter 14, is a key symbol in the novel, its exact significance is appropriately ambiguous and so has provoked much critical debate. In contrast to what he calls the absolutist ("chronometrical") morality of Christianity, Plinlimmon endorses a relative ("horological") value system, which would seem to warn against the kind of self-sacrificing course of action to which Pierre has just dedicated himself. Perhaps most importantly, however, the tract fails as a vehicle of communication. "[D]ivorced from context and experience, Plinlimmon's pamphlet cannot resonate with its intended reader; it leaves Pierre perplexed and untouched" (Silverman 361). With this pamphlet, Melville anticipates or foreshadows not only Pierre's subsequent authorial failure to communicate but, ironically, his own as well.

THEMES

In keeping with its domestic setting, Melville's psychological study of the title character revolves in many ways around his complex family relations. Pierre both rebels against his family and seeks to protect it; he also ironically destroys it. Since the novel's first publication, readers and critics alike have been dismayed by its implications of incest; however, it is important to recognize that Melville's interest is not in writing a book about incest. He merely uses this thematic strand as a means "to explore the nature of human morality: the means by which a person makes judgments and life decisions, and the effects those decisions have on the person making them" (Grenberg 126). The suggestions of incest, first raised in depicting the unhealthy relationship that Mrs. Glendinning has created with her son, reappear in Melville's depiction of the relationship that subsequently develops between Pierre and Isabel. Although he has no proof of the truth of Isabel's story about being his half-sister, and in fact comes to doubt this kinship in the end of the novel, he accepts her somewhat incredulous story at face value for much of the book. She offers no supporting evidence of her claims—not even producing the handkerchief that first led her to knowledge of her father's surname. Isabel's passionate nature stirs both Pierre's altruism and awakens him to his own sexuality. Because of his lack of experience, his conflicting emotions cause him to act impulsively instead of with the forethought that might have made a wiser decision possible, resulting in a course of action that could have saved Isabel without requiring his abandonment of Lucy and without resulting in the tragic deaths of all four of the major characters.

Despite his wrong-headed decision, Pierre still might have survived if he had been able to come to terms with himself and the real world he discovers outside the sheltered realm of Saddle Meadows; however, the truth of human existence eludes his comprehension. "One of the novel's primary themes is the dissolution of form and meaning; neither self nor reality can be grasped or imaged as a stable unity. Each remains tangled and ambiguous, frustrating and entangling the interpreter or writer" (Bellis 144). Even "in committing himself to Isabel Pierre is not, as he purports to believe, committing himself to Truth but to a further if different level of illusion" (Gray 122). Unable to face the complexities of his motivations, he grows more and more disillusioned about the possibility of meaning and belief: "'I am a nothing,'" he declares. "It is all a dream—we dream that we dreamed we dream" (*Pierre* 319).

Pierre's authorial struggle to find form and meaning that he can communicate reflects Melville's own frustrations with his publishers, critics, and readers. In the theme of authorship, which is centered in Chapters 17 and 18 of the novel but extends to its conclusion, Melville condemns the commercialism of his profession. "What sells best, what is most easily published and most highly regarded by critics," he argues, "is that literature which most nearly conforms to prevailing standards of taste, morality, and religion." Further, although every true artist seeks to be a truth-teller, "whatever truth there is, or 'might be,' remains inaccessible to humanity" (Grenberg 138). Melville thus views at least Pierre's heroic struggle to communicate meaning—if not the possibility of finding it—as inevitably doomed. Impelled, like Melville himself, by the contradictory pressures of "the burning desire to deliver what he thought to be new, or at least miserably neglected Truth to the world; and the prospective menace of being absolutely penniless, unless by the sale of his book, he could realize money," Pierre comes to spurn his aspirations as tainted: "With the soul of an Atheist, he wrote down the godliest things; with the feeling of misery and death in him, he created forms of gladness and life" (*Pierre* 329, 393). Dismayed by "the everlasting elusiveness of Truth," he finds himself a "prisoner of letters" (393, 394).

In part because of the book's autobiographical elements and its depiction of the literary artist's irresolvable paradox, many argue that it remains unclear whether Melville agrees with his protagonist's conclusions about the world and the inevitability of his fate. In his depiction of the city, Melville reveals reality as he saw it, presenting God's silence in this "inherently maddening world and humanity's tragic inability to adapt to it." As a result, it can be argued that *Pierre* "defines the absolute skepticism with which Melville viewed the possibilities of man's creating an 'original relationship with his universe'" (Grenberg 137). Although the world is often cold and inhospitable, however, opportunities for human fellowship exist for Pierre. Ultimately, it is his inability to recognize and accept his divided nature, rather than that nature itself, that causes Pierre's downfall, and his utter lack of self-awareness, in the end, is what most isolates him from others and empties his life of any possibility of form or meaning. Thus convincing evidence exists for the view that Melville does not stand in Pierre's shoes but rather in those of the narrator, who, like Ishmael before him, survives to ponder the significance and to tell the tale.

HISTORICAL CONTEXT

Influenced by the thinking of Immanuel Kant, Thomas Carlisle, and Samuel Taylor Coleridge, American transcendentalism was a small but extremely influential religious movement of the mid-nineteenth century that had its roots in the intellectual and literary enclave of Concord, Massachusetts. In a lecture that he gave in Boston in January 1842 and subsequently published, Ralph Waldo Emerson defined transcendentalism as "Idealism as it appears in 1842" (201). In 1849, Melville attended one of Emerson's Boston lectures, and he subsequently read some of his essays. Although he took issue with Emerson's optimistic view of humanity, he respected his intellectual acumen and breadth of vision. In *Pierre*, Melville incorporates his most extensive challenge to the philosophical underpinnings of transcendentalism. In line with transcendentalist notions espoused not only by Emerson but also by Henry David Thoreau and Walt Whitman, Pierre desires to do "something transcendently great" and aspires to let his own divinely inspired intuition guide him in his search for absolute truth (*Pierre* 331). Melville specifically connects transcendental prophesy and the idea of authorship. "[W]hatever its dramatization of the intensely procreative and subjective bases of art, *Pierre* finally challenges what Lawrence Buell defines as the distinguishing feature of 'literary Transcendentalism,' the writer's 'basic faith...that if only he looks far enough inward ... he will reach the unconscious universal'" (Duban 185). "Swayed to the universality of thought," Pierre misguidedly seeks an absolute Truth (*Pierre* 329). Melville's view of truth is far too tenuous, complex, and ambivalent to condone any such literary objective, which he finds not only naïve but dangerous. In his experience, as reflected in Pierre's, "Silence is the only Voice of our God" (*Pierre* 240).

In addition to debunking the transcendentalist belief in an open link between God and human intuition and exposing the danger of literature that has its foundation in such notions, Melville also takes issue with Emerson's view of love. "Inspired by love, Pierre acts precipitously and hazardously to correct the social injustices suffered by Isabel. But rather than appreciating the degree to which his decision is influenced by passion, he subscribes, instead, to the Emersonian tenet that 'there can be no excess to love... in the purest sense'" (Duban 169). In his self-delusion, Pierre clings to the notion that Isabel and he "will love with pure and perfect love of angel to an angel" (*Pierre* 184). Melville uses Pierre's fate to warn of the destruction that can result from being guided solely by what he deems the all too fallible dictates of the human heart.

ALTERNATE READING: FEMINIST CRITICISM

Feminist criticism is concerned with the condition of women in society and advocates equal rights for men and women. Operating from the knowledge that gender is culturally determined, feminists critique male-dominated (patriarchal) societies, which they argue marginalize or discount women by limiting their opportunity for self-definition and self-actualization. Feminist literary criticism examines the way gender is constructed in literature to reveal cultural values and norms. In particular, feminist critics concern themselves with exposing stereotypical representations of gender by examining the depiction, position, and treatment of female characters within a literary text. In their examination of literary history, feminists also argue that texts by women writers traditionally have been excluded from the canon of American literature because of accepted standards and conventions of what is "good" in terms of both content and form that reflect and perpetuate male dominance.

Pierre opens itself to a feminist reading because three of the four major characters in the novel are women. Significantly, it is the first of Melville's books to include American women as developed characters that are integrated into the text. Despite its apparent "derision of the false schemes popular novelists impose upon experience," feminists have argued that "*Pierre* reproduces a symbolic sexual economy, derived from allegory and romance, in which women appear largely as projections of male consciousness. Variously pathetic and menacing, domineering and servile," the female characters do not share in Pierre's intellectual quest (Lackey 68). Rather, these characters embody the sources of the male artist's discontent, identifying it as the type of story that one feminist critic has called "the melodrama of beset manhood" that governs prevailing notions of American literary tradition (Baym, "Melodramas" 130). In his struggle against convention to create an "original writing," Pierre, as a fictionalized American author, must battle the distractions, temptations, and obstacles of the women around him (*Pierre* 404). Both Isabel and Lucy support Pierre in his literary objectives, but although they are the original sources of his inspiration, they eventually become mere appendages and burdens to him, with no active role as partners in his mission. He repeatedly repulses their offers to assist him. Lucy complains at one point: "'there is no need of this incessant straining. See, Isabel and I have both offered to be thy amanuenses;—not in mere copying, but in the original writing; I am sure that would greatly assist thee.'" To which, Pierre tellingly responds, "'Impossible! I fight a duel in which all seconds are forbid'" (404). As the narrator observes, "On either hand clung to by a girl who would have laid down her life for him; Pierre nevertheless, in his deepest, highest part, was utterly without sympathy from any thing divine, human, brute, or vegetable…. Pierre was solitary as at the Pole" (392–93). From a feminist perspective, these women, serving only to embody Pierre's dilemma, become virtually invisible.

The domineering and manipulative Mrs. Glendinning gains power generally reserved for men only through her husband's death; however, it is in domestic affairs that she continues to exercise the most influence, devoting her central concerns to guarding the morality of Saddle Meadows. For instance, she conspires with the ineffectual minister to ensure that Delly Ulver will be evicted from the community for her sexual misdeeds. In escaping her influence, Pierre recognizes the gendered injustices that have befallen both Delly and Isabel and revolts against such social inequity by establishing a radically unconventional domestic arrangement in the city. However, these stereotypically drawn women—the servile Delly and the pathetic Isabel—remain powerless in his care, still objects rather than acting subjects who can define themselves in the world. Notably, the virtuous Lucy acts independently in renouncing the sterile artificiality of domestic convention to join Pierre's new family unit. Unmoved by the threats and entreaties of her mother, brother, and suitor, she stands firm in her conviction to determine her own destiny. Without the bold intervention of Pierre, however, she would have been bodily dragged back to the confines of Saddle Meadows by male force. And once safe within Pierre's walls, she subordinates her voice to his.

In comparing *Pierre* to women's novels of the same time period, feminist critics have observed that Melville's women characters "do not have the autonomy or credibility of many popular domestic heroines," while recognizing at the same time that the novel "engages and takes in quite startling directions some of the women's novels' challenges to patriarchal notions of marriage, family, and the home" (Kelley 96). For today's readers, *Pierre* "offers a radical reading of the gender roles and domestic structures that have produced profound distress in middle-class culture," revealing "the fault lines in the American family, not simply in extremis—in patterns of incest, abuse, betrayal, and the hypocrisy and silence that surround them—but also in the enormous and seemingly artificial labor required to maintain the illusion of ordinary, day-to-day respectability" (Kelley 110). Although Isabel and Lucy, as well as Delly, remain victims without the possibility of full lives, Melville uses these women characters to reflect gendered inequities and abuses in nineteenth-century American society. As Pierre leaves their home for the last time, he passes first Isabel, who sits "petrified in her chair, as one embalmed" and then Lucy, a "marble girl," who sits equally unstirring as if "enchanted" or "tranced" (*Pierre* 415). In his last wish for them, Pierre perhaps reveals Melville's as much as his own inability to fashion a better world: "'For ye two, my most undiluted prayer is now, that from your here unseen and frozen chairs ye may never stir alive'" (415). Tragically, he gets his wish, as even in death they mirror his desires.

6

The Piazza Tales

Faced with the disappointing reception of *Moby-Dick* and *Pierre*, as well as the mounting financial pressures that accompanied his purchase of Arrowhead and move to the Berkshire Mountains, Melville turned to magazine writing from 1853 to 1856. This new venue not only "offered Melville the opportunity to earn a prescribed and steady income" but also enabled him to reach a large number of readers receptive to his literary interests and social concerns (Post-Lauria 163). Of the short stories and sketches he wrote during this period, seven appeared in *Putnam's Monthly Magazine* and seven were published by *Harper's New Monthly Magazine*. In addition, Melville serialized the longer *Israel Potter* in *Putnam's* from July 1854 to March 1855. Another tale, "The Two Temples," which was rejected by *Putnam's*, was never published during the author's life. Melville wrote one additional story, "The Piazza," to introduce *The Piazza Tales*, which reprinted five of his magazine pieces originally published in *Putnam's*: "Bartleby, the Scrivener: A Story of Wall-Street," "Benito Cereno," "The Lightning-Rod Man," "The Encantadas, or Enchanted Isles," and "The Bell-Tower." This collection "offers not only some of the finest examples of Melville's short fiction but also the full range of narrative experiments attempted by Melville after 1852" (Rodgers 40). Because the stories adhere to the popular narrative frames with which his mid-nineteenth-century readers were familiar, they outwardly facilitated easy reading and interpretation. Through his well-known custom of concealment and penchant for ambiguity, however, Melville also invited readers of his day, as well as ours, to probe deeper for imaginative understanding.

"THE PIAZZA" (1856)

"The Piazza," the last short story Melville is known to have written, was created by the author to introduce his collection of tales and to provide a framework from which to view the other five stories. More than a functional afterthought, however, the story has depths that perhaps can be appreciated fully only by the reader who takes the narrator's advice that "beauty is like piety—you cannot run and read it; tranquility and constancy, with, now-a-days, an easy chair, are needed" ("Piazza" 622). Fittingly, the story invites the type of absorption that is required to appreciate most of Melville's fiction, long or short.

Setting and Plot

The tale opens with the narrator's description of his removal "into the country ... to occupy an old-fashioned farm-house" in the Berkshire Mountains (621). So that he can properly enjoy his new surroundings, he determines, "A piazza must be had," and despite his neighbors' derision over his impractical choice, he has one constructed on the north side of his house, which affords him a view of Mount Greylock (622). Over the next year, he marvels extravagantly at the natural wonders around him, eventually coming to focus on "[o]ne spot of radiance, where all else was shade" in the distance on the mountainside (625). Lured by the magical illusion that was reinforced by his reading of A Midsummer Night's Dream, the narrator eventually decides to set out in Don Quixote–fashion to search "for rainbow's end, in fairy-land" (626). Instead of fairies, however, he finds Marianna, "a lonely girl, sewing at a lonely window," in a rotting, dirty cottage with only flies and wasps for company (629). Weary of life, Marianna is an orphan who resides with a brother who is seldom at home. Left alone, she relieves her oppressive isolation by imagining the "happy one" who must live down the hill where "the white shines out against their blue" in "the only house in sight" (630). Rather than disillusioning her by revealing that he is the one who dwells there, the narrator leaves Marianna to her "strange fancies" and returns home (631). There each day he continues to watch the shining illusion from his piazza; however, at night—in darkness—he is still "haunted by Marianna's face, and many as real a story" (634).

Characters

Keying on the tale's setting, as well as the fact that Melville himself added a piazza to the north side of Arrowhead, many critics have approached "The Piazza" as a semi-autobiographical sketch of his personal disillusionment after the public and critical failure of *Moby-Dick* and *Pierre*, as well as a statement of the author's artistic philosophy and method. Because the unnamed, melancholic narrator is drawn in such exaggerated strokes, however, he also serves as "a cliché, a walking advertisement for the excesses Melville saw in the transcendental imagination.... This narrator is a dilettante, an amateur artist who dabbles in the aesthetic possibilities of his surroundings" (Roundy, "Fancies" 540). Enthralled by the landscape that surrounds him, which he deems "[a] very paradise of painters," he amplifies the sublimity of nature with magical illusions that he paints with his imagination and that have little or no connection with reality (621).

Far from a fairy queen, Marianna is just "a pale-cheeked girl," thoroughly at odds with the narrator's fanciful projections. Although she flatly refuses to entertain the notions he has invented about her, however, she nevertheless nurses her own romantic ideals. The two characters' houses and their fanciful conclusions about each other can be seen as ironically mirroring each other, but there are also important differences between the two characters. Marianna recognizes, as the narrator does not, "that thinking her 'wakeful weariness' can be remedied by looking upon 'the happy being' in 'yonder house' is nothing but a 'foolish thought.'" Further, whereas he relies for his fancies on books that "chart the terrain of dream and fantasy, she, 'never reading,' speaks from first-hand experience." Finally, "while her weariness and isolation originate in the material reality of her experience— monotonous 'woman's work,' primitive living conditions, and enforced solitude—his weariness and isolation are primarily conceptual, the frustrated result of the male quester seeking the romantic sublime" (DeNuccio 65–66). As a result, although the two seemingly are desperate for human contact, they are unable to create a meaningful relationship because the narrator finds himself unable to integrate the fact of Marianna with his fiction of her (DeNuccio 67). By withholding his identity, he denies them both the possibility of human relationship that she represents.

Allegory and Symbolism

Through his self-consciously excessive use of romantic language and literary allusions, Melville creates "a purely aesthetic glaze" that supports the "shifting allegorical mode" of "The Piazza" (Slouka 5; Avallone 221).

Throughout the tale, he "manipulates threads of allusions to Dante, Milton, Spencer, Shakespeare, Emerson, Cervantes, and Scriptural writers—acknowledged briefly or not at all on the surface—into an elaborately woven tissue of obscure significance." Repeatedly, these allusions function to signal "the reader of the ironic discrepancy between the narrator's world and his interpretation of it" (Avallone 221–22). In particular, Melville undercuts fairyland visions reminiscent of Spencer and Shakespeare with circular imagery that suggests parallels to Dante's *Purgatory*. Similarly, allusions to religious scripture and Milton raise the issue of faith. For instance, the narrator compares the building of his house to the quarrying of "the Kaaba, or Holy Stone," and the image of "social pilgrims" journeying to this Moslem site at Thanksgiving ironically parallel the lonely narrator's quest ("Piazza" 621).

Melville also weaves specific symbols throughout the story to support its ironic implications. The piazza, his "box-royal," functions as the narrator's vantage point, a seat from which he can passively observe the show of life he constructs in his imagination, thereby shielding himself from the pain he associates with active participation in the world from which he has "removed" himself (634, 621). The Chinese creeper that climbs one of the posts of the piazza has "burst out in starry bloom," but it is nonetheless infested with "millions of strange, cankerous worms," symbolizing the ironic difference between appearance and reality and suggesting the blighted hopes of the narrator, who "could not bear to look upon" it (626). The reader once again recalls this symbol when Marianna later points outside her window to "two hop-vines" that, "side by side, some feet apart ... climbed two poles, and, gaining their tip-ends, would have then joined over in an upward clasp, but the baffled shoots, groping awhile in empty air, trailed back whence they sprung" (633). Like the two vines, Marianna and the narrator, because of their different perspectives, are unable to find union and so return alone from whence they came. The inversion of their upward climb also signifies their failure to find salvation and the difficulty of faith in such a world.

Themes

In theme as well as technique, Melville considers the importance of point of view in "The Piazza," concluding that where one stands determines one's "view of the world, of truth, of reality," as well as one's "scale of values, as a matter of course." What a person thinks he or she "sees, however, may well be illusory" (Fisher, *Going Under* 16). Such a conclusion has obvious general implications, but Melville seems particularly interested in developing its significance for the artistic process. He accomplishes this thematic objective by likening the narrator's physical journey to the aesthetic mission and by comparing the different perspectives of the narrator and Marianna in relation to that mission.

In initiating the quest motif, the narrator suggests the ambiguous relationship between truth and fiction by explaining that his "inland voyage to fairy-land" is "[a] true voyage; but, take it all in all, interesting as if invented" (624). The narrator, however, by rejecting purposeful action for passive spectatorship, suggests artistic failure in his inability to unify the two realms of his experience—real and imaginative. By contrast, Marianna, whose sewing can be seen as a creative act, represents the successful artist-figure by representing "the unifying imaginative power which is necessary to reconcile the seemingly discrete and antagonistic elements of reality" (Clark 79–80).

The story's concluding paragraph not only introduces the stories that follow but also makes a final comment on the relationship between truth and illusion in fiction: "But, every night, when the curtain falls, truth comes in with darkness. No light shows from the mountain. To and fro I walk the piazza deck, haunted by Marianna's face, and many as real a story" (634). The narrator's quest has ended in failure, yet he succeeds in telling the story even though he no longer believes in his ability to do so. With this final irony, Melville complicates still further the meaning of truth in storytelling.

"BARTLEBY, THE SCRIVENER: A STORY OF WALL-STREET" (1853)

The first of Melville's magazine stories, "Bartleby, the Scrivener: A Story of Wall-Street" first appeared in two installments in the November and December 1853 issues of *Putnam's*. Although the tale was published anonymously, "Melville's authorship was an open secret" in publishing circles (Newman 19). *Putnam's* paid Melville $85 for the story, which set a precedent for his requesting and receiving $5 per page for his subsequent magazine pieces, all of which were published anonymously or with pseudonyms. At his editor's insistence, Melville agreed to place "Bartleby" immediately following the title story in *The Piazza Tales*. Despite its popularity, however, the author received no additional income for the tale because the collection generated no royalties (Newman 19–20). Unlike most of Melville's stories, which have been generally acknowledged only since the 1960s, "Bartleby" has consistently been singled out for recognition since the Melville Revival of the 1920s. Of all of the author's short fiction, this story has received the most critical attention, although interpretations of it have varied widely.

Setting and Plot

The story, set in mid-nineteenth-century Manhattan, takes place mostly in the Wall Street offices of the narrator, with the conclusion occurring in New York City's historic jail, commonly referred to as the Tombs. As in "The Piazza," Melville uses an unnamed bachelor as his first-person narrator, this time an attorney, who hires Bartleby as a scrivener to assist him in his growing practice by copying legal documents. The story relays Bartleby's progressive withdrawal from life and the baffled lawyer's reaction. This withdrawal begins with Bartleby disengaging from his professional responsibilities, which he signals by replying, "I would prefer not to," when the narrator asks for help (643). These words increasingly become the scrivener's response to all of the normal activities of life, including eating. Unable to solicit an explanation from his employee or convince him to alter his behavior, the attorney becomes so unnerved by Bartleby's silence and inertia that he finally takes the desperate step of moving his practice to escape the man. He continues, however, to be troubled by the moral responsibility he feels for the scrivener. When the new tenant of the narrator's former offices finds Bartleby intractable in his preference not to move, he has the police remove the scrivener from the premises. The narrator visits Bartleby in the Tombs but is still unable to convince him to eat or return to human activities. Returning some days later, he finds the scrivener dead and "[s]trangely huddled at the base of the wall, his knees drawn up and lying on his side" (671). A few months later, the narrator learns that Bartleby was formerly employed as "a subordinate clerk in the Dead Letter Office at Washington." This discovery elicits the lawyer's final comment, "Ah, Bartleby! Ah, humanity!" (672).

Characters

In commencing to describe Bartleby to the reader, the storytelling narrator sets himself an impossible task because "[t]he scrivener's personality, inner drives, and sensibilities will remain relatively unknown quantities" to him. In effect, he seeks "to align or harmonize his clerk with something he himself knows or can respond to, and these attempts continually fail. Although the lawyer never realizes it, the 'chief character…to be presented' will not be Bartleby, but himself" (Bickley 30). As if to signal this fact, the story begins with the narrator's self-portrait, in which he defines himself as "an eminently *safe* man," who has to this point been able to live by the adage that "the easiest way of life is the best," doing "a snug business among rich men's bonds and mortgages and title-deeds" ("Bartleby" 635). Although some critics deem him a weak and self-serving "fraud who is not fully aware of his own duplicity," the inclination of more recent scholarship has been to characterize the narrator's tone in describing himself as one of "self-directed irony" and to see his response to Bartleby as motivated by a humane and compassionate "recognition of the bonds of a common humanity" (Dillingham, *Short Fiction* 20; Sandberg 69, 77).

The "pallidly neat, pitiably respectable, incurably forlorn" and "singularly sedate" Bartleby who first arrives at the lawyer's office remains to the end essentially unknowable, an enigma of human suffering ("Bartleby" 642). However, the lawyer's other three employees—Turkey, Nippers, and Ginger Nut—are laughably and actively eccentric in name as well as behavior. In function, they add much needed comic relief to the tale and further support the view of the attorney as a tolerant and kind man. The young and ambitious Nippers suffers from indigestion, which makes him bad-tempered and unproductive in the morning; the elderly, alcoholic Turkey, who drinks to intoxication at the noon hour, becomes similarly useless each afternoon. Because these two men alternate their "paroxysms," however, the narrator rationalizes keeping them by reconciling himself to getting the equivalent of one fully productive employee from their half-days of efficiency (640). To complete his staff, the lawyer has hired Ginger Nut as his office boy in response to the wishes of the lad's father, "a carman, ambitious of seeing his son on the bench instead of a cart, before he died" (641). Because the 12-year-old boy's principal duty is to serve as "cake and apple purveyor for Turkey and Nippers," the reader suspects that the narrator acts more as the boy's benefactor than his employer.

Symbolism

With his choice of subtitle, "A Story of Wall-Street," Melville introduces the central symbol of the tale. This initial reference to walls represents capitalistic enterprise on one level, but it is "primarily intended to draw the reader's attention to the way walls function in the story, including the closed-in aspect of both the inside and outside of the Narrator's offices, the walls both physical and emotional between the characters in the story, and the walls of the prison where Bartleby finally dies" (Sandberg 66). The narrator uses a folding screen to shield himself from Bartleby, who spends his time staring through one of the office windows, all of which command "an unobstructed view of a lofty brick wall, black by age and everlasting shade" ("Bartleby" 636). The office door, mentioned repeatedly, is kept locked, foreshadowing not only the prison walls but also death itself, which will be the final barrier to communication between the two men.

The "pale plaster-of-paris bust of Cicero" that is prominently displayed in the lawyer's office links with the white imagery used to describe the colorless Bartleby to emphasize his isolation and inanimate nature (643–44). In addition, the story incorporates a mixture of financial and food imagery to suggest the counterfeit values and lack of true sustenance in the material world. In the Tombs, for instance, the narrator gives money to Mr. Cutlets, the grub-man, to prepare meals for Bartleby, who in turn declines Mr. Cutlets's invitation to eat with him and his wife by explaining, "I prefer not to dine to-day.... It would disagree with me" (670). Ironically, Bartleby, who "lives without dining," dies a few days later, just as Mr. Cutlets announces, "'His dinner is ready'" (671).

The epigraph that follows this scene elaborates on the story's symbolic treatment of the failure of human relationship and communication through the image of the dead letter, which Melville uses to represent Bartleby and his fate. The narrator himself makes this connection in his exclamation when he learns of Bartleby's former place of employment: "Dead letters! Does it not sound like dead men?.... On errands of life, these letters speed to death" (672). Nevertheless, although the scrivener dies, his fate is self-willed. He purposefully cuts himself off from society, declining to live in such a world as Wall Street represents. Bartleby's decision to end his life has been interpreted by some critics as a Christlike sacrifice, by others more secularly as the impetus to the narrator's awakening conscience, and most recently as a personal choice in conflict with societal values. Regardless, however, the story's final line, rather than signaling only resignation, may suggest that hope for humanity still exists in the ability to learn from Bartleby's ambiguous lesson.

Themes

On one level "Bartleby" can be read as a critique of materialism through its representation of the sterile environment of "Wall-Street" and the narrator's underlying discontent in spite of his financial success. From this perspective, Bartleby, in his passive resistance, actually serves as an active protest against the human isolation that has evolved from urbanization and the accompanying depersonalization of business enterprise. Unlike the narrator, who maintains the façade of propriety by adhering to the rules and reaping the economic benefits of his corporate practice, Bartleby refuses to take part in such a world, a world where life can have no real meaning. Beneath his outward show of contentment, however, the narrator's self-mocking tone suggests that he recognizes his own isolation and fears that the resulting loss of human relationship has rendered his own existence as meaningless as Bartleby's, giving it a death-in-life quality that makes the scrivener's choice of literal death less incomprehensible if no less tragic.

From a different perspective, "Bartleby" can also be interpreted as an exploration of one human's responsibility to another who prefers to die rather than to continue living. The lawyer attempts to save Bartleby, but he fails to do so and eventually despairs of trying. "Bartleby's narrator suggests that witnessing intense affliction tests the parameters of one's sensibility" (Garland-Thomson 794). His response to the scrivener evolves from pity to repulsion as he decides, "[T]he scrivener was the victim of innate and incurable disorder. I might give alms to his body; but his body did not pain him; it was his soul that suffered, and his soul I could not reach" ("Bartleby" 653). "Perhaps the fetal position of resignation and surrender that the dying Bartleby resorts to at the Tombs suggests the narrator's projection onto Bartleby of his own forced concession, his impotence before the problem of redeeming unfitness—of curing the world through curing his copyist—that he took on with such reluctance and compulsion" (Garland-Thomson 794). In such a situation, Melville seems to ask, what, if anything, can or should be done to alleviate the anguish of another human being? In the end, might acceptance and understanding have been the better response to Bartleby's desire to end his life?

In contemplating the ultimate effects of human isolation, Melville also uses doubling as a thematic device to deepen the story's psychological implications. Most obviously, Turkey and Nippers mirror each other. The struggle that ensues between the lawyer and Bartleby, however, might also represent an internal conflict within the narrator alone. In this sense, the copyist is but a psychic projection that gives voice to the narrator's repressed self-doubt. "The lawyer's entire narrative is freighted with his shocked recognition that Bartleby is very much like himself, with his fear that he might become exactly like Bartleby" (Grenberg 172). As he himself observes, both of them are "sons of Adam" (652). "The lawyer's struggle to rid himself of Bartleby is a struggle to survive in the face of overwhelming evidence that survival is pointless, and perhaps the permeating irony of the lawyer's situation is that, for him, survival, life itself, is reduced to a Bartleby-like negative preference—a preference not to die" (Grenberg 173–74). The lawyer, in this sense, is not able to rid himself of Bartleby because the two are one, and his final comment—"Ah, Bartleby! Ah, humanity!"—broadens the tale to make the scrivener not only a double for the conflicted narrator but for all of humanity as well.

"BENITO CERENO" (1855)

"Benito Cereno" originally appeared in three installments in the October, November, and December 1855 issues of *Putnam's*. Melville's source for the story was Chapter 18 of Amasa Delano's *A Narrative of Voyages and Travels*, which was published in 1817. This chapter describes and documents the American Captain Delano's quelling of a mutiny by the slaves onboard a Spanish ship that he encountered off the coast of Chile in 1805. Although he remained faithful to most of the particulars of this historical account, Melville made a few significant changes. In particular, he changed the date of the uprising, renamed the two ships involved, and added some significant scenes and imagery to develop further the intrigue and his thematic intent.

Point of View

One of the major keys to the story's success lies in Melville's manipulation of point of view. "In recreating his source materials as art, Melville worked a variation of his characteristic rhetorical mode, first-person ironic narration." To maintain "the immediacy and familiarity of the first-person technique," while simultaneously "hinting at Delano's incomplete view of reality," the author "settled on a limited-omniscient narrator, one privileged to enter Delano's mind alone, but also permitted to draw partially aside the masks that conceal the identities of" other characters (Bickley 101). Although he withholds knowledge of the true situation until the end of the story, Melville nonetheless intends for the reader to recognize Delano's perceptions as unreliable since he introduces the man as "a person of a singularly undistrustful good-nature, not liable, except on extraordinary and repeated incentives, and hardly then, to indulge in personal alarms, any way involving the imputation of malign evil in man" ("Benito Cereno" 673).

Setting and Plot

The story, which in Melville's version takes place in 1799, opens with Captain Delano's ship, the *Bachelor's Delight*, at anchor in the harbor of St. Maria near the southern tip of Chile. Coming to the aid of the *San Dominick*, a dilapidated Spanish slave ship that seems about to run onto a reef, Delano meets its captain, the young but sickly Benito Cereno, and learns that Alexandro Aranda, the owner of the slaves on board, is dead. Most of the rest of the story consists of Delano's detailed observation of the strange and puzzling behavior of the ship's crew. In particular, he is troubled by the lack of discipline among the slaves and perplexed by the unusually close relationship between Cereno and Babo, the slave who seems to attend him so solicitously, never leaving the Spaniard's side. Only when Delano prepares to leave the ship, and Cereno suddenly jumps into the boat beside him, does the American realize that an insurrection, led by Babo, has occurred, leaving the slaves in command of the *San Dominick*. During the fight that ensues, Delano saves Cereno and recaptures the ship. To clarify the events aboard the *San Dominick,* the story concludes with extracts from depositions at the subsequent trial of the black mutineers in Lima. A final postscript informs the reader that the melancholy Cereno has died shortly after retiring to a monastery. Babo's head, meanwhile, has been set upon a stake in the public square of Lima.

Characters

Amasa Delano's subjective responses to Cereno, Babo, and the rest of the crew of the *San Dominick* create the focus of the story, suggesting that Melville is more interested in states of mind than in dramatic action. "Another Melvillean 'bachelor,' good-natured Delano is naively confident about the world, and about his own God-given potentialities as a leader of men of will and benefactor of those weaker than himself" (Bickley 102). Early critics often interpreted him as a benign if somewhat obtuse figure, but the consensus of more recent scholarship is that Melville uses Delano as a critique of northern antebellum thought in terms of the sentimental racism of his day (Zagarell 247). Operating from an ideology that sees blacks as docile and inferior, he shakes off all outward signs to the contrary. Most often he thinks of blacks in terms of animal imagery. For instance, he describes a nursing black woman as "like a doe" with "her wide-awake fawn,'" while Babo has a "rude face...like a shepherd's dog" ("Benito Cereno" 704, 678). As the narrator explains, "Captain Delano took to negroes, not philanthropically, but genially, just as other men to Newfoundland dogs" (716).

Because he cannot conceive of blacks as humans and so capable of masterminding the diabolical plot that Babo has devised, most of Delano's suspicions center on the Spanish captain. By nature, whites, after all, are "the shrewder race" (706); however, the American's chauvinistic attitude also surfaces in his view of Cereno, whose unaccountable laxity he excuses by reminding himself that "as a nation . . . these Spaniards are an odd set" (710). Cereno is described from Delano's perspective as "a prey to settled dejection," suffering from a "debility, constitutional or induced by the hardships, bodily and mental, . . . too obvious to be overlooked." The American rightly concludes that his mind has been "unstrung if not still more seriously affected" but fails to comprehend the true cause of the Spaniard's malaise (679). Even at the end, Delano is incredulous that Cereno, the aristocratic enslaver who has now experienced the horrors of slavery firsthand, cannot forget the past: "'You are saved,' cried Captain Delano, more and more astonished and pained; 'you are saved; what has cast such a shadow upon you?'" Cereno's response, "'The negro,'" brings only silence from the uncomprehending American (754).

Assisted by the physically powerful Atufal, it is Babo who plans and executes the slave uprising that breaks Cereno's spirit and then keeps Delano befuddled as to the true state of affairs on the *San Dominick*. More than any other character in this story, Babo has elicited a full range of critical responses over time. Some have viewed him as the "manifestation of pure evil" (Feltenstein 247); others have excused his diabolical violence as the justified and even inevitable reaction to the intolerable condition of slavery. In the most nuanced readings, however, Babo, Delano, and Cereno are each seen as both victims and perpetrators of the ideology of slavery. Babo, after all, is the least sympathetic of the three major characters, and his savagery exceeds that which is necessary merely to secure his own freedom, instead serving to brutalize and enslave others as he himself was. A striking contradiction to stock views of blacks, Babo, who remains stoically silent through most of the tale, displays a sharp and cunning intellect and a courageous defiance that extends even beyond his death as his "head, that hive of subtlety, fixed on a pole in the Plaza, met, unabashed, the gaze of the whites" and looked even beyond in the direction of the now dead bodies of both Aranda and Cereno ("Benito Cereno" 755).

Symbolism

The massive rope knot that one of the sailors tosses to Delano as he walks the deck of the *San Dominick* suggests the tangled threads that the reader must "slice through to the core of the story" (Nicol 25). Most obviously, the three main characters represent different cultures and attitudes. The Yankee Delano, in his naïve and self-righteous innocence, signifies the "New World" of America, and the noble Spaniard Cereno, with his empty sword scabbard, suggests the impotence of the outmoded aristocratic values and rotting imperialism of "Old World" Europe. The two are joined, however, by the African Babo with all the political ramifications that the slave trade suggests. Allied with Babo is Atuful, a former African king, now chained and padlocked in slavery, "an emblem of the physical plight of all slaves" and ironically a foil for Cereno, who although he wears the key to Atuful's padlock around his neck, is actually a prisoner himself rather than the jailer he seems (Nicol 26).

A central symbol in the story, the stern piece on the *San Dominick* provides a further statement on the ambiguity of appearances and the nature of slavery. This shieldlike "relic of faded grandeur" depicts "a dark satyr in a mask, holding his foot on the prostrate neck of a writhing figure, likewise masked" ("Benito Cereno" 676). "Nearly the whole tale is compressed in this symbol: slavery, an Old World inheritance, is a man with his foot on another's neck; the satyr is part man, part beast; the figure held down is writhing … ; and finally both are masked, as in this story the truth is masked from Delano," as both the whites and blacks on the *San Dominick* wear masks of authority and submission, respectively, and as brutality is masked as docility (Vanderhaar 190). At the end of the story, this image is repeated in Delano's boat when the American clutches Cereno with one hand "while his right foot, on the other side, ground the prostrate" Babo, writhing like a snake at the bottom of the boat, his dagger pointed "at the heart of his master" ("Benito Cereno" 733, 734). Although Babo is a killer and must be subdued, Melville "hints that it is really Delano figured in the satyr, that Delano wears the mask of benevolence which in reality hides a moral vacuum, and Babo, snake-like bent on his vindictive purpose, symbolizes slavery—The snake in the American garden of Eden" (Vanderhaar 190–91).

Offsetting the stern piece is a mysteriously shrouded figurehead that, except for the chalked inscription "'*Seguid vuestro jefe*' (follow your leader)," is covered by canvas as Cereno boards the Spanish ship ("Benito Cereno" 676). After Babo is subdued, however, the canvas covering comes loose, revealing "death for the figure-head, in a human skeleton" that Cereno recognizes as Aranda, whom the slaves had murdered and impaled on the front of the ship. This phrase, "follow your leader," was meant by Babo "as a warning to the Spanish sailors that they would meet Don Aranda's fate if they did not succumb to black control of the ship. Yet insofar as 'Benito Cereno' is a story of retribution, it was the Spanish who perpetrated the first evil of enslaving the blacks." Similarly, Delano's unquestioning acceptance of the system of slavery suggests "the New World follows its leader, the Old World," despite the democratic "ideals upon which the American republic was founded" (Vanderhaar 189).

Themes

The tableaux that Melville creates in opening "Benito Cereno" initiates "the forthcoming ambiguities and veiled tensions between blackness and whiteness" that will reinforce the story's thematic focus on slavery (Bickley 105). Melville repeatedly invokes gray imagery in setting the scene for his tale: "The sea . . . was sleeked at the surface like waved lead that has cooled and set in the smelter's mold. The sky seemed a gray surtout. Flights of troubled gray fowl, kith and kin with flights of troubled gray vapors among them were mixed. . . . Shadows present, foreshadowing deeper shadows to come" ("Benito Cereno" 673). Rather than resorting to a simplistic representation of white as good and black as evil, Melville instead suggests that the truth, here as elsewhere, is ambiguously gray. Neither side in this story—black or white—is presented as entirely good or entirely evil, and Melville seems to warn us that appearances in such matters often prove to be deceiving. Furthermore, the real tragedy may be that no one seems to learn the true meaning of human compassion as a result of their experiences aboard the *San Dominick*. Cereno and Babo, who exchange their roles of master and slave, both die—the former a spiritually broken man and the latter defiant to the end. Neither is the wiser for having experienced the other's reality. Likewise, although Delano survives, he gains no self-knowledge, remaining willfully ignorant and safe behind the mask of benevolent goodwill that cloaks his fundamental inhumanity. Melville offers the reader no easy answers in "Benito Cereno."

Historical Context

In particular, two of the changes that Melville made to the story point to his interest not just in abstract evil but in the institution of slavery. In 1799, San Domingo, now known as Haiti, was the scene of a slave revolt that extended over the entire island. By changing the date of Delano's account to 1799 and renaming the Spanish ship the *San Dominick*, Melville was drawing historical connections, as well as making a political comment on the more immediate antebellum tensions within the United States that ultimately led to the Civil War.

"THE LIGHTNING-ROD MAN" (1854)

Since it was first published in August 1854, "The Lightning-Rod Man" has drawn mixed reactions. The tale may have been biographically inspired, as Melville reportedly had "an encounter . . . with a real lightning-rod salesman, who chose times of storms to pursue his trade" (Leyda, Introduction xxvi). One of Melville's shortest—and some would say flimsiest—stories, it nevertheless can be approached on three levels: as comedy, as allegory, and as satire.

Setting and Plot

The story, which is set in the narrator's cottage "among the Acroceraunian hills" of Greece, can be quickly summarized ("Lightning" 756). A peddler visits the narrator during a thunderstorm and tries unsuccessfully to sell him a lightning rod for protection. Unconvinced by the salesman's spiel about the dangers of lightning, the narrator eventually loses his temper. A fight ensues, during which the narrator breaks the salesman's rod before tossing him out. Thereafter, however, as the narrator remarks in closing, "the Lighting-rod man still dwells in the land; still travels in storm-time, and drives a brave trade with the fears of man" (763).

Characters

To narrate this tale, Melville uses another first-person, nameless man— presumably a bachelor—who seems like a man of good spirits as his unexpected guest arrives while he is enjoying the storm's "grand irregular thunder" and "glorious" bolts of lightning (756). It is only through the narrator's eyes that we see the salesman, who, in appearance, "seems like an escapee from some gothic tale" (Fisher, *Going Under* 120). The man has a "lean, gloomy figure. Hair dark and lank, mattedly streaked over his brow. His sunken pitfalls of eyes were ringed by indigo halos, and played with an innocuous sort of lightning: the gleam without the bolt" ("Lightning" 756). Despite the visitor's strange appearance, the narrator demonstrates his graciousness by inviting him into his home and urging him to dry off by the hearth. When he discovers the man's profession and intent, however, he also shows his firmness of mind and self-reliance by refusing to succumb to the fear tactics on which the salesman relies to promote his product. Although the host acts somewhat condescendingly to his uninvited visitor, calling him "Jupiter Tonans" repeatedly, he otherwise evidences not only playfulness but also remarkable patience in his responses, resorting to physical violence only after the stranger springs upon him with the rod pointed at his heart. He seems, in fact, an average man dealing with trying circumstances as best he can. The salesman, by contrast, becomes increasingly excited, agitated, and demanding as the conversation progresses. By the time he leaps at the narrator, he is actually foaming and "blackening in the face," calling his uncooperative customer an "[i]mpious wretch" with "infidel notions" (762).

Allegory and Symbolism

"The Lightning-Rod Man" can be enjoyed on the literal level for its comic, tongue-in-cheek handling of the ubiquitous door-to-door salesman routine gone awry. By using the Acroceraunian hills as his setting, however, Melville immediately "places the tale in a world apart from reality" because this range of mountains, in classical mythology, is associated with the throne of Jupiter (Verdier 275). Clearly, it is possible to interpret the story as a religious allegory because of its language and imagery. The narrator, in such a reading, represents self-reliant faith as he tells the salesman, "The hairs on our heads are numbered, and the days of our lives. In thunder as in sunshine, I stand at ease in the hands of my God" ("Lightning" 762). A pagan-Christianity opposition is invoked by the numerous references to Jupiter and the salesman's horror at being called "that pagan name" (758). The salesman's language is also extravagantly religious, littered with exclamations such as "good heavens," "for heaven's sake," and "merciful heaven." Further, he continually commands the narrator to "hark" to his warnings and accept the "only true rod," suggesting that he represents organized, evangelical religion (758–59). To sharpen his attack, Melville draws the salesman in Satanic terms both through his physical appearance and by the metal rod he carries, which "terminates at the top tripodwise, in three keen tines" (756). At the story's end, this instrument becomes a "tri-forked" weapon aimed at the narrator's—or faith's—heart, completing the image of the rod as the Devil's trident or pitchfork.

It is also possible to interpret the tale as a satire on the state of American civilization. In such a reading, the salesman and his rod would symbolize scientific and technological progress, waging a war of commercialism against nature as represented by the storm. The narrator refuses to put his faith in the latest gadget, however, convinced that the magnificent powers of nature will never be controlled by manmade devices.

Themes

"The Lightning-Rod Man" can be read from both religious and secular perspectives. As a religious allegory, it considers the issue of faith in terms of good and evil. Although the Devil is thwarted in this specific instance, the narrator's concluding remark suggests that "evil and temptation will always be present, and each [person] must meet and defeat temptation" alone (Verdier 279). As a satire of science and commercialism the story also presents a confrontation of value systems in terms of good and evil. In this case, the opposition depicted "satirizes the gadgetry of civilization with the contrast between the sharp, ironic wit of the narrator and the scientific pitch of the salesman" (Shusterman 165). Whether the lightning-rod man represents evil in a general sense or stands for a more specific evil that Melville saw in Calvinistic Christianity or American progressiveness, he will continue to seek potential victims. Melville's point is that the customer must beware. Regardless of the product, the "protection racket" peddled by fast-talking scam artists—be they ministers, salesmen, or devils of another nature—represents false security at best.

"THE ENCANTADAS, OR ENCHANTED ISLES" (1854)

Although the identity of the true author was recognized at once, "The Encantadas" originally appeared under the pseudonym Salvator R. Tarnmoor in the March, April, and May 1854 issues of *Putnam's*. This pseudonym is almost certainly an allusion to the landscape painter Salvator Rosa, as "Melville himself acknowledged a relationship between 'The Encantadas' and the eighteenth-century artist known for his gloomy and menacing portrayals of nature" (Newman 187). In both form and content, "The Encantadas" is the most unusual of Melville's short fiction. Mixing travel, geography, adventure, history, and philosophy, it consists of "a loosely organized series of sketches, with no very intense unity among them" (Arvin 241). Left to their own devices, however, most "readers find an internal coherence" and "a 'final effect' of aesthetic wholeness" by closely considering the interplay of structure, theme, and symbols in the work (Newman 193).

Setting and Plot

Set in the Galápagos Islands that Melville visited twice during his days as a seaman and rover, "The Encantadas," like Melville's early novels, presents a "travelogue-like description of an exotic, faraway place. The first-person narrator guides the reader about this group of Pacific islands, "pointing out their dismal features and recounting stories, both comic and tragic, about some of the former inhabitants" (Dillingham, *Short Fiction* 76). No sustained plot binds this series of 10 sketches, however, and the overall tone and effect are much darker and intense than in Melville's early work. "Strongly visual," Melville moves "steadily from general to particular" as "he first presents the islands to the imagination as a whole, and then proceeds to amplify, analyze, and criticize" (Fogle 93).

The first four sketches present an overall impression of the Galápagos by relaying "some general history, topography, and geography of the isles" (Grenberg 155). The narrator introduces this archipelago with an image of "five-and twenty heaps of cinders." As he explains, "It is to be doubted whether any spot of earth can, in desolateness, furnish a parallel to this group," which lays "[l]ike split Syrian gourds left withering in the sun, . . . cracked by an everlasting drought beneath a torrid sky" ("Encantadas" 764–65). After presenting the islands in general terms, "[t]he fifth and six sketches offer the first cursory glimpses of pirates, explorers, and sailors who [have] touched upon the islands," before the final four sketches deal specifically with some of the former inhabitants (Grenberg 155). To strengthen the bleak sense of enchantment that pervades the work and creates its subtitle, Melville prefaces the various sketches with 24 epigraphs, most of which are taken from Edmund Spencer's *The Faerie Queen*.

Characters

In serving as the reader's tour guide of this isolated locale, the narrator is the only human to provide continuity throughout the sketches. "He is somewhat sententious, prone to exaggeration and contradiction," but not totally lacking in humor (Beecher 89). Stressing that the islands are mainly characterized by "their emphatic uninhabitableness," he claims, "Man and wolf alike disown them"; thus, "[l]ittle but reptile life is here found. . . . No voice, no low, no howl is heard; the chief sound of life here is a hiss" ("Encantadas" 765). Eventually, however, in sketches seven through nine, the narrator "relates the stories of two bachelors and a widow, each a sojourner on the Encantadas who came to grief there" (Sappenfield 126).

The subject of the seventh sketch, the Dog-King of Charles' Isle, is a "Creole adventurer from Cuba," a mercenary, "who by his bravery and good fortune" gained sole possession of Charles' Isle for his role in the Peruvian war for independence ("Encantadas" 788). "Faced with isolated acts of insubordination among the eighty souls whom he has lured to his promised land, he declares martial law and rules tyrannically" until a full-scale mutiny erupts (Beecher 92). Battling the mutineers with his "disciplined cavalry company of large, grim dogs," the Dog-King is finally banished, and the rebels set up a republic that serves to be "no democracy at all, but a permanent *Riotcracy*, which gloried in having no law but lawlessness" ("Encantadas" 789, 791).

The Chola widow Hunilla, who is the subject of the eighth sketch, is the most fully drawn and sympathetic character in "The Encantadas." Left on Norfolk Isle with her husband and brother by a French captain who fails to return as promised, Hunilla witnesses the drowning of her companions and is later abused and abandoned again by whale boaters. Finally rescued by chance, she narrates her tale of endurance with quiet composure and dignity. As the narrator observes, "She but showed us her soul's lid, and the strange ciphers thereon engraved; all within, with pride's timidity, was withheld" (797). Forced to leave all but two of her dogs behind when there is no room for them, the widow "never looked behind her; but sat motionless.... She seemed as one, who having experienced the sharpest of mortal pangs, was henceforth content to have all lesser heart-strings riven, one by one" (805). In Melville's depiction of her, Hunilla "has an adaptability and a resourcefulness in the face of adversity," surviving loss and victimization at the hands of others without letting such tragedies "permanently immobilize her" (Canaday, "'Encantadas'" 65).

The hermit Oberlus, as depicted in the ninth sketch, offers a sharp contrast to Hunilla's response to adversity. Deserted on Hood's Isle "about a half century ago," Oberlus, the narrator explains, "struck strangers much as if he were a volcanic creature thrown up by the same convulsion which exploded into sight the isle." His nature was "[s]o warped and crooked ... that the very handle of his hoe seemed gradually to have shrunk and twisted in his grasp" (807). The narrator concludes that "[t]he long habit of sole dominion over every object round him ... must have gradually nourished in him a vast idea of his own importance, together with a pure animal sort of scorn for all the rest of the universe" (808–9). According to legend, his attempts to capture and enslave others, were continually frustrated until he finally departed from Hood's Isle by trickery and guile in a stolen boat, leaving behind a letter of embittered protest about his mistreatment in life. Subsequently thrown into a South American jail, Oberlus there for a long time "was seen; the central figure of a mongrel and assassin band; a creature whom it is religion to detest, since it is philanthropy to hate a misanthrope" (814).

Allegory and Symbolism

Not just a place, the islands that Melville describes in "The Encantadas" allegorically represent a condition of existence, a fallen world similar to that of Dante's *Inferno*. "But this *Inferno* is not neatly stacked away into the underworld; it is centrally situated in the real world" (Newbery 51). In describing this locale, Melville "repeatedly endows the physical features of the islands with base human attributes or compares them to broken or spent human artifacts" (Beecher 91). The vegetation, for instance, is "ungrateful," the mist is "gray" and "haggard," and the landscape in general is "woe-begone" ("Encantadas" 765, 766, 768). Tortoises, the most prominent creatures on the island, are images of "[l]asting sorrow and penal hopelessness" (768).

The tortoise serves as the central, unifying symbol of "The Encantadas." "Ancient, venerable, scarred, and yet with a bright underbelly, the tortoise embodies at once the darker and livelier aspects of life," the interplay of good and evil in the world (Canaday, "'Encantadas'" 61). From another perspective, the tortoise again represents duality. This figure, in its unswerving insistence on crawling straight forward without turning aside for obstacles, represents heroic endurance, but it also suggests an inflexibility that can prove obstinate and self-defeating. Hunilla and Oberlus illustrate both types of such perseverance in the face of the capricious, unpredictability of life. Hunilla suggests the tortoise's positive side in her heroic resolve and eventual triumph. Oberlus, however, is "the fullest human embodiment of the Encantadas, more representative than Hunilla in his dual character of misery and wickedness. He is at once pitiable and evil," an oppressor and oppressed in his insistent and unswerving will (Fogle 110).

In this lost island world, delusions are central to the air of enchantment. In particular, Melville uses his depiction of the island known as Rock Rodondo to create the motif of delusion. "[S]olitary and alone," this rocky mount, "rising straight from the sea ten miles from land," is almost impossible to climb but offers "a noble point of observation" to those who are able to reach the summit and survey "the whole mountainous group to the south and east" ("Encantadas" 773). The narrator describes its changeable aspect, observing that even now at "[t]his moment, doubtless, while we know it to be a dead desert rock, other voyagers are taking oaths it is a glad populous ship" (777). At another point, the narrator compares Rodondo "to a lighthouse and reinforces the implication that the isle is associated with human life and perhaps safety. But when the viewer approaches the isle, he finds that the distant picture was false: the rock is barren and uninhabited except for an array of hostile sea fowl" whose droppings "cause the white sail-like appearance" (Howington 69–70). The Encantadas—like Oberlus and the Dog-King—betray and deceive, suggesting the difficulty in perceiving truth in nature or humanity.

Themes

With "The Encantadas," Melville continues his consideration of the themes of good and evil, appearance and reality, life and death. In this consideration of humanity's inhumanity in a fallen world, Melville suggests that either the nature of the world is delusive, or that the nature of humanity is such that humans delude themselves by failing to see through appearances. Endurance is perhaps the best possible response in a death-in-life world like the Encantadas, where "[v]ictims are enticed, deluded, and left to wonder at capricious nature, or suffer at its hands." As with the lesson of Hunilla, "along with the victimization of life goes an ultimate recognition of it, and a stoic adaptation to its trials, which somehow elevates the victim above his [or her] fate" (Howington 75). Like the ironic epigraphs that precede each of these 10 sketches, the tropic isles of the Encantadas seem to promise freedom, ease, and tranquility, all of which prove illusory in the end. These isles are but a stony wasteland that offer little, if any, hope for redemption. For although the tortoise may have a bright side, it must be turned on its back to discover it, a position that, for this animal, represents helplessness and ultimately death.

"THE BELL-TOWER" (1855)

When "The Bell-Tower" was first published in August 1855, it was the fifth of Melville's tales to appear in *Putnam's* since 1853. The story's setting and atmosphere suggest the possible influence of Edgar Allan Poe, but Nathaniel Hawthorne's allegorical "Ethan Brand," "The Birth-mark," and "The Artist of the Beautiful" seem most likely to have influenced the shaping of the piece. No source has been found for the opening three epigraphs "*From a Private MS.*," and critics are divided as to whether the obscure footnote at the end of the tale was Melville's or added by the publisher.

Setting and Plot

The story opens with a view of "the black mossed stump" of the Bell-Tower, designed and built by the renowned architect Bannadonna, and then proceeds to recount the history of the tower ("Bell-Tower" 819). In an unnamed state in early-Renaissance Italy, Bannadonna creates a structure, 300 feet high, that combines a bell tower and a clock tower in one. While casting "the great state-bell" for the edifice, Bannadonna strikes one of his workers dead for showing fear of the boiling metal (820). The townspeople pardon this act of rage, excusing it as evidence of the artisan's "esthetic passion"; however, they do not observe the human "splinter" that falls "into the seething mass," creating a flaw in the bell (821). Beside the bells in the belfry, Bannadonna places Talus, a mechanical device that he has created amidst much secrecy and that is designed to move along a track and strike the clasped hands of 2 of the 12 sculpted maidens that signify the hours. The artisan works to perfect the expression of Una, the maiden signifying the first hour, as a crowd stands below to witness Talus in his first sounding of the hour. Instead, however, the mechanical figure strikes dead Bannadonna, who unknowingly blocks the automaton's path in his absorption with Una. At his funeral, as a live bell-ringer swings a rope to strike the hour, the state-bell cracks from the flaw in its metal and crashes onto the plain. One year later, the whole structure is leveled by an earthquake.

Characters

Throughout the tale, Melville uses a third-person narrative voice, which, although it often reflects the opinions of the community, offers little direct insight into the protagonist Bannadonna's thoughts and motivations. Bannadonna, "the great mechanician" and "unblest foundling," is described as having a "firm resolve" that "no man in Europe at that period went beyond." Wealthy and celebrated, "[h]is repute assigned him to be architect" when "the state in which he lived voted to have the noblest Bell-Tower in Italy" ("Bell-Tower" 819). A man of science, this "practical materialist" fails in his attempt to master nature (831). The magistrates and other officials, for their part, show mixed attitudes toward Bannadonna. While they stand in awe of his skill and daring, they harbor doubts and suspicions about "the foundling's secrets" (830) and fear he is overreaching the possible, crafting a bell that is too heavy to hang and a tower so high that no one but he will dare to climb to its summit. Never, however, do they attempt to stop him, as he strives to create a structure meant to bring them, as well as him, honor and recognition.

Allegory and Symbolism

"The Bell-Tower" has been described as "Melville's one attempt to write a pure allegory" (Grenberg 177). As a result, its symbols are "more regular than is usual with Melville, more formal and consistent" (Fogle 63). The tower, as the central symbol, "is likened to Babel which, in the Bible represents men's futile attempt to outdo God, the Father, and the consequences of such action" (Costello and Kloss 255). The tower in its vertical form, Bannadonna in his attempt to create the one-of-a-kind edifice, and Una all signify the number 1 and its implications of both pride and isolation. The imagery associated with these symbols is also sexually charged. The tower itself is an obvious phallic symbol. As the narrator explains, "To the sound of viols, the climax-stone rose slowly in air, and, amid the firing of ordnance, was laid by Bannadonna's hand upon the final course. Then mounting, it he stood erect, alone, with folded arms, gazing upon the white summits" ("Bell-Tower" 820). The narrator also observes that "[i]n the one erection, bell-tower and clock-tower were united, though, before that period, such structure had commonly been built distinct," suggesting that the joining of the two—the masculine tower and the feminine bell—represents an incestuous act (820). "That Bannadonna's crime is an incestuous one is indicated by his refusal to accept what may be regarded as natural limitations" (Costello and Kloss 255).

The epigraphs and the image of the blackened stump that begin the story, as well as Una's "fatal" expression, all forewarn the reader of the solitary Bannadonna's doom, while the magistrates, with their feeble warnings and suspicions about the tower and its creator, represent the traditional wisdom that has become outmoded in this new age of science and advancement ("Bell-Tower" 824). Talus, the robot, was intended to be "a new serf, more useful than the ox, swifter than the dolphin, stronger than the lion, more cunning than the ape, for industry an ant, more fiery than serpents, and yet, in patience, another ass" (830). This combination of traits, however, makes him unswervingly loyal in carrying out his master's will, which ironically results in Bannadonna's death as he seeks to perfect his unnatural creation. In death, Bannadonna lies at the feet of Una, who in her association with the heroine of *The Faerie Queene* embodies eternal truth. Fittingly, it is nature herself who completes the tower's destruction on the anniversary of its creator's death.

Themes

In the first half of the nineteenth century, science and technology began to dominate American life, vying with religion as a source of meaning and understanding. Following up on the resulting tensions probed comically in "The Lightning-Rod Man," "The Bell-Tower" somberly reflects the uncertainties of the day regarding the possible repercussions of science crossing natural boundaries that had previously been considered inviolate. In his depiction of the tower and Bannadonna, "the great mechanician, the unblest foundling," Melville draws associations between the Renaissance, a new "age that has no recognizable ancestors," and the technological revolution of his own day (Vernon 265). Framed by the presence of nature in its opening and closing imagery, the intervening narrative presents the inevitably doomed attempt of humanity to exceed its limitations by assuming godlike powers.

To support the central theme of human technology versus nature, Melville uses supporting motifs of time, slavery, and pride. In "Banna-donna's attempt to burst through human limitations, the limitation of time becomes a chief obstacle." Combining the roles of scientist, technician, and artist, Bannadonna "looks upon all of his creations as his time-extensions, capable of providing him with earthly immortality" (Vernon 268–69). Recognizing no bounds to his ambition, he terrorizes his workers, driving them relentlessly and even killing one as an example of the fate that will befall those who do not bend to his will. A slave to his own obsession, he enslaves others—both human and mechanical—to serve him in achieving his objectives, suggesting the dehumanizing dangers of technology. He seeks, as the narrator observes, "to solve nature, to steal into her, to intrigue beyond her, to procure some one else to bind her to his hand; these, one and all, had not been his objects; but, asking no favors from any element or any being, of himself, to rival her, outstrip her, and rule her." Misguided in his obsession, "[h]e stooped to conquer. With him, common sense was theurgy; machinery, miracle; Prometheus, the heroic name for machinist; man, the true God" ("Bell-Tower" 831). Such misplaced and overweening pride, in Melville much the same as in Hawthorne, can only lead to destruction, replicating again and again the fallen and seemingly irredeemable condition of humanity.

The stories collected in *The Piazza Tales* illustrate the wide range of narrative frames that Melville used in his magazine stories. These frames, as Bruce Bickley and John Bryant have variously identified, include the travelogue ("The Encantadas"), the gothic tale of mystery ("Benito Cereno" and "The Bell-Tower"), the romantic confessional ("The Piazza"), the character sketch ("Bartleby"), and the then popular Yankee peddler story ("The Lightning-Rod Man"). "The fact that Melville undertook to reprint a series of magazine pieces in book form perhaps emphasizes his financial difficulties during this period of his life for which so few biographical facts are known" (Sealts, "Publication" 59). However, although *The Piazza Tales* did not solve Melville's financial problems, the collection does underscore the fact that Melville was still a prolific and creative writer, willing to try new forms and work within a tighter compass in response to the changing reading habits of mid-nineteenth-century America.

7

Other Magazine Tales

In addition to the stories collected in *The Piazza Tales*, Melville wrote 10 other pieces of fiction that appeared in *Harper's New Monthly Magazine* and *Putnam's Monthly Magazine* between 1853 and 1856. Illustrative of the range and merit of these works are "I and My Chimney," which was originally published by *Putnam's*, "The Paradise of Bachelors and the Tartarus of Maids," which first appeared in *Harper's*, and the longer *Israel Potter*, which was serialized by *Putnam's* in nine installments before being published in book form.

"I AND MY CHIMNEY" (1856)

Written sometime during 1855, "I and My Chimney" was published in the March 1, 1856, issue of *Putnam's*. Surprisingly, of Melville's short fiction, the tale reportedly ranks only behind "Bartleby" and "Benito Cereno" in critical attention (Fisher, *Going Under* 199). The tale has been interpreted variously as a personal essay, a spiritual autobiography, "a thoroughgoing symbolic expression of Melville's basic epistemology," and "an illustration of his deep concern with political, social, and economic questions of his day" (Woodruff 283, Sowder 128–29). The enduring popularity of the tale has been explained in terms of its themes, which, according to some critics, "strike deep into the collective American psyche to a level that makes them recurrently contemporary" (Fisher, *Going Under* 212). Others, however, have observed that this continuing attention "could just as well be part of the growing awareness of the accessibility of Melville's work, so that sociologists, artists, philosophers, theologians, psychologists, as well as cultural historians, can find in the apparently inexhaustible symbolism of 'I and My Chimney' a reflection of their own compelling concerns" (Newman 251).

Setting and Plot

Because the story takes place in a country home and describes the relationship between an elderly man, who narrates the tale, and his wife, critics have generally assumed that the setting is the foothills of the Berkshire Mountains, where Melville lived from 1850 to 1863. At least one critic, however, has argued against this assumption, claiming that the setting could just as well be a plantation home in the antebellum South (Sowder 130). Although the home's geographic location may be debated, the plot revolves around a dispute between the narrator and his wife over the brick chimney that forms the architectural centerpiece of the house. The wife wants to remove the chimney so that a hallway can be added to make the rooms more accessible. The man, however, who regales the reader with an extended description of the chimney's attributes, refuses to part with it. When Hiram Scribe, an architect and stonemason, is summoned for consultation, he and the wife try to convince the narrator that there is a secret compartment in the chimney, which may be filled with treasure hidden there by a mysterious ancestor, Captain Julian Dacres. Scoffing at such foolish speculations, the narrator bribes Scribe with $50, getting in return from him a certificate that attests that the chimney is not unsound and has no secret closet in it. As the story ends, the narrator and his chimney—now seven years later—are still under attack. He remains vigilant, however, in standing guard against all threats, and closes his narrative with the steadfast avowal, "I and my chimney will never surrender" ("Chimney" 1327).

Characters

Melville draws the story's unnamed male narrator and his wife as contrasting studies. The narrator clearly aligns himself and his affections with his chimney—"two grey-headed old smokers," "old settlers here," and "both rather obese," he observes (1298–99). He, in fact, declares, "my chimney is my superior," and he enjoys nothing more than the sedentary pleasure of smoking beside it. In stark opposition to his companionable relationship with the chimney, a relationship that he values for its "settled" stability, he describes his marital relationship as one of continual discord (1321). In contrast to his own admiration for "oldness in things," his wife, he claims, "takes to nothing but newness" (1308–9). The man characterizes his wife as beset by a "terrible alacrity for improvement," which he views as just "a softer name for destruction" (1326). Although not without a sense of humor, the narrator views with skepticism the opinions of outsiders such as Scribe and increasingly isolates himself from the inhospitable world around him. Confiding at the end of the story that "[i]t is now some seven years since I have stirred from home," the man acknowledges that friends "think I am getting sour and unsocial" (1327). The wife, for her part, remains just as dedicated to her project of renovation as the husband is to resisting it. As he explains, "Scarce a day I do not find her with her tape-measure, measuring for her grand hall.... Assailed on all sides, and in all ways, small peace," he laments, "have I and my chimney" (1326).

The narrator depicts the other characters in the story as in league with his wife in her "mad project" to remove the chimney and thereby destroy his peace of mind (1326). After explaining that his two daughters, Anna and Julia, "take after, not me, but their mother," he depicts them assisting his wife in taking measurements for the hallway (1325). "Anna," he explains, "holds a yard stick on one side, and Julia looks approvingly on from the other" (1326). The narrator claims that the chimney "cannot be really comprehended except through what he calls the 'higher mathematics.'" As a result, he views his wife and daughters "as practitioners of a lower mathematics.... They measure, they calculate, and then draw rigid and simplistic conclusions" (Dillingham, *Short Fiction* 278, 279). From the narrator's perspective, Scribe most fully represents this type of limited understanding. The narrator quickly senses that Scribe is a con man motivated only by the financial gain he stands to make in removing the chimney. Furthermore, despite three visits to inspect the chimney, Scribe's errors in measuring and calculating, coupled with how easily he is bought off in the end, convince the reader that the narrator is not mistaken in his low estimation of the architect.

Allegory and Symbolism

"I and My Chimney" has invited many different allegorical readings. The conventional interpretation, posed first in 1941, views the story as a representation of Melville's and his family's concern about his mental health. The chimney, in this reading, represents "the heart and soul of Herman Melville," and the domestic argument about the chimney's possible "unsoundness" leads to calling in an expert to make an examination and diagnosis (Sealts, "'Chimney'" 147). The biographical support for such a reading includes Melville's refusal to sell Arrowhead, his home in the Berkshires; his family's concern over his response to the failure of his recent books to garner critical or popular success; and the related financial stress that he was under at the time he wrote this tale. It can also be argued that the mysterious ancestor Dacres, who built the house and the possible "secret closet" inside the chimney, is based on Melville's memories of his father, who suffered a mental breakdown before he died. In the narrator's refusal to consider that Dacres's "secret closet" lies within his chimney, he denies his own fear that he may have inherited his father's disposition to mental disorder. Because of her domineering nature, the wife in the story is judged to be patterned after Melville's mother, who was also living at Arrowhead at the time. This conclusion is also supported by a notation that Melville's wife Lizzie made about the character: "'All this about his wife, applied to his mother—who was very vigorous and energetic about the farm, etc.'" (qtd. in Sealts, "'Chimney'" 144).

It has also been conjectured that the model for Scribe may be Oliver Wendell Holmes, a physician, as well as a writer and a neighbor of Melville's in the Berkshires, who is believed to have treated him for an attack of sciatica in 1855. Further echoing Melville's preoccupation with his back is the fact that the narrator likens the chimney to a spine when he asserts, "To take out the backbone of anything, wife, is a hazardous affair" (1313). Thus, the chimney may actually stand for the narrator's back rather than his heart or soul. If so, the questionable soundness of the chimney would reflect the narrator's physical, rather than mental, health and so represent a humorous treatment of Melville's own—or any reader's—fears of growing old and infirm.

Closely related to this approach to reading "I and My Chimney" are others that focus on the story's sexual humor by arguing that the narrator is really concerned about impotence and castration rather than a bad back or insanity. Here "the chimney's identification with the man's phallus and the wife's dissatisfaction with the chimney would seem to suggest that the wife is not interested in sex"; however, "nothing can be further from the truth" (Pearce 85). By depicting the wife as young as a "mare" in spirit if not in actual years, Melville suggests that the woman's interest in sex has not flagged ("Chimney" 1307). Instead, her campaign to "remove" the chimney arguably reflects her wish to castrate her husband, who stubbornly guards the chimney, which is "the only thing that this man retains power over in his household" (Pearce 86).

Although the sexual imagery is hard to deny, it does not preclude the possibility that philosophical and political ideas may be at the heart of the story. In recent years, the sharp contrast between the narrator's love of "oldness" and his wife's love of "newness" has been identified as representing a number of conflicting value systems and world views that Melville observed in his day. For instance, the husband and wife have variously been interpreted as standing for English conservatism and American liberalism, traditionalism and modernism, empirical realities and transcendental idealism, Catholicism and Protestantism, and even the antebellum North and South.

Themes

Given the many different allegorical and symbolic associations that "I and My Chimney" invite, Melville's overarching intention may be to expose the fallacy of viewing the world in dualistic terms. The two main characters, in their polar oppositions, reflect the difficulty in reconciling world views, as well as the danger of oversimplifying the human condition or the complicated values and belief systems that operate in modern society. Clearly, Melville's personal allegiances tended in the direction of the narrator; however, as a critical thinker, he realized both the attractions and limitations in these opposing views. As a consequence, he ultimately seems to reject not only the wife's moral immaturity and idealism, but also the husband's cynical isolation and unquestioning adherence to tradition. In the process, he also critiques Scribe's "scientific method to probe final causes or ultimate meaning" (Woodruff 292).

"THE PARADISE OF BACHELORS AND THE TARTARUS OF MAIDS" (1855)

First published in the April 1, 1855, issue of *Harper's*, "The Paradise of Bachelors and the Tartarus of Maids" is generally considered the best of three formally structured bipartite stories—commonly called diptychs—that Melville wrote (the others being "The Two Temples," which was not published during Melville's lifetime, and "Poor Man's Pudding and Rich Man's Crumbs"). Named after an ancient writing tablet with two hinged panels, the diptych, as a story form, draws its point and effect in the relationship of opposition that exists between its two parts.

Setting and Plot

The first half of the story is set in London at a lavish bachelor dinner inspired by Melville's 1849 visit to London. While there, he visited Temple Church and then dined one night with male companions in Elm Court,

Temple, subsequently using the phrase "The Paradise of Bachelors" to describe the evening in his journal. Drawing from the mystery, myths, and legacy of the Knights Templar from the Crusades, Melville paints a lush and cloistered environment in which the narrator is invited to dine with nine present-day Templars, now lawyers, of the Temple-Bar in London. After much feasting and drinking, the men pass around "an immense convolved horn, a regular Jericho horn" containing "a mull of snuff" before drifting off, "two by two, and arm-in-arm," "some going to their neighboring chambers to turn over the Decameron" ("Paradise" 1264–65). Finally, only the narrator lingers behind. When asked by his host what he thinks "of the Temple here, and the sort of life we bachelors make out to live in it," he replies "with a burst of admiring candor—'Sir, this is the very Paradise of Bachelors!'" (1265).

In the second half of the story, inspired by Melville's own winter excursions in the Berkshires, the same narrator describes his sleigh ride to buy envelopes at a paper mill located in a valley dubbed Devil's Dungeon. Upon inspecting his surroundings, he observes, "This is the very counterpart of the Paradise of Bachelors, but snowed upon, and frost-painted to a sepulchre" ("Tartarus 1269). Entering the mill, he finds himself in a spacious room where, sitting "[a]t rows of blank-looking counters," are rows of "blank-looking girls, with blank, white folders in their blank hands, all blankly folding blank paper" (1270). Given a tour of the building by a youth named Cupid, the narrator inspects the "great machine" that manufactures the paper and learns about the paper-making process (1274). Later, the mill owner, Old Bach, explains that he only hires "maids," because married women "are apt to be off-and-on too much" (1278). Taking his leave of Devil's Dungeon, "wrapped in fur and meditations," the narrator thinks again of Temple-Bar and then exclaims, "Oh! Paradise of Bachelors! And oh! Tartarus of Maids!" (1279).

Characters

Melville uses the unnamed first-person narrator, identified as a seedsman in the second sketch, to tie together the two halves of the diptych. His observations and conclusions about both scenes make their relationship clear as a study in opposing lifestyles that are part of the same world picture. During the course of the story, the narrator moves from naivety in his uncritical embrace of the bachelors' opulent way of life to disillusionment and complicity in his realization of the implications of the maidens' oppression. Serving as the reader's guide through this process of growing comprehension, the narrator remains essentially a voyeur who lacks the necessary strength of character to change his values or even to criticize openly what he observes (Rowland 391).

The waiter who serves at the bachelor dinner is dubbed Socrates by the narrator. Through this character, Melville allows the reader to see an "outsider's" perspective, which raises doubts about the reliability of the narrator's impressions and suggests that authorial irony may underlie the exaggerated description of the lavish scene. The narrator declares that the waiter is a "venerable man" and a "surprising old field-marshal," who "[a]midst all the hilarity of the feast, intent on important business...disdained to smile" ("Paradise" 1262). However, "[t]he implications are that what the narrator mistakes for Socrates' decorum is actually disgust" (Browne, "Views" 45). Even the waiter's name supports the conclusion that the story's tone is wholly ironic. Rather than effecting clarity and understanding through the Socratic method of dialectical inquiry, this Socrates "brings comforts to cloud the mind" of those he serves, men who have no interest in or aptitude for intellectual inquiry or insights (Fisher, "'Tartarus'" 95).

In the "Tartarus" section of the tale, the guide Cupid also "belies his name. He looks right, but by word and deed shows himself a heartless little devil. He knows what makes this particular world go 'round and it certainly is not love" (Fisher, "'Tartarus'" 95). Cupid's nonchalant responses to the narrator's concerns about the maidens' working conditions and the "blank" product they produce, reveal a startling lack of social conscience or human empathy. For instance, when the narrator inquires why the maids are "'so sheet-white,'" Cupid, "with a roguish twinkle, pure ignorant drollery, not knowing heartlessness," replies, "'I suppose the handling of such white bits of sheets all the time makes them so sheety.'" Although the narrator recognizes Cupid's "cruel-heartedness," he strives to excuse it as a result of simple ignorance, as well as his being "usage-hardened," rather than imputing his attitude to a more pervasive and systemic failure of modern society ("Tartarus" 1274).

Cupid's boss Old Bach, by name, word, and deed, also is clearly oblivious to his own gendered insensitivity regarding the working conditions of the women he employs. For him, these women have no identity, purpose, or value beyond that which he derives from their physical labor. In addition, his name connects him back to the bachelors in "Paradise," ensuring that the reader considers the two sections of the tale in relation to each other in determining their symbolic and thematic meaning.

Allegory and Symbolism

"The Paradise of Bachelors and the Tartarus of Maids," like "I and My Chimney," has generated much critical commentary that focuses on the allegorical and symbolic elements of the tale. A few critics have viewed the two halves as representing a contrast between the Old World of Britain and the New World of America, with the British side being the way of life that Melville finds decidedly superior. The majority of critics, however, argue that such a surface reading fails to account for the obvious ironies in the tale and, as a result, fails to discern the deeper significance of Melville's social commentary. As the narrator explains, without yet realizing the implications of his comment, "The genuine Templar is long since departed" ("Tartarus" 1258). These bachelors live empty lives without substance or purpose. In fact, as "shirkers of the responsibilities of life, Melville's 'bachelors' . . . fail to commit themselves to life and thus actually do evil" (Browne, "Views" 43). Although the symbols supporting such a reading remain ambiguous until the second half of the tale, they gain both power and clarity when the story is considered as a whole.

The overabundance of rich food and alcoholic drink that the bachelors imbibe represent their lack of restraint and moderation. Significantly, the climax of the festivities suggests just how insubstantial and debased this domain of male prowess has become. The "Jericho horn," fittingly brought to the table by Socrates, "is in every way a bugle calling the dispossessed and poor to arms. The walls of this bastion are bound to come tumbling down. The vulnerability of these people is demonstrated by the fact that the horn contains only snuff; only a smoke screen of power is needed to topple them" from this hedonistic "Paradise" (Browne, "Views" 45).

By locating the maids in "Tartarus," the lowest region of the world in Greek mythology, Melville draws an immediate contrast to the bachelors' heavenly realm. He then uses seasonal and color imagery to emphasize their stark lives of oppressive servitude. The sketch is dominated by descriptive terms of winter coldness, ice, and snow. Incorporating the ambiguity of whiteness that he used in Moby-Dick, Melville complicates the maidens' innocence and virginity with repeated suggestions of sterility.

The "Tartarus" section of the tale is replete with undeniable sexual symbolism. Surprisingly, these symbols, which clearly would have been shocking to nineteenth-century readers, went undetected in Melville's day, but recent commentary has often focused on them as crucial in interpreting the tale's full meaning. The majority of modern readers "have noticed that the trip into Tartarus follows the contours of the anatomy of a giant female and that the horse's journey and the workings of the paper mill are described in terms of copulation, gestation, and birth" (Newman 297). The seedsman rides through a frigid winter landscape in a sleigh drawn by his horse Black. Racing "downward madly," he enters the womblike Devil's Dungeon, "a great, purple, hopper-shaped hollow," through "the

Black Notch." Once there, he visits a paper mill that is powered by the "strange-colored torrent Blood River" ("Tartarus" 1266). The reproductive process of the machinery in the mill, which is also explicitly described, turns pulp to paper in "'only nine minutes.'" The paper grows "more and more to final firmness" until, as a former nurse stands in attendance, "an unfolded sheet of perfect foolscap," that is "still moist and warm" drops down, accompanied by "a scissory sound . . . as of some cord being snapped" ("Tartarus" 1274–75).

Although the sexual allusions in the "Paradise" section are muted, they are nevertheless central to connecting the two sides of the story and drawing convincing conclusions about the whole. "Melville's references to Boccaccio's *Decameron,* to the song, 'Carry Me Back to Old Virginny,' to the serving man named Socrates, and to the 'Jericho horn' used as a mull for snuff, have all been interpreted as suggesting the impotency and latent homosexuality of the bachelors" (Newman 298). Further, the narrator's obvious anxiety in witnessing the reproductive process at the factory may point to his own fears of impotence and castration. His pointed recollection of the bachelors of "Paradise"—both as he arrives at and departs from the mill—suggests he feels inadequate and threatened in the presence of females, longing instead for the all-male companionship that he found in London.

Themes

Contrary to what most of Melville's canon of works has led critics to believe, the pervasive sexual symbolism in "The Paradise of Bachelors and the Tartarus of Maids" suggests he may have been sensitive to the gendered inequities of Western society. Women in "Tartarus" are doomed to serve men and unable to escape the biological burdens associated with child-bearing. When the narrator questions the inevitability of the paper-making process, Cupid replies, "'It *must* go. The machinery makes it go just *so;* just that very way, and at that very pace you there plainly *see* it go. The pulp can't help going.'" Further, "[t]he implication here is that the bachelor's way of life is only possible because he is selfishly using women as wage-slaves and domestic drudges as well as sexually" (Leavis 205–6).

In addition to its feminist theme, the tale also "expresses imaginatively the emotional impact" of what Melville saw as an impending "general crisis for humanity: the widespread existence of a mechanistic, life-deadening, freedom-denying set of values emphasized in America by increasing industrialization" (Fisher, "'Tartarus'" 83). Some argue that all levels of symbolism merge in the end of the story to create a cry that echoes that of the lawyer narrator at the end of "Bartleby." Although as social protest, the tale arguably seeks improved living and working conditions for all, Melville's sympathy clearly lies with the females who are involuntarily committed to the means of production (Browne, "Views" 47). The issues raised by "The Paradise of Bachelors and the Tartarus of Maids" are still being argued today by feminists and humanists in general. This fact explains why the tale is among the most anthologized of Melville's short stories and supports the claim of the continued relevance of his social commentary in the twenty-first century.

ISRAEL POTTER (1855)

Like "The Paradise of Bachelors and the Tartarus of Maids," *Israel Potter* was inspired by Melville's 1849 trip to London. While there, he acquired a copy of the *Life and Remarkable Adventures of Israel R. Potter*, the memoir of an obscure Revolutionary War figure that had been ghostwritten and published by the printer Henry Trumbull in 1824. During this same visit, Melville noted in his journal that he had bought a 1766 map of London to use in case he decided to "serve up the Revolutionary narrative of the beggar" (qtd. in Bach 40); however, it was not until 1854 that the writer followed up on this possibility. The first installment of the narrative appeared in the July 1854 issue of *Putnam's*, appropriately carrying the subheading "A Fourth of July Story," and G. P. Putnam and Company followed up by publishing the serial in book form in March 1855. Blurring historical fact with fiction, Melville took some liberties with his source materials in creating *Israel Potter*, which parodies elements of biography, adventure story, historical romance, and sentimental novel. Although the tale has generated little critical attention, its satirical portraits of recognized Revolutionary figures have drawn much praise.

Setting and Plot

In his version of the life of Israel Potter, Melville relocates Potter's birthplace and youth from Rhode Island, where the actual Potter was born and raised, to the Berkshire Mountains of Massachusetts. After quarreling with his father, the youth leaves home to try a variety of occupations without success. Returning home for the second time during this period, he works as a farmer until his militia is called up to fight in the American Revolution. After recovering from being wounded in the Battle of Bunker

Hill, Potter volunteers for naval service. Captured by the British off the coast of Boston, he is taken to England by prison ship.

Although its subtitle, "His Fifty Years of Exile," suggests that *Israel Potter* will delineate the adventures of the title character's entire life, Melville compresses his treatment of Potter's early life in colonial America, as well as most of his years in exile, choosing to focus most of his attention on the first few years of the protagonist's struggles after being separated from his homeland. In this major section of the novel, Melville recounts a series of adventures that chronicles Potter's many experiences of escaping from captivity of one sort or another during his first five years of exile. During these adventures, he travels to Paris as a courier for Squire John Woodcock, a British sympathizer to America, to deliver secret communications to Benjamin Franklin. While staying with Franklin, he meets Captain John Paul Jones, with whom he shares his room for the night. Returning back to England, Potter is next secreted in a hidden compartment within the home of Squire Woodcock and must make his own escape when his host unexpectedly dies. Slipping through a secret passage, he changes into the Squire's clothes, posing as his ghost to exit the house. Soon thereafter he is shanghaied into the service of the British Navy but is eventually rescued by a man-of-war commanded by his old acquaintance Jones. As a result, he ends up assisting Jones in the famous battle between the *Bon Homme Richard* and the *Serapis* before being trapped on a British frigate. Eventually, after finding a place for himself as part of the crew of this ship, he observes Ethan Allen, chained in captivity, when they stop at Falmouth. Again escaping, Potter labors for 13 weeks in a brickyard a few miles from London before moving into the city. There he endures in abject poverty for 45 years, mending chairs for a trade, marrying, and fathering 11 children, 10 of whom die. Finally, in 1826, his one remaining son and the American counsel help him fulfill his dream of returning to America. Arriving there on the fourth of July in the midst of a commemorative celebration of the Battle of Bunker Hill, he finds nothing remaining of his memories of home. He dies soon thereafter.

Characters

Israel Potter is an "everyman" figure, a common man who despite his courage and ingenuity is continually gulled by circumstance. "[H]e is dupe and trickster by turns and seems," in the end, "to suffer more than he gains from life (Rosenberry, *Comic Spirit* 173–74). Although, as the protagonist, he is centrally present throughout the narrative, he seems in most respects "not only a minor figure but the book's least interesting character"

(Obuchowski 456). Ultimately, his true significance lies in the comparison of his life with those of the three major historical figures who cross his path.

The first and foremost of these national heroes is Dr. Benjamin Franklin, depicted satirically by Melville "as a slightly humorous, overbearing, prudential autocrat." Franklin "systematically assumes the role of a teacher" to Potter by lecturing him on a variety of subjects: "undue suspicion, gratitude, exactness in pecuniary matters, seriousness in funerals and business transactions, frugality in regard to both money and food, extravagance, and idleness" (Bach 43). "The Franklin of Melville's creation represents a duality which is irreconcilable. As he preaches thrift, he seems surrounded by an aura of luxury" (Jackson 199). Reflecting on Franklin's treatment of him, Potter shrewdly observes, "'Every time he comes in he robs me ... with an air all the time, too, as if he were making me presents. If he thinks me such a very sensible young man, why not let me take care of myself?'" Perusing the pamphlet of maxims that Franklin has left for him to read, Potter concludes, "'Oh confound all this wisdom! It's a sort of insulting to talk wisdom to a man like me. It's wisdom that's cheap, and it's fortune that's dear'" (*Israel Potter* 486). Realizing the dichotomy between his own world and Franklin's, Potter smarts under the presumptions inherent in the doctor's "wisdom."

While Franklin is presented as "everything but a poet," John Paul Jones is described as "a bit of the poet as well as the outlaw" (*Israel Potter* 479, 489). Dramatic and egotistical, he is consumed with his search for a ship for which there will be "no leader and no counselor but himself." Described as "a disinherited Indian Chief in European clothes," he wants nothing more than to "rain down on wicked England like fire on Sodom" (*Israel Potter* 488, 490). Recalling Ahab's monomania in *Moby-Dick*, Jones repeatedly demonstrates "that he is willing to sacrifice the safety of his crew in his mad pursuit of the seemingly invincible British" (Bach 45).

Although Potter never actually meets Ethan Allen, he clearly has much more in common with this man than with either Franklin or Jones. Both are exiled captives struggling for their lives. Their treatment and outcomes differ, however. Allen is treated with "inexcusable cruelty and indignity" by the British, who look upon him as "a common mutineer" (*Israel Potter* 594, 595). Nevertheless, in the end, he is returned to America and "in due time, at New York, honorably included in a regular exchange of prisoners" (*Israel Potter* 596). In contrast, Potter's treatment by the British is for the most part humane, but as a common soldier, rather than a distinguished officer, he is ultimately abandoned and forgotten by both America and England.

Allegory and Symbolism

Formally, the book is structured as an allegory that likens Potter's lengthy exile, through the significance of his first name, to those of the displaced Jews. As Melville explains in the first chapter, "for more than forty years, poor Potter wandered in the wild wilderness of the world's extremest hardships and ills" (432). Because of the comic antics, however, as well as the fact that the reader is told of the ultimate outcome at the beginning of the book, the reader "tends to follow the events of Israel's life with detachment and a sense of anticlimax" (Obuchowski 460). Only in the closing chapters does Melville engage the reader's sympathy by describing the intense poverty that Potter suffered for decades after his earlier adventurous escapades.

Israel's "career as a wandering exile from the promised land" represents humanity's "failure to achieve earthly happiness," connecting with the biblical "expulsion of Adam and Eve from the garden of Eden" through the garden imagery that appears in the novel. Unlike Adam and Eve, however, Potter "does not descend into an unpeopled world" (Keyssar 13, 15). Significantly, he flees to the city of London because "crowds are the security, ... the true desert of persecuted man" (*Israel Potter* 598). Further, Potter's "identity as a fugitive is determined by his fear of capture and imprisonment." As a result, the "symbolism of captivity, immurement, and enclosure is highly developed" in the text (Keyssar 16). The hidden compartment in Squire Woodcock's house, the brickyard pit, and the sewers of London all serve as virtual tombs, from which Potter is resurrected only through his own ingenuity.

This dual motif of confinement and escape is repeatedly supported by Israel's symbolic changing of clothes. "At least seven instances of clothes changing are explicitly mentioned by Melville, and each represents, to some extent, a shift in Potter's role, function, or destiny." Potter assumes the clothes—the identity—of others to stay alive. However, "it becomes increasingly clear ... that these identities represent a denial of life's rewards and the continuance of an existence that is hardly human." In addition, the fact that Potter's "relations to other characters are greatly influenced by the appearance of his clothing is a further commentary upon the role of social status in determining fate" (Keyssar 19–20).

Potter also represents not just any common man but specifically the common American, and in doing so, he stands in the role of son to the land of his birth. The tension inherent in such a relationship is obvious from the beginning, when Potter leaves home after arguing with his father about his wishes to marry a young woman of whom the father disapproves.

Throughout the years of his exile, Potter is befriended by various other father figures, all of whom use him for their own purposes and then leave him to his own devices. Although authority and privilege are vested in these fathers, they continually fail their responsibilities to their son, just as America has. Further, through his detailed portraits of the three national heroes—Franklin, Jones, and Allen—Melville seems to represent all that he feels has gone wrong with American values and attitudes. Franklin's hypocrisy, Jones's barbaric savagery, and Allen's class privilege all suggest Melville's belief that America, even at the time of its founding, had already lost sight of the democratic and idealistic dreams on which it was supposedly built.

Supporting this conclusion is the fact that Melville frames his story of Israel Potter with the Bunker Hill Monument, the symbol of American patriotic values and the American dream of freedom. Addressing and dedicating the novel "To His Highness the Bunker-Hill Monument," he asserts that he is presenting this tribute to Potter, "a private of Bunker Hill," so that his name can become part of the record of the Revolutionary War (*Israel Potter* 425). Melville drives home the satiric intent of this dedication, suggested already by the choice of the word "Highness," in the scene of Potter's return to America on July 4, 1826. Arriving on a day of national celebration, he observes a parade in honor of Revolutionary heroes and is nearly "run over by a patriotic triumphal car in the procession" (*Israel Potter* 613). The crowd of patriotic celebrants neither recognize Potter as a hero nor care about his life story, suggesting that national heroism has become an abstract and empty concept for Americans.

Melville presents his most symbolic commentary on Potter's heroic response to life in the chapter that depicts the pit of the brickyard in which the protagonist toils as a "bondsman in the English Egypt" (*Israel Potter* 602). As he tends the kiln, Potter observes that there are three types of bricks, distinguished by their proximity to the fire: "The furnace-bricks were haggard, with the immediate blistering of the fire—the midmost ones were ruddy with a genial and tempered glow—the summit ones were pale with the languor of too exclusive an exemption from the burden of the blaze" (*Israel Potter* 601–2). "Only those bricks which are in the middle are the good ones. Not broken by life's poverty and adversities, not detached and therefore indifferent, but truly and completely and democratically committed, they are the best bricks for the wall of humanity" (Browne, "Israel Potter" 96). "Potter is associated with that middle layer of bricks, but more specifically with those middle bricks closest to the fire." His "strategic placement here testifies to Melville's recognition that man's humanity must be tested and tempered by the fiery kiln of experience"

(Carlson 86). It is a testimony to Potter's strength of character and courage that he is able to endure this test without giving in to despair and becoming, like the furnace-bricks, "burnt to useless scrolls, black as charcoal, and twisted into shapes the most grotesque" (*Israel Potter* 601).

Themes

With *Israel Potter*, Melville creates a vehicle to critique the traditional view of biography that ignores "the common man as a viable subject and productive force of history." By exploring the "complex tensions between greatness and commonness, genius and virtue, ideas and artifacts," he "suggests ways of integrating the common man into the events and texts of history" (Reagan 258). In probing these tensions, he develops several related themes.

From a universal perspective, Potter's story depicts the plight of the common person in a hostile world. Trust becomes impossible in such a setting. The pattern of Potter's life as a fugitive "emphasizes the existential fact that man, on earth, is fundamentally *alone*, that he is confined by the very fact of his existence in the world" (Keyssar 17). Balancing this theme of alienation, however, is the motif of endurance that suggests not only Potter's strength of character on an individual basis but also the hope for humanity that he represents on a broader scale.

More specifically, *Israel Potter* deals with the reality and myth of America by presenting a commentary on the evolution—or devolution—of American character and American ideals. As the conclusion of the novel makes clear, "America, intent upon celebrating its myth, ignores its social reality" (Keyssar 24). Like his renowned co-patriots, Israel embodies those characteristics of national character that have come to be regarded as components of the American ethos: he is fearless, chauvinistic, independent, self-reliant, adventurous, and resourceful. Unlike Franklin's "rags to riches" story, however, Potter's story ends with no reward for his steadfast courage, patience, humility, or industry. Through the example of this long-forgotten, common soldier, Melville suggests that the American dream is now just empty rhetoric for all but the privileged or fortunate few. Seeking his whole life to get back home, Potter finds in the end, that "[f]ew things remain" and so dies in virtual anonymity (*Israel Potter* 615). That he has one surviving son, however, suggests that some small hope remains that America will change its course and recover its lost values.

8

Deconstructing
The Confidence-Man

Melville began work on *The Confidence-Man* (1857) in 1855, while he was still submitting stories to *Putnam's Monthly Magazine*. Some scholars have claimed that the central character for this work is modeled on the figure of the traditional Yankee peddler of American folklore. More recent scholarship, however, has determined that the origin of Melville's character can, in fact, be traced to a "real life criminal so well known in the 1850s that many readers of *The Confidence-Man* could not have helped but connect him with the novel as they read it" (Bergmann 561). According to the research of Johannes Dietrich Bergmann, the term "confidence man" was coined in connection with this criminal, a swindler named William Thompson, who received much publicity in the press when he was arrested in 1849 and again in 1855. This original confidence man, operating under one of many alias identities, would approach a stranger, whom he pretended to know, and ask for the person's "confidence," which he then convinced the unwitting victim to prove in the form of a loan. Having secured this proof of trust by receiving a watch or money from the victim, Thompson would then disappear. Although he certainly was not the first swindler to prey on his victim's trust, Thompson was the first to use the word "confidence" in his deception, resulting in the origin of the appellation from which Melville drew in conceiving his novel and its title character.

Presumably drawing the connection to its source of inspiration, some of the early reviews of *The Confidence-Man* commented on it as "using a specifically indigenous American subject, an 'original subject,'" and "aiming at greater popularity than was usual with Melville's novels, if only because of its topic and title" (Bergmann 576). Overall, however, when the book "appeared in 1857 it was greeted by the English periodical press in a series of reviews which at once expressed an unusual enjoyment and revealed a profound incomprehension of the work" (Drew 418). Even during the Melville Revival of the 1920s and 1930s, *The Confidence-Man* was deemed an embarrassing and unreadable failure, which could be explained only in terms of its author's creative exhaustion and descent into bitter cynicism if not outright madness. Although its ambiguity still confounds critical consensus, the book in recent decades has finally found an audience with tastes more attuned to its form, style, and themes. As a result, *The Confidence-Man* has gained something of a cult following, and critics now consider it, if still Melville's most baffling text, then also his most modern. In recovering the novel from obscurity in 1949, Richard Chase deemed it "Melville's second-best achievement," and others since this time have been similarly impressed, citing it, for instance, as "the clearest example of the experimental novel—not only in Melville's writings, but in the whole of the nineteenth century, in America or Europe" (Chase, "Confidence" 136; Sten 285).

In large part, the experimental nature of *The Confidence-Man* can be attributed to its complex mix of genre, always present to some extent in Melville's writings, but here carried to new extremes. In fact, the book's fragmented form has caused many to resist classifying it as a novel at all. Those who prefer to categorize it as a prose satire point to Melville's emphasis on abstract and intellectual ideas through his use of "a series of dialogues, whose speakers are stylized" (Kern 30). Others point to the same emphasis on dialogue as evidence of the text's dramatic method, as well as to the use of "reversals of character and action" and the protagonist's protean performance in which he assumes a variety of shapes and disguises (Dubler 308). Further, the novel adheres to the three dramatic unities, derived from Aristotle, which stipulate that for unity of effect a play must develop a single action that occurs in one location and within the confines of a single day. *The Confidence-Man* also exhibits a number of elements associated with the picaresque, a popular eighteenth-century form that features humor in detailing the episodic adventures of a roguish hero of low social standing who lives by his or her wits in a corrupt society. To a lesser extent, Melville uses elements of the romance that recall the metaphorical and symbolic qualities of *Mardi*, and he also incorporates some verse—and even nursery rhyme—into the text. In its final resistance of generic labels, *The Confidence-Man* shows Melville to be ahead of his time in searching for a new form to transcend the traditional limits of the novel.

POINT OF VIEW

In keeping with the dramatic aspects of the novel, the narrative voice in *The Confidence-Man* is removed from the action, so that for long stretches of time, the dialogue has center stage. Acting almost as a director who sets the actors in motion, this third-person unnamed narrator rarely intrudes by making judgments, which serves to reinforce the ambiguity in the text. Rather, "[t]he whole story is told entirely from without, by someone who merely observes and reports" (Buell, "Last Word" 17). At times, the narration achieves an omniscient or biased effect, as when one character is presented as "unmindful of another pensive figure near" or when another character "half divines" that he has been misled (*Confidence-Man* 38, 978); however, "such hints are infrequent, contradictory (like the two just given), and inconclusive. As a result, the reader is enticed into a continuous guessing game" (Buell, "Last Word" 17). At times, the narrator directly addresses the reader, most notably in digressions about the relationship between life and fiction, but also in descriptive comments about the characters. On such occasions, through his use of equivocation and wordplay, he often misleads the reader, causing some critics to claim that the narrator is "the most important character we meet" and "the ultimate Confidence-Man" (Roundy, "*Confidence-Man*" 10, 11). "When he does play omniscience he often provokes our suspicion of the character in question, though he never offers proof of ill-intent; and when he professes ignorance about a particular character, the effect is strangely the same" (Sten 290). In short, although the narrator is never completely unreliable, the reader cannot depend on him to resolve the text's inconsistencies.

Only a few scholars have pondered the reason behind the evolving attitude toward point of view that Melville displays in his prose fiction. Although his early novels depended almost exclusively on the voice of a first-person participant, he eventually moved to embrace the perspective of a third-person observer, a change that culminates in the detached and anonymous narration of *The Confidence-Man*. This shift may bespeak only his growing maturity and artistic sophistication. Alternatively, it may suggest a "philosophical withdrawal on Melville's part, a resignation in the belief that the world cannot be altered or even understood" (Buell, "Last Word" 28).

SETTING, PLOT, AND STRUCTURE

The action of *The Confidence-Man* takes place in the span of one day—significantly April 1, April Fool's Day—a date with implications that Dix, Edwards and Company, Melville's American publisher, capitalized on by releasing the book on this day in 1857. The setting is similarly confined to one location, a Mississippi steamer named the *Fidèle*. Leaving St. Louis after boarding its passengers "[a]t sunrise," the riverboat begins its journey of 1,200 miles down the Mississippi River to New Orleans (*Confidence-Man* 841). At the end of the day, the novel draws to a close in darkness.

Lacking a cohesive, coherent plot, the novel is instead characterized by a pattern of repetition and reversal whereby a succession of encounters occur between confidence men and their victims. The book can be divided into two main sections. In the first section, composed of the first 23 chapters, seven principal confidence men are introduced. With the exception of the first such character, a deaf mute who promotes charity, "[a]ll seem basically out for money," although "there is a development of sorts in the [increasing] sophistication of their lines of appeal" (Buell, "Last Word" 18). In the second section of the book, the focus is on just one confidence man—Frank Goodman, the cosmopolitan, whose role is reversed. Instead of seeking money, he claims to seek friendship. Instead of succeeding as the earlier confidence men do, his overtures are met by apathy, suspicion, distrust, and even outright hostility. In the first part of this section, the reader is even temporarily misled to consider another character, Charlie Noble, as the confidence man. Ultimately, however, these reversals are incomplete. The cosmopolitan talks the barber William Cream into taking down his sign, which reads, "No trust" (i.e., no credit). Drawing up a contract promising to reimburse the barber for any losses that may result, Goodman walks out without paying for his shave. The barber then tears up the contract and rehangs his sign. In the final chapter, the cosmopolitan enters the gentlemen's cabin, where he meets an old man who is reading the Bible. They agree that distrusting man—God's creation—is like distrusting God, the creator. Then, when the old man asks where his life preserver is, the cosmopolitan hands him a stool, turns out the light, and "kindly" leads him away. The novel concludes with the final enigmatic statement, "Something further may follow of this Masquerade" (1112). This final word, as well as the statement's overall suggestion of incompletion, connects with the full title of the novel, *The Confidence-Man: His Masquerade,* to reinforce the conclusion that the novel has actually recounted the encounters of not multiple confidence men but rather just one such figure with multiple masks.

Ultimately, despite its mazelike configuration, the novel can be seen to repeat one basic pattern: "the encounter in which trust is solicited, then given or denied, under circumstances sufficiently ambiguous that the reader is encouraged to infer, but not permitted to know, the motives of the solicitor and the wisdom of the solicited. This central situation is embellished" not only by repetition and the reactions of bystanders, but also by four anecdotal stories narrated by characters within the main storyline and three narrative digressions on the art of fiction (Buell, "Last Word" 20).

In keeping with the overall texture of the book, the interpolated stories incorporate removals and reversals. The first tale relates the vicious acts perpetrated on John Ringman, one of the guises of the confidence man, by his wife Goneril, which eventually cause him to take up a life of wandering until he learns of her death. Although Goneril seems to represent evil, doubt arises because the story is told by the confidence man, at one remove, through the narrator. When Charlie Noble relays the story of Colonel John Moredock, the Indian-hater, the question arises as to whether Moredock, whose obsessive hatred for all Indians is incited by the murder of his family, "is represented as a hero or a villain, or even as an absurdist, serio-comic fabrication" (Cook 184). This story also has the effect of being told second-hand because Noble claims he is relaying his recollection of the remembrance of Moredock by his father's friend, the author James Hall, who was an actual nineteenth-century author of such accounts. The cosmopolitan relays the third story, which features Charlemont, a wealthy and popular bachelor living in St. Louis, who is financially ruined at the age of 29 in the span of a single day. Disappearing without explanation, this "gentleman-madman" eventually recovers from his financial reversal by making another fortune in Marsailles. Returning to St. Louis nine years after his bankruptcy, he is accepted back into the fellowship of friends but still refuses to explain "the one enigma of his life" other than to say that it occurred when he resolved to save the world "from a sin by prospectively taking that sin" upon himself (*Confidence-Man* 1039–40). The final story concerns the misfortunes of China Aster, a candle maker from Marietta, Ohio, who accepts from a friend a $1,000 gift—later termed a loan—to expand his business. Unable to repay the debt when his business fails, he loses all and dies. This last tale is told by one of the intended victims of the confidence man, Egbert, who disclaims the spirit, if not the moral, of the story by assuming the words and "maudlin" style of "the original story-teller" (*Confidence-Man* 1063).

Interspersed with these stories are three digressions on narrative strategy, which comprise Chapters 14, 33, and 44 of the novel. In these chapters, the narrator discusses "issues of consistency, realism, and originality in fictional characterization" (Cook 199). The digressions relate directly to Melville's method in The Confidence-Man and also indirectly support the structure of the overall narrative. In Chapter 14, Melville uses a sudden revelation by one of the characters as the pretext for his defense of inconsistency in fictional characterization as reflecting the inconsistency of actual life experience. Characters who are transparent, or whose apparent contradictions turn out to be resolvable, he argues, are incompatible with the true complexities of human society. Serving as a preface to the enigmatic story of Charlemont, Chapter 33 again begins by defending the apparent criticism of how "unreal" his presentation of a character—the cosmopolitan—has been to this point in the novel. This time, however, the discussion is concerned not with the importance of art's fidelity to life, but instead with its seeming opposition—the invocation of the imaginative realm in achieving art's objective to entertain and delight. Taking its impetus from the barber's remark that the cosmopolitan is "QUITE AN ORIGINAL," the final authorial reflection elaborates on originality in fictional characterization (Confidence-Man 1096). The narrator claims that a truly original character "is like a revolving Drummond light, raying away from itself all around it" (1098). Nevertheless, by ending the chapter with the narrator's assertion that he has been endeavoring "to show, if possible, the impropriety of the phrase, Quite an Original, as applied by the barber's friends," Melville mystifies his meaning by undercutting this revelation's association with his own protagonist (1098). He further adds to the ultimate ambiguity of this specific discussion, and the novel as a whole, by using the digression as a set-up for the next chapter—the final chapter of the book—which ends in darkness when the cosmopolitan turns off the light.

CHARACTERS

At the onset, the passengers on the Fidèle are described as "[n]atives of all sorts, and foreigners.... In short, a piebald parliament, an Anacharsis Cloots congress of all kinds of that multiform pilgrim species, man" (Confidence-Man 848). The sheer variety of representation prepares the way for "a bewildering proliferation of [individual] characters and descriptions." Often the characters "lack names. They are instead identified by epithets like 'the hook-nosed man,' 'the other,' and 'the stranger.' But a single epithet can apply to more than one character," as in the case of "the stranger," and "individual characters also accrue multiple epithets" (Renker 71). Appearing first is a deaf mute, who writes maxims about charity on the slate that he carries. This pale "man in cream colors," whose cheek is "fair, his chin downy, his hair flaxen, his hat a white fur one," contrasts starkly with Black Guinea, the beggar, who is next introduced and described as "a grotesque negro cripple" with "an old coal-sifter of a tambourine," "knotted black fleece," and a "good-natured, honest black face" (*Confidence-Man* 841, 849). Some passengers speculate that Guinea's blackness is a painted-on mask. "'He's some white operator,'" muses a man with a wooden leg, "'betwisted and painted up for a decoy'" (853). However, other passengers, notably a Methodist army chaplain and an Episcopal clergyman, support the beggar's authenticity.

Another manifestation of the confidence man is John Ringman, "the man with the weed," who is mourning his dead wife Goneril and who may "be a great sage or a great simpleton" (865). Ringman asks another passenger, the merchant Henry Roberts, for a bank note and momentarily tempts him to buy some Black Rapids Coal Company stock. A man in gray appears to solicit contributions for the Seminole Widow and Orphan Asylum. He is followed by John Truman, the president and transfer agent of the Black Rapids Coal Company, who carries a "ledger-like volume" and sells stock to a college man, Henry Roberts, and a coughing miser with the promise of multiplying their investment (*Confidence-Man* 889). In his next configuration, the confidence man is an herb doctor, who identifies Truman to the miser as coming from St. Louis and then sells him one of his miracle cures. He fails, however, to convince Pitch, a disillusioned backwoodsman from Missouri, to buy from him. Pitch, nevertheless, falls prey next to the Philosophical Intelligence Officer. This incarnation of the confidence man convinces Pitch not to replace the boy who works for him with a machine. He then disappears after taking the Missourian's money based on a promise to produce another boy in whom trust would be warranted. In the second half of the novel, Frank Goodman, the dapper cosmopolitan, converses with a number of potential victims, most notably Charlie Noble, the mystical philosopher Mark Winsome, and Winsome's more practical disciple Egbert. Unable to separate them from their principles or money, the cosmopolitan finds success with the barber William Cream instead.

ALLEGORY AND SYMBOLISM

The Confidence-Man, with its frontier setting and constantly shifting cast of disparate and vivid characters, represents the character of American society. The riverboat and its passengers symbolize the "dashing and all-fusing spirit of the West, whose type is the Mississippi itself, which, uniting the streams of the most distant and opposite zones, pours them along, helter-skelter, in one cosmopolitan and confident tide" (*Confidence-Man* 848). With its link to the cosmopolitan, who will figure as the most developed image of the confidence man, this early comment suggests that the title character, in particular, reflects the characteristics of the "melting pot" image of American society. On the level of universal allegory, however, the ship can also be seen as a microcosm of the world, where life is compared to a masquerade and where the confidence man becomes a representative example "of that multiform pilgrim species, man" (848).

The name of the ship, *Fidèle*, which means faith, immediately brings religious elements into Melville's tale, as does the character of the mute, who chalks onto his slate well-known Bible verses from the thirteenth chapter of First Corinthians. "Throughout his various enterprises, the double-crossing Confidence-Man blandly preaches the Christian doctrine of faith, hope, and charity, because it helps him in his business" (Thompson 298). Critics disagree, however, as to just who the confidence man represents in his allegorical relationship with his fellow travelers in life. He has been variously interpreted as the returning Christ, as a devil disguised as a Christian, and as an indictment of American society in terms of race, economics, and politics; however, each of these interpretations of the confidence man, in one way or another, fails to cohere. "For instance, if he is Christ, then why is he actively swindling people, and why does the ending seem so sinister? If he is the devil, then why is he conning people for such trivial sums, and why, in the final chapter, does Melville describe him as 'eying the old man with sympathy'?" Further, Melville continually drops clues that "lead either to intricate dead ends or ambiguous revelations, and often they fail to materialize at all" (Lamb 503).

The figure of Black Guinea illustrates the type of interpretive riddle that the novel repeatedly configures. As the only nonwhite actually to appear in the book, his obvious contrast with the apparent "lamb-like" innocence of the mute, who immediately precedes him, suggests that Melville may be drawing on black-and-white color stereotypes to represent the contrast between good and evil, Christ and Satan (*Confidence-Man* 844). The crippled Guinea's connection with the devil "accords with legends of the devil as crippled by his fall from heaven or as disabled by his cloven hoof." He "is even metaphorically given the horns of the devil when" another passenger "puts 'his large purple hand on the cripple's bushy wool, as if it were the curled forehead of a black steer'" (Cook 67). Guinea also suggests the devil's association with sexual temptation when he moves among the passengers with his "black face rubbing against the upper part of the people's thighs" (*Confidence-Man* 849). Guinea's comparison to a "half-frozen black sheep" and his human suffering, however, "also suggest

Christ's symbolic role as the Lamb of God" (*Confidence-Man* 850, Cook 63). All in all, it is unclear whether Guinea is a mock-diabolic figure or a parody of Christ's life and teachings.

Looking beyond the religious inferences to those of historical and political significance, Guinea still remains an ambiguous figure. In physical description, he "evokes an antebellum stereotype of the Negro as a child-like dependent who would be helpless in white society if freed from slavery," seemingly typifying the degraded "black man as a permanent alien in white America" (Cook 35). With the suggestion that, as a confidence man, Guinea is actually a white man in black-face makeup, however, it becomes increasingly unclear if "Melville is degrading the black through stereotype or whether he is indicting the white man for his oversimplification of the black character." Guinea is at the same time depicted as "a grinning darky, a deserving object of the white man's abuse" and "as a white man assuming the stereotypical characteristics of the darky … an indirect criticism of the whites who see the Negro as formula" (Grejda 128–29). As a result, he ultimately seems "an ambiguous index of racial injustice" (Cook 36).

Because of the maze of such interpretive impasses that Melville devises, the book ultimately deconstructs any overarching, consistent interpretation, either as an allegory or as a more densely symbolic text. Even the novel's conclusion in darkness, interpreted by the most cynical of Melville's readers as apocalyptic doom, is undercut by the final enigmatic sentence that suggests a continuation of some sort. For some readers and critics, this "breakdown" in coherence represents the novel's failure. Increasingly, however, critics have argued that Melville's fragmented, multivoiced masquerade succeeds, rather than fails, *because* of its inconsistency—that such inconsistency is fundamental both to the author's intensions and to his achievements in *The Confidence-Man*. Such critics argue, in part, that "the novel's meaning lies in its disordered appearance and not in any hidden, comprehensible order" (Lamb 501).

Because of its failure to adhere to an overall allegoric or symbolic design, critical opinion is still divided as to the overall verdict to impose on the novel; however, virtually all agree that Melville, within *The Confidence-Man*, draws some brilliant caricatures fashioned from identifiable biographical models. For instance, the renowned actress Fanny Kemble has been suggested as the model for Goneril, and Edgar Allan Poe was almost certainly the inspiration for the "crazy beggar" who approaches Mark Winsome and Frank Goodman with his "rhapsodical tract" as they discuss mummies (Oliver, "Goneril"; Hayford, "Poe"; *Confidence-Man* 1049). Much attention has also been given to Melville's critique of American transcendentalism, the idealistic philosophical and religious movement fashioned by Ralph

Waldo Emerson from the European philosophy of Immanuel Kant and others. In *The Confidence-Man*, the mystic Mark Winsome "resembles Emerson in posture and physical appearance. Moreover, the mystic's conversation bears a relationship, in general and in many particulars, to the ideas and phrasing of Emerson's *Nature*" (Oliver, "Melville's Picture" 62). Both Winsome and his protégé Egbert, who seems modeled after Henry David Thoreau, are described with words such as "coolly," "chill," and "icy" to suggest the actual deficiency of heart and human warmth that Melville sensed in both the abstract tenets of transcendentalism and the behavior and personalities of its adherents.

Also drawing much critical attention, as well as the opinion that the episode forms the center of the novel, is Melville's ambiguous treatment of "Indian-hating." Reflecting the same interpretive ambiguity already discussed regarding the representation of the confidence man, this interpolated story has received various readings as a result of the difficulty in determining Melville's tone. Some critics claim that Melville, despite his personal views of Indians, uses them as symbols of diabolic evil, arguing that to hate the devil is the duty of good Christians such as Moredock, although most have difficulty viewing this character's obsessive dedication to vengeance as heroic. Others argue the reverse, insisting that it is Indian-hating itself that represents evil and that Moredock is in no sense heroic. A more nuanced reading interprets the tale as "a tragic study of the impracticability of Christianity, and, more obviously, a satiric allegory in which the Indians are the Devils and the Indian-haters are dedicated Christians, and in which the satiric target is the nominal practice of Christianity" (Parker, "Metaphysics" 166). Arguing from a different perspective, a more recent study claims that the real purpose of the tale is to emphasize "the centrality of the Indian-hater to American society. He is not a marginal figure who can be disowned; he is the defining center of American attitudes toward the native." The Indian-hater "validates the white community's self-image of civilized Christianity, because he permits the community overtly to disown his actions (as unchristian, uncivilized), even as he serves its material and political interests" (Matterson 30, 33). In the story, diabolic actions occur on both sides of the line separating white "civilization" from Indian "savagery," suggesting that this boundary is just a cultural construction rather than a natural distinction.

THEMES

As the ambiguous characterization of Back Guinea and the tale of the Indian-hater illustrate, Melville goes well beyond a simplistic or even coherent level of allegorical or symbolic correspondence in *The Confidence-Man* to probe the linked themes of good and evil, appearance and reality, and the difficulty—if not impossibility—of both certain knowledge and faith. In doing so, he depicts the human condition in the context of specific cultural issues related to life in mid-nineteenth-century America. In the book's opening, for instance, the mute's pleas for "charity" are offset by the barber's announcement of "No Trust," typifying "the basic opposition between Christian and commercial values found throughout the novel." This juxtaposition "points to the contemporary belief that in the absence of traditional forms of authority, only the ethics of Christianity could keep a democratic society like America from disintegrating into a collection of autonomous individuals driven by predatory self-interest" (Cook 26–27). That American society is at risk is further emphasized through the riverboat setting, which during this time period was notorious for its association with the vices of gambling and drinking.

Melville exposes a number of other social issues that defy easy understanding or resolution. First of all, the topic of race and slavery is prominent in the novel, most obviously through the depiction of Black Guinea and the Indian-hater. The man in gray's charitable appeal on behalf of the Seminole Widow and Orphan Asylum also develops the theme of race, combining it with a critique of nineteenth-century philanthropic or reform movements and the role of the clergy and their lay followers in supporting such enterprises. Then, "in the appearance of the herb doctor, Melville launches a prolonged attack on the national faith in 'nature' by means of a critique of its patent medicine industry." This growing industry and the associated claims made by its zealous salesmen were "evidence of the optimistic tenor of nineteenth-century American life and a reminder of the marketability of that optimism" (Cook 42, 43). Furthermore, Melville expands his depiction of American business by using the interplay between the Philosophical Intelligence Officer and Pitch to consider different views of industrialization and the complicated conflict it poses between human beings and machines. In all of these cases—and others—Melville shows the difficulty in distinguishing between good and evil and appearance and reality within the context of an increasingly complex American society that he fears is becoming just a masquerade of authentic life. In such a world, knowledge is uncertain, and faith—in both its religious and secular forms—becomes difficult, if not foolhardy. Ambiguity rather than truth underlies all the masks of the confidence man, suggesting both Melville's darkening view of human society and his role as a writer within such a world.

The theme of writing permeates the novel in the digressions on the relationship between fiction and life. The figure of the author also opens the novel in the first appearance of the confidence man. "This character, whose lack of a voice makes him a writer by necessity, instigates a crisis in interpretation that will preoccupy the entire novel merely by inscribing" on his slate the traditionally accepted truisms that underlie Christian belief: "Charity thinketh no evil," "Charity suffereth long, and is kind," "Charity endureth all things," "Charity believeth all things," and "Charity never faileth" (Sussman 32, *Confidence Man* 842–43). Representing the plight of Melville himself by this time in his career, the mute, in writing these lines, is perceived by his "readers" as an author whose "writing was of much the same sort" (*Confidence-Man* 842). However, these repetitiously bland and boring platitudes of accepted wisdom, when considered in the context of the sequence of encounters to follow, ultimately test and confound any stable relationship between words and meaning.

In its tone, style, and thematic concerns, *The Confidence-Man* appeals to present-day sensibilities in ways that mid-nineteenth-century readers failed to appreciate. Where Melville's contemporaries viewed the book as proof of the author's madness, many of today's readers are content to see the world's madness instead. "For us, Melville's strained humor is camp: it is the strain, not the humor that amuses. Today, we are quite used to understated visions of the apocalypse, to literary put-ons, to self-cancelling ironies, for modern writers have made these things unremarkable" (Brodtkorb 421). More than 150 years after its initial publication, the book is strikingly applicable to twenty-first-century concerns. In its representation of human nature in continuing and irresolvable existential crisis, *The Confidence-Man* offers its readers both aesthetic and philosophical challenges that invite re-reading and reconsideration.

ALTERNATE READING: READER RESPONSE

"More than any of Melville's other works, *The Confidence-Man* lacks the neat resolutions that we" traditionally have come to "expect from narrative fiction and instead demands" our active and purposeful involvement and assistance as readers (Sten 289). As a result, the book invites critical attention to the reader's role and response. Reader-response criticism often defines reading as a transactional process between a reader and a text in which meaning is as dependent on the reader as it is on the text. Although there are a variety of different concerns and approaches that are associated with this mode of literary criticism, the primary focus is to analyze the effect that a text "has on a reader and the strategies that produce that effect. Interpretation of meaning is assumed to be an act of reading, thereby making the ultimate authority not the writer or the text but the reader. A literary work becomes, then, an evolving creation, as it is possible for there to be many interpretations of the same text" (Dobie 121). To keep the approach from becoming overly subjective and personalized, the focus is on informed or competent readers who operate under a set of shared reading conventions. Nevertheless, all texts include interpretive gaps that the reader must fill, a process that is complicated by the fact that "sometimes an author can use recognizable conventions to 'fool' the reader" (Dobie 123).

The Confidence-Man provides an extreme example of just this type of reading transaction. By repeatedly subverting his readers' expectations, Melville forces his audience to play the same sort of confidence game that the characters in the novel play. In this type of literary contest, the "'author' is the implied initiator of the game, the strategist inferred from the sequence and direction of the play.... But 'the reader' is also a construct, the ideal Other for whom the test is posed, against whose expectations and likely calculations all the ruses and hints have apparently been laid" (Bruss 154). In *The Confidence-Man,* the interplay between reader and author becomes self-conscious as a result of the overstated form in which the game is played out. Melville lures the reader into a false sense of security through his use of a pattern of repetition in which the confidence man attempts to dupe his victims. The frequency of role switching and other reversals and removals, however, thwarts the reader's ability to anticipate and comprehend the individual "moves" or their overall significance to the "game."

In this literary competition, Melville seems to "hold all the cards." "Failed communication is a presupposition woven into the book's rhetorical design, its teasing interruptions and extravagant digressions," and the author continually "twits his impatient and inattentive readers, toying with their demand for a coherent story and consistent fidelity to nature" (Bruss 167). Unable to determine meaning, the reader's conditioning nevertheless mandates adherence to the rules of reading. Although the allegorical and symbolic framework of the text is insistent, however, the clues repeatedly lead the reader to false starts and dead ends. Eventually, the reader "is tempted to take refuge from mounting confusion by adopting an attitude of absolute skepticism. But this move is blocked as well" because total skepticism fares no better than total faith on the *Fidèle* (Bruss 169). Virtually all readers of Melville's novel, sophisticated and naïve alike, ultimately experience a crisis of confidence for "there is no meeting ground in *The Confidence-Man*; reciprocal moves cancel each other out" (Bruss 169).

For this reason, *The Confidence-Man* is increasingly cited as Melville's most controlled novel. It is also his most controlling text. "Melville controls us in this conundrum which he has written because we do not know enough to make basic and essential decisions. And yet, even when we are in his control, he leaves us alone in our quandaries" (Gaudino 138). In turning the tables on his readers in such an unrelenting fashion, Melville perhaps was responding to his own despair at feeling impelled to write conventional novels that followed the rules if he wanted to find a receptive audience. Difficulties of communication between characters in the novel are mirrored by the difficulty that Melville had repeatedly experienced with his own readers in his attempt to sell his books while still remaining committed to the need to use his fiction to analyze the human condition. With this sardonic masquerade, Melville holds up a double-sided mirror that reflects the game that both life and novel writing had come to represent to him. Having expanded the form of the novel to—and perhaps beyond—its limits, he now leaves the stage of prose fiction for a lengthy intermission to take up the challenges and opportunities of a new art form—poetry.

9

Melville as Poet: *Battle-Pieces* and *Clarel*

Except for his final work of prose fiction, *Billy Budd*, which itself may have begun as a ballad, Melville devoted the final 34 years of his writing life to the craft of poetry. His poetry received little attention during this period, as his reputation faded and he dropped increasingly from public view. Even since Melville's death, this posture of poetic dismissal has been slow to change. One of the first even to acknowledge Melville's poetry, F. O. Matthiessen, writing in 1941, nonetheless dismissed it as adding "little to his stature as an artist" (494). Robert Penn Warren essentially concurred with this conclusion five years later when he called Melville a "poet of shreds and patches" who "did not master his craft" (144). In 1955, Randall Jarrell added his opinion by asserting, "Melville is a great poet only in the prose of *Moby-Dick*" (101). Only gradually since this time has the negative consensus been revised, and even today, Melville's poetry is not always addressed in edited collections of critical essays on the writer. The tendency has been to consider Melville's poetry writing as a hobby of his later years. As one critic observes, however, "The poetry that a great novelist writes over the last thirty years of his life cannot be without interest. Critics of that novelist neglect such writing at their peril" (Hook 179–80). In recent years, fewer and fewer critics seem willing to take this risk.

As a result, despite the qualifications and lack of enthusiasm for his poetry that accompany its recognition, Melville has frequently been cited as the third best American poet before 1900 (behind his contemporaries

Walt Whitman and Emily Dickinson). Within his poetry, he incorporates an extraordinary range of poetic speakers, stances, and locales; however, even at his most political and social, he writes "from a conviction of the loneliness of thought in human life," resulting in a "consequent rhetorical aloofness" that "estranges many readers" (Vendler 583). Like his fiction, his poetry exposes the moral ambiguities of the human condition in general and of American history in particular. Precisely for this reason, perhaps, "the poet Melville has not been incorporated into American culture in the way that Whitman and Dickinson have." Although just as heretical as Melville in their outer reaches, "Whitman is more conventionally patriotic, more anecdotal, more colloquial, more genial, and more personal; Dickinson is briefer, less forbidding, less historical" (Vendler 583). Melville's poetry, above all, shows a depth of reflective thought that justifies its serious consideration on its own merits rather than only in comparison to his own novels or to the poetry of others.

Inspired by his Mediterranean travels in late 1856 and early 1857, Melville's first collection of poetry went unpublished, although individual poems subsequently may have been incorporated elsewhere. Before his death in 1891, Melville published four volumes of poetry: *Battle-Pieces and Aspects of the War* (1866), *Clarel* (1876), *John Marr and Other Sailors* (1888), and *Timoleon* (1891). In the final years of his life, he also wrote the unpublished collection of poems, "Weeds and Wildings," for his wife. Of this work, *Battle-Pieces*, his collection of Civil War poetry, has received the most scholarly attention to date, with inevitable comparisons to Whitman's *Drum-Taps*, but the epic poem *Clarel* has recently garnered significant attention as well.

BATTLE-PIECES AND ASPECTS OF THE WAR (1866)

Because Melville was 42 years old and suffering from poor health when the Civil War broke out, his experience of this national crisis was largely confined to what he read about it. His only actual exposure to the war front occurred in 1864 when he visited the Army of the Potomac in Vienna, Virginia, and accompanied the troops on one scouting mission. Thus *Harper's Weekly* and the *Rebellion Record*, a compilation of newspaper accounts of the war, served as his primary sources when he decided to compile a collection of Civil War poetry, which he inscribed "to the memory of the three hundred thousand who in the war for the maintenance of the union fell devotedly under the flag of their fathers" (*Battle-Pieces* iii).

Although Melville probably wrote a few of the poems before the end of the war, most of the 72 poems that make up the collection appear to have been written between the Confederates' surrender at Richmond, Virginia, in April 1865, and the publication of the volume by Harper and Brothers in August 1866. Beginning in January 1866, four of the poems were published in *Harper's New Monthly Magazine* in advance of the book. That Melville was not yet finished with the entire manuscript at this time is evident by the fact that the next to the last poem, "Lee in the Capitol," was inspired by the Confederate General Robert E. Lee's testimony before the Reconstruction Committee of Congress on February 17, 1866. Melville himself attests to the retrospective nature of the collection in the preface, where he explains, "With few exceptions, the Pieces in this volume originated in an impulse imparted by the fall of Richmond" (*Battle-Pieces* v). Thus the book forms a meditation in a full range of emotions and moods that were evoked by Melville's contemplation of this critical period in American history.

By the very title of the collection, Melville emphasizes the "representational problem" of such a summary undertaking "by inviting us to look for 'the war' in the 'pieces' and 'aspects' as they appear in the volume" (Sweet 165). In the preface, Melville elaborates on this issue by explaining, "The aspects which the strife as a memory assumes are as manifold as are the moods of involuntary meditation—moods variable, and at times widely at variance. Yielding instinctively, one after another, to feelings not inspired from any one source exclusively, and unmindful, without purposing to be, of consistency, I seem, in most of these verses to have but placed a harp in a window, and noted the contrasted airs which wayward winds have played upon the strings" (*Battle-Pieces* v). However, "[n]ot only are the poems in the collection products of emotion recollected in tranquility, as the winds of memory stir the strings of poetic imagination; they are also 'Pieces'" in the sense of "a series of pictures in a gallery" (Dryden, *Monumental* 67). Throughout this poetic series of intensely visual images, the pieces work collectively, while simultaneously standing separately in recognition of the fragmentation that resulted from a war that split not only the nation, but families within the nation and individual psyches.

Although Melville dedicated the volume to the Northern soldiers, the sympathy with which he treated the South and his concern for reconciliation, as well as his violation of traditional conventions of verse-making, provoked harsh comments in a majority of the reviews. Of the original 1,260 copies that were published, only 486 copies were sold by February 13, 1868.

Setting, Plot, and Structure

Battle-Pieces takes as its canvas the entire compass of the U.S. Civil War. The book as a whole "can in a sense be regarded as one sustained action, a chronological sequence responding to significant points in the war." The dates that Melville affixes to the titles of many of the poems "refer not to composition, but to the place of narrated events within the unfolding drama of the war" (Rosanna Warren 104). Opening the collection with "The Portent," Melville considers the December 2, 1859, hanging of the radical abolitionist and martyr John Brown, an event that occurred as a consequence of the 15 deaths that resulted from his unsuccessful attempt to seize guns and spark a slave uprising by raiding the federal arsenal at Harper's Ferry, Virginia (now West Virginia). Brown's incendiary act was seen by both the North and South as proof of the inevitability of war. Set in italic type and separated from the other poems in the book by a blank page, "The Portent" was not listed in the table of contents of the original edition of *Battle-Pieces,* all of which suggests it serves "as a kind of epigraph to the rest of the poems" (Cox 298). As its title makes clear, the poem, like the figure of John Brown himself, is "a sign or omen, one designed to foreshadow the representations of 'events and incidents of the conflict' that constitute the collection, as well as to suggest their 'natural order'" (Dryden, *Monumental* 69–70).

The remaining 71 poems in the collection are grouped into three sections. First is an untitled sequence of 52 poems that feature particular events—mostly battles—and personalities. The events chronicled here begin in the fall of 1860 and end with Appomattox, Lincoln's assassination, and victory celebrations of the spring of 1865. Next is a section of 16 poems entitled "Verses Inscriptive and Memorial" that memorialize the war dead in a variety of scenes that often cannot be identified by region or allegiance. This section concludes with "The Returned Volunteer to his Rifle," which depicts a Northern soldier reminiscing to his "tried companion" of the war, his rifle, as he returns home to the Hudson Valley (183). At this point, Melville adds three final poems in an unnamed section marked off from the preceding poems by separate title pages. The first of these three, "The Scout toward Aldie," has puzzled readers by its seeming misplacement, since—though undated—it takes the reader back in time to battle. By far the longest poem in the collection and directly inspired by Melville's visit to the front, this poem arguably serves as "a poetic reflection of Melville's concern that the war may not truly be over" (Cox 305). The only poem to depict guerilla warfare, it magnifies the barbaric horrors of war and then serves "to elevate Robert E. Lee in preparation for making him spokesman for the poet's politics," by using the Major's actions in this poem to mimic Lee's restraint in turning away from guerrilla tactics at the end of the war (Dowling 2). Melville cements this subtle link by following "The Scout toward Aldie" with "Lee at the Capitol," a poem in which

Lee, contrary to the historical record, counsels the North to use moderation in its posture toward the South. "Meditation," the final poem in the collection, uses the form of a dramatic monologue to plea for forbearance and harmony while simultaneously questioning the likelihood of resolving the complex issues of Reconstruction and emancipation without resorting again to violence.

After this final poem, Melville appends some explanatory notes to contextualize specific poems. He then concludes the volume with a reflective prose "Supplement" in which he struggles to find the positive lessons of the Civil War and, in keeping with the tenor of the final poems, moves beyond the partisanship suggested by the book's opening inscription by stressing that Reconstruction should be carried out without vengeance against the South. Taken together, the preface and "Supplement" function as somber bookends to the poetry they bracket.

Characters

"Melville orders his poems to follow the course of the war, but the deeper movement of *Battle-Pieces* resides in its play of voices" (Milder, "Reader" 13). In recreating the scenes of war, he emphasizes local details and places his characters within these particularized settings, frequently giving them voice in dramatic monologues. Although most of the poems feature military figures in battle, Melville also uses nonmilitary characters throughout the volume. Prominent among these characters are famous figures such as John Brown and Abraham Lincoln, both of whose deaths are contemplated. Providing historical context for battle scenes, other civilians on the home front register their voices in poems like "The House-Top" and "Formerly a Slave." In "The House-Top," a dramatic monologue about the New York draft riots of July 1863, Melville depicts Irish immigrants as "rats—ship-rats/And rats of the wharves" who are "Fear-bound, subjected to a better sway/Than sway of self," as they riot against "The Town" (86). "'Formerly a Slave'" was inspired by Elihu Vedder's painting *Jane Jackson, Formerly a Slave*, which Melville viewed at the National Academy of Design in 1865. In his verbal portrait, the poet claims that this woman, although representing the "sufferance of her race," is "not at strife" because she is content that "Her children's children they shall know/The good withheld from her" (154). In the final two lines, Melville observes that "Her dusky face is lit with sober light,/Sibylline yet benign" (154). By associating the woman with light and the mythical Sibyl of ancient Greece and Rome, Melville suggests the woman's vision of the future may be prophetic.

The men who fought in the war, however, are the principal characters in *Battle-Pieces*. Melville infuses the poems with portraits of Union generals such as Philip H. Sheridan, whose victory at Cedar Creek is celebrated with majestic imagery, and William Tecumseh Sherman, whose "March to the Sea" is depicted in ironic pastoral imagery that exposes the shocking destruction that was left in his path. General Ulysses S. Grant receives the most attention, emerging "as a sustained character, and not simply as a symbol, in the progression of these poems." Tracing Grant's career and progress toward national prominence "in the movement between 'Donelson,' 'Shiloh,' 'Chattanooga,' and 'The Armies of the Wilderness,'" Melville simultaneously "questions the representational power of word and photograph" as the poems move from idealistic expectations and visions of pastoral beauty "into the technological horror of the war as a whole" (Williams 155–56).

In contrast to his prolonged but ambivalent treatment of Grant, Melville imbues Grant's Southern counterpart, Robert E. Lee, with dignity and magnanimous nobility in defeat. Called to testify before his former enemies, he pleads for human decency toward the South while "No word he breathes of vain lament" ("Lee in the Capitol" 229). Two poems are also dedicated to the memory of the Southern General Stonewall Jackson, "stormer of the war," who "not the North shall care to slur" because of his stoic dedication and "gentle ways" ("Stonewall Jackson [Ascribed to a Virginian]" 81). In striving to sort through the conflicted feelings that this brave hero's death has evoked, Melville writes, "Even him who stoutly stood for Wrong,/How can we praise? Yet coming days/Shall not forget him with this song" ("Stonewall Jackson: Mortally Wounded at Chancellorsville" 79).

In addition to renowned figures such as these, Melville also peoples his poems with anonymous officers of varying ranks. "On the Photograph of a Corps Commander," for instance, opens with a traditionally heroic image that, although it may represent Grant, is not identified by name: "AY, man is manly. Here you see/The warrior-carriage of the head/And brave dilation of the frame" (105). In contrast, "The College Colonel" dramatizes the situation of a young officer who has just emerged from the infamous Libby Prison in Richmond, Virginia, where he witnessed the true horrors of war and realized its meaning for the first time. The poem opens with an image of the wounded colonel leading his men: "He rides at their head;/A crutch by his saddle just slants in view,/One slung arm is in splints, you see,/Yet he guides his strong steed—how coldly too" (120). As the poem makes clear, however, "It is not that a leg is lost,/It is not that an arm is maimed" that has crippled this man. Rather, his spirit has been broken as

"Lean brooding in Libby, there came—/Ah heaven!—what *truth* to him" (121).

Also included in *Battle-Pieces* are striking images of the common soldier, both alive and dead, alone and in mass. In the early days of war, the Union troops march forward with youthful enthusiasm and zeal: "In Bacchic glee they file toward Fate" as "all they feel is this: 'tis glory" ("The March into Virginia" 23). In the long narrative poem "Donelson," Melville juxtaposes euphoric journalistic reports of victory with italicized depictions of the soldiers who struggled and fell on the ravaged warfront: "*They faltered, drawing bated breath,/And felt it was in vain to dare;/Yet still, perforce, returned the ball,/Firing into the tangled wall/Till ordered to come down. They came;/But left some comrades in their fame,/Red on the ridge in icy wreath/And hanging gardens of cold Death*" (38). In closing the volume of poems, Melville emphasizes the fratricidal nature of the strife, as well as its psychic toll, with "Meditation." Appended to this dramatic monologue is a note advising the reader that the speech that follows is "attributed to a Northerner after attending the last of two funerals from the same homestead—those of a National and a Confederate officer (brothers), his kinsmen, who had died from the effects of wounds received in the closing battle" (*Battle-Pieces* 239). Seeking to understand the war and its effects, the man reflects, "Mark the great Captains on both sides,/The soldiers with the broad renown—/ They all were messmates on the Hudson's marge,/Beneath one roof they laid them down;/And free from hate in many an after pass,/ Strove as in school-boy rivalry of the class" (243). With such sentiments, this survivor struggles to find confidence in the promise of peace and reunification.

Symbols

In much the same way that the volume of poems itself is "constructed of 'pieces' that may or may not cohere, so are the individuals in this world frequently fragmented within the context of the struggle for social wholeness. In this respect the individual body becomes the ironic casualty in the attempt to reform or retain the integrity of the social body; the genuine wound to the flesh both reflects and, the poetry hopes, ultimately heals the symbolic wound to the country" that the war represents. The symbol of the body is introduced with the book's first poem, "The Portent," in which John Brown's body serves "as both a parodic crucifixion and potent mystery that foreshadows the violence and sacrifice of the coming conflict" (Clark Davis 109). The sacrificial implications of the symbolic body are emphasized throughout the collection. The hero of "Lyon," for instance, courageously leads his inexperienced soldiers into battle as a "seer" who "foresaw his soldier-doom,/Yet willed the fight./He never turned; his only flight/Was up to Zion,/Where prophets now and armies greet brave Lyon" (27). Although this poem, dated "August, 1861," can be read as a reflection of the idealistic confidence that such sacrifices are justified, questions mount about the legitimacy of dying to resolve the country's political conflicts as bodies of soldiers from both sides of the conflict increasingly pile up on battlefields.

Melville's symbolism, however, is not devoid of hope for the country's future. Offsetting the image of Brown's body in "The Portent" is the allegorical female figure in "America," which closes the first and longest groupings of poems in *Battle-Pieces*. Representing America, this "lorn Mother," stands "speechless" and "Pale at the fury of her brood" when the war breaks out and "Valor with Valor strove, and died" (160–61). Falling into a deathlike sleep in her despair, she is troubled by nightmare visions of what the future may hold; however, she awakens with a "clear calm look." With "hope grown wise,/And youth matured for age's seat," she stands with "Law on her brow and empire in her eyes," as "the shadow, chased by light,/Fled along the far-drawn height,/And left her on the crag" (162). Although this imagery is not entirely untroubled in its suggestion of empire-building and isolation, it points to the country's awakening—or projected awakening—from the dark gloom and evils that have threatened its very existence.

Sometimes Melville eliminates the actual body and replaces it with a photograph, thereby distancing us from the war and its participants and suggesting the difficulty of their true representation. By using the motif of the photograph, he asks us to "look beneath the immediate surface, beneath the artificiality Melville associates with the photograph and beneath the seeming order of the written word, to reconstruct a new version of the Civil War" (Williams 151). "On the Photograph of a Corps Commander" presents a "cheering picture" consistent with the romantic notions of war and manhood that the collection of poems as a whole disavows (105). "In writing *Battle-Pieces*, Melville was conscious that he was critically representing extant verbal and visual representations of the war." Several poems, such as "Donelson" and "The House-Top" "versify and otherwise manipulate (without apology) previously published journalistic accounts" to "demonstrate the mystifying political effects of the prevalent journalistic and poetic tendencies to aestheticize" and thereby legitimize the war (Sweet 181).

The Civil War was the first war in which photography was used as a means of documentation and reportage. When it became impossible to present a positive image of battlefields strewn with corpses and other scenes of the war, the recuperative powers of nature were often invoked to suggest the regenerative aspects of death. Melville, too, invokes nature as a symbol in *Battle-Pieces* but often to ambivalent if not outright ironic effect. The body of "Weird John Brown" with his "streaming beard" swings above the pastoral Shenandoah valley ("The Portent" 11). As the troops march forth in "The March into Virginia," Melville observes the "green" recruits who in their innocence misconstrue their mission: "No berrying party, pleasure-wooed,/No picnic party in the May,/Ever went less loth than they/Into that leafy neighborhood" (23). Writing retrospectively, Melville's irony comes through in his wordplay between "berrying" and "burying," which foreshadows the historic reality they are marching toward at the Battle of First Manassas. In "The Scout toward Aldie," all pretense of belief in nature's recuperative powers seems lost as "Men fall from their saddles like plums from trees!" (*Battle-Pieces* 219).

Consistent with Melville's love for the sea, several poems in *Battle-Pieces* reflect symbolically on war ships and naval battles. In "A Utilitarian View of the *Monitor*'s Fight," the ironclad ship—the *Monitor*—becomes a comprehensive symbol of the dehumanizing mechanization of war, as well as of nineteenth-century American technology in general. The contrast between the ironclads (the New World) and the wooden ships that preceded them in service (the Old World) is depicted in "The Stone Fleet" and "The *Temeraire*." With the retiring of the *Temeraire*, which Admiral Lord Nelson commanded in the 1805 Battle of Trafalgar, Melville mourns the decay of values caused by technology: "Your bulwarks to the years must yield,/And heart-of-oak decay./A pigmy steam-tug tows you,/Gigantic to the shore." As this ship is dismantled to make way for progress, "The rivets clinch the iron-clads,/Men learn a deadlier lore" ("The *Temeraire*" 60). This "deadlier lore" is depicted for the reader in "In the Turret," where Melville explores the personal effects of fighting within a machine in which the men are "Sealed as in a diving-bell" that may become their "welded tomb" (55, 56). With such images, Melville ponders the human price involved as war enters the modern era of technology.

Melville also uses the image of the Capitol dome as a symbol of society's changing values. During a trip to Washington in March 1861, Melville "witnessed the construction of a new Capitol dome to be made from iron to replace the old one which was destroyed by fire" (Jalal 82). In "The Conflict of Convictions," the *"rust on the Iron Dome"* suggests the tarnishing of the American dream of freedom and democracy on which the country was founded (16). The American tragedy of the Civil War, for Melville, ultimately seems to lie in its destruction of the past and its ideals and values, as he fears the "Founders' dream shall flee" despite the outcome (17).

Themes

As the symbols of the warships and Capitol dome suggest, "the theme of an America corrupted by materialism and utilitarianism, and descending into civic barbarism, is a recurrent one" in *Battle-Pieces*, as well as in Melville's poetry as a whole (Hook 185). Echoing some of the concerns about the corruption of American society by commercialism and self-interest that he revealed in *The Confidence-Man*, Melville turns his mirror this time on the savage violence and dehumanizing effects of modern warfare, as well as the political agendas that made the Civil War and its aftermath so costly for the country in terms of lost lives, human suffering, and disillusionment. Such devastation, he fears, will thwart the country's further development and change its course of direction.

The theme of knowledge, as well as the end of innocence that such knowledge brings, reverberates in the poems. In the early poems, this knowledge is foreshadowed in the repeated emphasis on the youth of the soldiers being called to duty in the name of patriotism. In "The March into Virginia," for instance, Melville observes, "All wars are boyish, and are fought by boys,/The champions and enthusiasts of the state" (22). By contrast, however, in "The College Colonel," the young warriors of the Colonel's regiment return home, "Not as they filed two years before,/But a remnant half-tattered, and battered and worn" (120). The poet depicts pain and suffering as brutal "payments that war extracts"; however, it is "what happened to the spontaneity, the promise of youth," that truly haunts Melville (Kimbell 310). In his depiction of the colonel, we see "A still rigidity, and pale—/An Indian aloofness lones his brow;/He has lived a thousand years/Compressed in battle's pains and prayers" (120). The sacrifice of youth that the war has exacted moves Melville beyond partisanship to suggest the culpability of these youths' elders in sending their sons forward in the name of "Heaven" and "Honor" rather than arming them with an adult understanding of the realities before them. In "On the Slain Collegians," he reflects, "Each went forth with blessings given/By priests and mothers in the name of Heaven;/And Honor in both was chief./Warred one for Right, and one for Wrong?/So be it; but they both were young—/Each grape to his cluster clung,/All their elegies are sung" (158–59). As he observes with ironic pastoral imagery, "Each bloomed and died an unabated Boy;/Nor dreamed what death was—thought it mere/Sliding into some vernal sphere" (159). With grim retrospective knowledge, Melville grieves as the experiences of war move these boys prematurely from youth to maturity, from innocence to experience, from life to death.

As he probes these linked themes of knowledge and the testing of youth, Melville also contemplates the meaning of heroism. Moving beneath the flawless surface of the "Photograph of a Corps Commander," Melville creates ambivalent tensions in his depiction of generals such as Grant, who most forcefully personifies the modern state and its warfare. Most telling of the impossibility of considering such coldly calculating and heartless leadership heroic is one of the italicized observations in the second section of "The Armies of the Wilderness": *"Were men but strong and wise,/Honest as Grant, and calm,/War would be left to the red and black ants/And the happy world disarm"* (99). Unlike the sanitized, still image of the Corps Commander, Melville's evolving multidimensional portrait of Grant tells "the reader that modern man, that the 'modern hero,' has himself been turned into a mechanical instrument whose disinterest precludes the possibility of depth and of a soul" (Williams 165).

War in any era speaks to the human condition. "The Civil War for Melville enacted in stark reality the doom that he had prophesied for America in some of his earlier works … , but when it broke upon the country he concluded, as he wrote in 'The Conflict of Convictions,' that 'Wisdom is vain, and prophecy'" (Kimbell 315). Debunking the glory of heroism in war, *Battle-Pieces* ultimately pleas for reconciliation and reunification of the fractured country. Observing that "it is right to rejoice for our triumph, so far as it may justly imply an advance for our whole country and for humanity," Melville uses the "Supplement" to drive home his message of tolerance and compassion. In these final remarks, he urges, "Let us be Christians toward our fellow-whites, as well as philanthropists toward the blacks, our fellow-men. In all things, and toward all, we are enjoined to do as we would be done by" (*Battle-Pieces* 264, 268). Ending on such a note of universal significance, *Battle-Pieces* still speaks to the hard lessons of war that repeatedly are learned too late.

CLAREL (1876)

Whereas *Battle-Pieces* foregrounds the struggle of the human body at war, *Clarel: A Poem and Pilgrimage in the Holy Land* revolves around the frustrated battle of the human spirit for fulfillment. Inspired by Melville's own visit to the Middle East in late 1856 and early 1857, this complex narrative poem was published by G. P. Putnam and Sons at the expense of Melville's Uncle Peter Gansevoort in June 1876, 20 years after the poet's own pilgrimage and 10 years after the publication of *Battle-Pieces*. Although writing and preparing the poem for publication had sorely taxed Melville, both creatively and emotionally, he was seemingly indifferent to its reception, asserting in the inscription, "I here dismiss the book—content beforehand with whatever future awaits it" (*Clarel* iii). Neither did Melville underestimate his public. Readers and critics were equally dismayed by the poem's inordinate length and its heavy philosophical and religious preoccupations. *Clarel* was withdrawn by Melville in March 1879, when he ordered the publisher to destroy the remaining copies. Presumably still untouched by the fate of his most ambitious poem, however, Melville, with wry humor, described *Clarel* in 1884 as a "metrical affair, a pilgrimage, or what not, of several thousand lines, eminently adapted for unpopularity" (*Letters* 275). This unpopularity continued virtually unabated for the next hundred years. "*Clarel*, it is safe to say, will never become a popular poem with the public…. Its awesome size, constricted verse, and occasionally obscure subject matter discourage even some Melville enthusiasts" (Kenny 69). In recent years, however, there is growing respect for the work among literary scholars, who increasingly acknowledge that *Clarel* must be incorporated into any serious contemplation of Melville's contributions to American literature.

Setting, Plot, and Structure

A narrative poem of more than 18,000 lines, *Clarel* is organized into four books that tell the story of Clarel, an American divinity student of unknown background who travels with other pilgrims from Jerusalem across the desert to the Dead Sea and Mar Saba and back again through Bethlehem. Through his pilgrimage, Clarel seeks to reconfirm the faith in Christ that he has lost: "'Can faith remove/Her light, because of late no plea/I've lifted to her source above?'" (*Clarel* 1: 6). Having found no answers in "blind theology," Clarel is, through this pilgrimage, making one final attempt to recover his belief in Christianity. Arriving in Jerusalem, however, he is immediately disappointed by the dust and weeds and "blank, blank towers" that do not meet his romantic expectations of the Holy Land (1: 4). He meets Nehemiah, an eccentric old American who, like Clarel, has fallen into disbelief, and through Nehemiah is introduced to a Jewish woman named Ruth. Falling in love with Ruth, he plans marriage to her, but because of Hebrew religious strictures must limit the time that he spends with her during their courtship. Accordingly, he falls into companionship with other foreigners in Palestine, who invite him to journey with them through the Middle East. When Ruth's father Nathan dies and she is precluded from seeing Clarel during the subsequent mourning period, he decides to accept the invitation. The first book ends as they leave on their pilgrimage into the Wilderness.

The second book, set in the Wilderness, covers their four-day journey to the Dead Sea, ending with their arrival and the drowning death of Nehemiah. By the time they leave the Dead Sea at the beginning of the third book, Clarel has become disillusioned by his conversations with the others and by Nehemiah's death, and he finds it difficult to believe in the possibility of a happy future with Ruth, whose features he has trouble recalling. After three days of trying to escape his troubles amidst the colorful and pleasing diversions of Mar Saba, Clarel begins seriously to ponder the celibate life of the monks as a more fitting life for him than marriage to Ruth, but such reflections only increase his anxiety and sense of conflict. As the pilgrims prepare to leave Mar Saba, Clarel finds Mortmain, another of their company of pilgrims, dead. Because Mortmain is considered a heretic by the monks, he must be buried outside the monastery walls.

Journeying on to Bethlehem, the setting for the fourth book, Clarel rooms with a businessman from Lyon, whose interest in sensual pleasures dismays him. Completing their circular journey on the next night, the pilgrims reenter Jerusalem. As they do so, they pass a cemetery where two graves are being prepared. Learning that these graves are for Ruth and her mother Agar, who have died from fever and grief over the death of Nathan, their father and husband, Clarel remains while the bodies are buried. Five days later, after the last of his companions depart, Clarel is left alone. Wandering throughout Jerusalem during Holy Week, he tries unsuccessfully to find consolation in the religious commemoration of Christ's crucifixion and resurrection. At the poem's end, he joins another group of pilgrims during Pentecost as they walk along the Via Crucis, the road taken by Christ on his way to his own execution. In the epilogue, Clarel is urged to keep heart and believe that, as Faith says, the spirit will rise above the dust.

Characters

Clarel, the youthful hero of the poem, "is more a problem than a person, passive and inarticulate and with a tendency to fade into the background, at times actually seeming to vanish. And yet he is the figure around which the poem's other characters converge" (Dryden, *Monumental* 104). Described by Melville as "pale, and all but feminine," he is "earnest by nature, long confined/Apart like Vesta in a grove/Collegiate," and marked by a "cultivated narrowness" in his religious doubts and disconnection from both God and humanity (*Clarel* 1: 3, 6). Far from an experienced quester, this "Young Doubter" "draws most of his experience from books and clearly lacks both sexual maturity and the ability to balance or harmonize a restless intellectualism with emerging erotic desires" (Clark Davis 126).

Through the numerous other characters that gather around Clarel, Melville articulates a variety of philosophical and religious attitudes and beliefs. Nehemiah serves as an early guide and Christian example to Clarel, seemingly "Emerging from the level heaven,/And vested with its liquid calm," his faith and actions (*Clarel* 1: 32–33). Another pilgrim, an Italian hunchbacked figure named Celio, serves as Nehemiah's counterpart, recreating "the absence of Christ while offering a distant companionship, if not guidance to the mental seeker" (Dryden, *Monumental* 104). Ruth's appearance intensifies Clarel's search for his own sexuality, and the tension between his sensual attraction to her and his search for spiritual fulfillment forms an important part of the poem's dialectic. The deaths of all three of these companions suggest the unresolved nature of Clarel's search for fulfillment and his inability to synthesize the different aspects of his nature.

"Mortmain, the disillusioned Swedish idealist, and Ungar, the wounded half-Indian and former Confederate officer, reflect varying degrees of monomania and metaphysical discontent. Ungar especially comes to represent the madness of physical pain that leads to bodily denial and a distortion of the search for truth" (Kenny 140). Other significant characters include Rolfe, Vine, and Derwent, all of whom "demonstrate some degree of the balance between body and mind" that Ruth's mother Agar also maintains. In "their attempts to maintain true to their own visions," they "offer Clarel the clearest examples "of the kind of energy and activity necessary to avoid overcommitment to a single idea" (Kenny 144). The poem, as a whole, is dominated by the religious and philosophical discussions among these diverse characters, rather than by the actual pilgrimage that it traces. In the end, the circular rhetoric and discursive wanderings preclude resolution or closure.

Symbols and Themes

Melville invests the wanderings of these pilgrims with allegorical significance through the biblical allusions that many of their names suggest. The deeper meaning of the poem, however, resides in its symbolic depth, which draws from an impressive knowledge of Christian and Hebrew scripture, as well as numerous other sources, in furthering his concern with the human condition and the possibility of faith in the modern world. Through his depiction of the Holy Land, Melville represents "the lifelessness and desiccation of the land itself, the palpable sense of physical blight with its intimation of lost promise and waste." The landscape through which Clarel and his companions search for traces of the divine "presents an image of bodily loss," suggesting "a profound inability to invigorate either its own soil or those who dwell or walk upon it. Lifelessness and impotence pervade the poem's world" (Clark Davis, 127–28). Clustered images of dust and stone join with that of the sea to depict nature as a wasteland from which escape seems impossible: "Sands immense/Impart the oceanic sense:/The flying grit like scud is made:/Pillars of sand which whirl about/Or arc along in colonnade,/True kin be to waterspout" (*Clarel* 1: 216). These controlling images "produce the sterile atmosphere proper to Melville's portrayal of man's tragic existence. The image of the Cross similarly runs throughout the poem, like an iron rod binding the pilgrims to the bleak facts of reality." Symbolic of pain and sorrow, the Cross "must be carried or endured, not as a redemptive act guaranteeing immortality but simply because there is little else in life except suffering" (Kenny 108–9).

Clarel's life remains essentially unchanged as a result of his pilgrimage, which he, in fact, seems destined to continue without hope of any earthly knowledge or reward. In the end, Melville seems to conclude that grand ideas such as the pilgrims debate "have little positive impact on human happiness; they do Clarel no more good than they do the wounded veterans of the war" in *Battle-Pieces*" (Short, "Form" 557). The overwhelming impression that the poem as a whole imparts is bleak. However, "[t]hrough his contact with other religions, beliefs, and faiths," Clarel "is able to comprehend both the diversity and the similarities among peoples, so that at the sad conclusion of the poem he is suffering both alone and as part of the great cosmic train (Potter 210). In addition, for the first time in his writings, Melville suggests some small hope of redemption in the poem's epilogue: "Then keep thy heart, though yet but ill-resigned—/Clarel, thy heart, the issues there but mind;/That like the crocus budding through the snow—/That like a swimmer rising from the deep—/That like a burning secret which doth go/Even from the bosom that would hoard and keep;/Emerge thou mayst from the last whelming sea,/And prove that death but routs life into victory" (2: 298). With these words, Melville moves toward the notion of transcendence of the spirit over the physical body that will reach its fullest statement in *Billy Budd*.

Alternate Reading: Genre Criticism

Through genre analysis, a literary critic seeks to gain insight into a writer's use of a specific type—or genre—of artistic composition by studying it in terms of its distinctive style, form, or content. Although genres traditionally have been considered relatively stable and pure categories, the concept of genre and its study have been reconceived in recent years. Rather than merely categorizing surface features of a text in prescriptive terms, genre analysis now conceives of text types as more fluid and dynamic in character and concerns itself more with the communicative purposes and roles of genres within different historical and social contexts. By applying or altering textual conventions, an author can use genre as an instrument of power to express ideas and values that adhere to or defer from dominant ideologies or systems of belief within a society.

By considering Melville's shift from novelist to poet, much can be discerned about the attitudes and beliefs of both nineteenth-century American society and its writers. In 1859, Melville's wife Lizzie wrote to her mother, "Herman has taken to writing poetry. You need not tell anyone, for you know how such things get around" (qtd. in Hand 326). With this warning, she expresses the prevailing attitude of the times, which viewed poetry as a nonremunerative and idle pastime, a tool of private reflection, the practice of which properly belonged behind closed doors and which certainly held no prospect for restoring a novelist's fading reputation, popularity, or pocketbook. As a serious writer, however, as well as a voracious reader of poetry and criticism, Melville knew that the writing of great poetry, although without prospect of financial reward, was "the surest way to achieve ultimate immortality in literature." As America sought to emerge from the shadow of England in terms of its literature, the idea persisted "that the great American literary work would be a poem.... Even throughout the decade after Melville published his last work of prose, the theory still prevailed that for a lover of literature the highest and richest rewards were to be found in poetry and that the greatest writers were poets" (Parker, *Herman Melville* 2: 403).

In moving to poetry, Melville undertook a concerted and long-term study of its craft. Reading the poetry of his peers, he found little to respect, as one of his marginal notations makes clear: "Harmonious modulations and *unvarying exactness of measure,* totally precluding sublimity and fire, have reduced our fashionable poetry to mere sing-song" (Leyda, *Log* 649). Determined that his poetry should stand apart as a vehicle to probe the same intellectual and philosophical concerns that his fiction addressed, he sought a style and form that would suit his content, one that was clearly at odds with the narrowly constrained conventions of nineteenth-century rhyme and meter. Rather than being summarily dismissed as "bad" poetry, Melville's verse should be considered in light of the fact that he was consciously working to innovate American poetry. Writing in 1955, one critic observed, "Indeed what he was doing with form was so new that it is new to us still, just as his highly personal symbolism and his unique metaphysical ambiguities are still new. Because they are, we are not yet clearly aware how often they actually do succeed, and we sometimes chalk them up as unjustified violences that have to be conceded" (Barrett 620). It is no accident that critical attention to Melville's poetry has grown in recent years as modern tastes and attitudes have evolved to embrace poetry not as a vehicle for expressing conventional sentiments in conventional ways but rather as a creative means to convey truths often at odds with traditional wisdom.

That Melville's successes as a poet of innovation were uneven, however, still seems clear. For instance, his typical adherence to traditional stanza patterns, inversions of syntax, and use of archaic words categorize his poems with the normative tastes of his day. Melville's harshly "unpoetic" diction, rhythmical unevenness, and use of near-rhyme in *Battle-Pieces*, however, suggest his affiliation with Whitman, whose 1855 *Leaves of Grass* long went unappreciated, and Dickinson, whose poetry even when published after her death eluded recognition until the second half of the twentieth century. "Melville, Dickinson, and Whitman were all uneven writers, at worst dully self-imitative of their own mannerisms. The deeper reasons for the neglect of Melville's poetry are probably the comparatively traditional character of its language and prosody relative to Whitman's and Dickinson's; its severe emotional restraint; and the deliberate entanglement of the larger narrative continuities of Melville's two most significant books of poetry" (Buell, "Melville the Poet" 136). Nevertheless, although Melville's poetry will probably continue to be judged inferior to that of Whitman and Dickinson, genre critics increasingly argue that it is still the work of a major poet, instead of a novelist who wrote some verse.

More than any other literary genre, poetry defies encapsulation. "Rather than a known, unchanging form against which individual efforts can be measured for adequacy, 'poetry' is merely a word, one 'of very disputed meaning.' Instead of dictating what a writer must do to be a poet, poetry is defined and continually redefined by what poets do." In the end, "the received opinion of Melville's poetry ... may well have its primary cause not in the poetry itself but in the reigning conception of the thing called 'Melville'" (Spengemann 571). Only when Melville's poems can be evaluated on their own terms and for their own merits, rather than as the work of the author of *Moby-Dick*, will it be possible truly to evaluate his contribution to American poetry.

10

Making Peace?: *Billy Budd*

After publishing *Clarel* in 1876, Melville continued to work at the New York Custom House until his retirement in December 1885. A $3,000 bequest from his sister Frances Priscilla enabled him to publish privately much of the poetry he wrote during his final years in two volumes of 25 copies each, *John Marr and Other Sailors* (1888) and *Timoleon* (1891). One of the poems originally intended for inclusion in *John Marr* was "a sentimental ballad called 'Billy in the Darbies,' the prison reverie of an old mutineer waiting to be executed." However, after writing "a prose preface to the ballad, he decided to hold it in reserve," and most scholars believe that this text formed the seed for Melville's final prose fiction, the novella *Billy Budd* (Robertson-Lorant 585). Although he was still writing poetry, Melville appears to have worked fairly steadily on this manuscript for several years, revising it extensively as he did so. On April 19, 1891, he recopied at least part of the ballad, penciling after it the notation "End of Book," which may have indicated that the poem was to end the novella or his impression that the work as a whole was now finished. At any rate, when Melville died five months later, this manuscript for *Billy Budd*, as well as other poetry in progress, was still on his desk.

The manuscript languished undiscovered among Melville's papers until it was found by Raymond Weaver, Melville's first biographer. As a result of Weaver's diligence, *Billy Budd* was finally published in 1924 as part of the first standard edition of Melville's writings. Because the manuscript was in such rough form when Weaver found it and because Melville's intensions for it are unknown there has been much controversy over the manuscript's transcription, resulting in several editions of the text. Weaver's edition, by his own admission, was freely edited for general readers. In 1948, F. Barron Freeman published the first scholarly edition of *Billy Budd*, which was intended to provide in a single text a literal transcription of the manuscript with editorial notations as to possible variants, as well as a general reading version. In 1962, to correct the shortcomings and errors in the Freeman edition, which was based in part on Weaver's work, Harrison Hayford and Merton M. Sealts Jr. published an independent transcription and analysis in two separate editions, a general reading text and a genetic (or literal) text. Significantly, the Hayford and Sealts transcription changes the name of the ship on which the story takes place from the *Indomitable* to the *Bellipotent*, based on their conclusion that Melville's inconsistency on this point suggests his intension to use the latter name. This edition is most often cited in recent scholarship, and it now serves as the basis for most commercially available editions.

SETTING AND PLOT

Billy Budd, Sailor (An Inside Narrative) takes place at sea in 1797, during the Napoleonic Wars. As the story opens, the title character is being impressed into naval service, which involves his transfer from the British merchant ship, the *Rights-of-Man,* to the man-of-war ship, the *Bellipotent,* where the subsequent action unfolds. Accepting his change of life without protest, he cheerfully takes to his new duties as a foretopman and quickly becomes popular with the crew. Even Captain Vere, the commander of the *Bellipotent,* looks with favor on his new sailor. The ship's master-at-arms, John Claggart, however, grows jealous of Billy's goodness and begins to contrive ways to thwart his efforts to adapt to his new surroundings successfully. An old seamen known as the Dansker warns Billy, "'Jemmy Legs' (meaning the master-at-arms) 'is down on you'" (*Billy Budd* 1379). The naïve Billy, however, reacts incredulously, as Claggart has always spoken kindly to him. The next day, when Billy spills some soup on the floor of the dining hall, Claggart, who is passing by as "the greasy liquid steamed just across his path," makes a joke of the accident, commenting, "'Handsomely done, my lad! And handsome is as handsome did it, too'" (1380). A few days later, a stranger awakens Billy and, making reference to their common plight in being impressed into the Navy, he tries to recruit Billy for a mutiny. Although Billy refuses and confides in the Dansker about the incident, he fails to inform a superior officer of the supposed plot.

Shortly thereafter, Claggart accuses Billy of being responsible for letting a frigate escape that the *Bellipotent* was trying to capture. Unconvinced of this accusation, Vere nevertheless calls both Claggart and Billy to his cabin to discuss the matter. When Claggart falsely accuses him of mutiny, Billy is unable to speak to defend himself because of a speech defect—a stutter—that affects him at times of emotional stress. In frustration, he lashes out physically, striking a single blow to Claggart's forehead, which kills him. Billy denies the truth of Claggart's accusation and explains, "Could I have used my tongue I would not have struck him" (1410). Vere believes the young sailor, but he nonetheless convenes a drumhead court-martial, which is an unusual act under the circumstances. As a result of the sole testimony of Vere and his avowal that Billy must be convicted for assaulting and killing a superior officer in spite of the situation, the three-judge court convicts the sailor and sentences him to death by hanging. Further, they acquiesce to Vere's insistence that the hanging must be carried out at once to prevent a real mutiny. In the morning, after Vere and Billy have met in private, Billy is hanged while everyone on board watches. Before his death, Billy calls out, "'God bless Captain Vere!'" (1426), and the crew echoes this blessing. During the actual hanging, his body remains still, rather than twitching in spasms, which some of the crew take as evidence of the supernatural. Returning to the rest of the British fleet, the *Bellipotent* engages with a French ship named the *Athée* (or *Atheist*). In the subsequent battle, Vere is wounded. He dies a few days later, murmuring "words inexplicable to his attendant: 'Billy Budd, Billy Budd'" (1432). A newspaper account from "a naval chronicle of the time" records a different representation of the events on board the *Bellipotent*, asserting that Billy was the "ringleader" of a mutiny and a depraved "assassin," rightfully executed for "vindictively" stabbing Claggart in the heart as he arraigned the man before the captain (1432–33). One of Billy's fellow foretopmen commemorates him in a ballad called "Billy in the Darbies," which ends the story.

HISTORICAL CONTEXT

Set in the broad historical context of the war against revolutionary France, *Billy Budd* blurs the line between fiction and fact by depicting in fictional form the fear of mutiny in the British Navy that resulted from two actual rebellions by sailors at Spithead and Nore in the spring of 1797. In the first of these two situations, the mutineers demanded seaman pay raises and better living conditions, which they succeeded in achieving, as well as a pardon for all involved. Inspired by the example at Spithead, the mutineers at Nore issued additional demands, including more shore leave, fairer distribution of prize money, and changes to the Articles of War. Not inclined to make further concessions, the Admiralty offered the mutineers nothing but a pardon for immediate return to duty. Expanding their initial grievance, the mutineers moved to blockade London; however, when they were denied food, many deserted, and the mutiny ultimately failed. The leaders of the outbreak were tried and hanged, and other participants were imprisoned or flogged. Although these two mutinies were suppressed, they resulted in new legislation to allow British naval officers more latitude and powers in dealing with any such outbreak in the future, a fact that is played out in *Billy Budd* through Captain Vere's protocol in handling the crisis aboard his ship.

Military historians have surmised that the mutinies of 1797, in large part, were caused by the British practice of impressment, whereby the Navy resorted to seizing men involuntarily to find enough sailors to operate their ships. Eventually, the British even began impressing sailors from American ships, which was one of the factors that led to the War of 1812 between America and Britain. By beginning *Billy Budd* with an impressment, Melville gains immediate sympathy for his title character while simultaneously raising doubts about the practices of the British Navy in wartime.

With this novella, Melville returns to many of the issues and conditions that he depicted first in *White-Jacket*, as he himself recognized in his dedication of the book to the fictional character of Jack Chase from *White-Jacket* fame. Although he uses a British context set back in time, he simultaneously connects with American readers of the late nineteenth century by recalling the notorious 1842 *Somers* mutiny, which had involved his own cousin, Lieutenant Guert Gansevoort. The three hangings that resulted from this mutiny provoked a national scandal, as well as Melville's own outrage, over what were considered "arbitrary violations of the natural rights of man" (Rogin 80). In *Billy Budd*, Melville specifically compares the undue pressure put upon the officers convened to hear Billy's case to that which occurred on the *Somers* and again indicts the resolution of the *Somers* incident, which unlike that of the *Bellipotent*, "was carried out though in a time of peace and within not many days' sail of home" (1417).

In addition, Melville connects his tale with American issues and conditions in the period of its composition between 1886 and 1891. At this time, "the United States, having fulfilled its manifest destiny to conquer the continent from ocean to ocean, now contemplated a globe divided and redivided by the great European empires.... To become a world power, America would need both overseas colonies and a large peacetime navy" (Franklin, "From Empire" 200). *Billy Budd,* in part, can be read as questioning the consequences of such objectives.

NARRATIVE FORM AND POINT OF VIEW

Melville's parenthetical designation of *Billy Budd* as an "inside narrative" literally instructs readers as to the character of the text they are about to read. Presumably, readers should assume that the events to be relayed have been "set down as by one privy to the actual facts of the case, and [that] the narrative is to be valued as a true account" (Berthoff 183). To emphasize the significance of perspective in interpreting the events that take place on the *Bellipotent,* Melville appends to the main narrative the official account of the incident from "the naval chronicle of the time, an authorized weekly publication." This account, we are told, was "doubtless for the most part written in good faith, though the medium, partly rumor, through which the facts must have reached the writer served to deflect and in part falsify them" (*Billy Budd* 1432). Thus this second account can "be called an 'outside' narrative" (Hunt 274). Further complicating the issue of perspective is the poem "Billy of the Darbies" that concludes the book. Although created to memorialize Billy Budd by "one of his own watch," this ballad was apparently composed long after the incident in a somewhat "rude utterance" that then circulated orally for some time among various shipboard crews before it "finally got rudely printed at Portsmouth as a ballad" (*Billy Budd* 1434). Although inspired by the story of Billy Budd, this version further blurs the line between fact and fiction, moving the narrative into the realm of legend by converting Billy from a concrete individual into a universal figure or archetype.

Because Melville specifically draws his readers' attention to the effect of point of view in how the events in question are interpreted, scholarship on *Billy Budd* has frequently considered the role and perspective of the narrator in the main narrative. Some have characterized this third-person omniscient voice as a naval historian, who "on several occasions clearly says he is writing a history.... The vantage-point from which the narrator looks back on the earlier age—the time of his or his contemporaries' 'grandfathers'—is that of post-Civil War America, as he makes clear when he nostalgically recalls the great sailing ships of old," as well as when he notes "that the 'dandified Billy-be-Damn' of the time before steamships is 'an amusing character all but extinct now'" (Lyon Evans 327). Thus, even this "insider" view is distanced in time from the narrated events. As a result, the narrator must admit at times to a lack of knowledge about what occurred and resort to speculation to fill in some of the resulting gaps.

He admits, for instance, that he does not know what happened during Captain Vere's last meeting with Billy and so offers only his own guess as to what they discussed. The narrator also has no factual knowledge about Billy's or Claggart's early lives.

Nevertheless, the narrator assures the reader repeatedly of his credibility and good faith. Admitting that "truth uncompromisingly told will always have its ragged edges," he insists that he is not writing "pure fiction" or dealing "with fable" but rather "with fact" (*Billy Budd* 1431). Although the narrator claims he has written an "adequate narration" and provided readers with a "better understanding of such incidents," several critics have concluded that Melville's narrator is unreliable not only because of his lack of knowledge, but also because he reveals a clear bias (*Billy Budd* 1419). For one thing, he "endorses and identifies himself with aristocratic values and the heroism of 'the ampler and more knowing world of a great warship'" (Garrison 33). Differentiating between "sailors" and "landsmen," he "considers himself and, although to a lesser degree, Vere superior to both. Sailors are 'without the faculty, hardly had the inclination' to understand Vere; they are 'well-meaning men not intellectually mature, men with whom it was necessary to demonstrate certain principles that were axioms to himself'" (Garrison 32). In "his sympathy for the officers' class and his deference to established authority," the narrator's sympathies seem aligned with Captain Vere (Evans 344). In particular, those who interpret the meaning of *Billy Budd* as ironic—that is, at odds with the narrative's face value—point to the narrator's unreliability to support their position that Melville's sympathies do not align with the point of view from which the story is told.

CHARACTERS

A later-day Jack Chase, Billy Budd is introduced by the narrator as "the 'Handsome Sailor' of the less prosaic time alike of the military and merchant navies. With no perceptible trace of the vainglorious about him, rather with the offhand unaffectedness of natural regality, he seemed to accept the spontaneous homage of his shipmates" (*Billy Budd* 1353). Twenty-one years old and of unknown heritage, his physical beauty is matched by his innocent and congenial spirit. Billy's only physical defect is a speech impediment that renders him speechless or causes him to stutter at certain crucial moments when he is excited or anxious. Emotionally and mentally, he is characterized by extreme naivety. Unable to perceive malice in others, he sometimes puts too much trust in human nature and so is easily manipulated.

Older and more experienced than Billy but also of unknown background, John Claggart is in his mid-thirties. A physically imposing figure, Claggart, who entered the Navy late in life, is tall and lean with a strong chin, pale complexion, and dark hair. As master-at-arms he serves on the *Bellipotent* as a sort of chief of police, a position to which he has advanced quickly through intelligence and determination. Because his role of keeping order requires him to report misconduct to the captain, he is not well liked by the crew. They suspect his secrecy about his past hides a criminal history. Taking an unreasonable dislike to Billy Budd, Claggart becomes obsessed by a desire to destroy him that is motivated by jealousy of the younger man's innocence, beauty, and goodness. The narrator explains that Claggart possesses "the mania of an evil nature, not engendered by vicious training or corrupting books or licentious living, but born with him and innate, in short 'a depravity according to nature'" (1384). He conceals his true nature, however, behind a complacent façade.

The Honorable Edward Fairfax Vere, the commander of the *Bellipotent*, is a bachelor of about 40 years old who comes from an aristocratic seventeenth-century family. A bookish man of high intellect and conservative philosophy, he has progressed to his current rank of captain through years of dedicated and distinguished service. Although his crew respects him as a good leader, they find him overly interested in abstract ideas and somewhat aloof and pedantic. An imminently decisive and practical man who is dedicated to doing his duty and serving his king, Vere also has a reflective and dreamy side, as suggested by his nickname of "Starry Vere." In handling the crisis precipitated by Claggart's death, Vere is personally troubled by his paternal feelings for Billy and the mitigating circumstances. However, he does not let his compassion for Billy influence his professional judgment, determining that his duty to uphold military law and protect the ship from mutiny requires him no latitude. The interpretation of *Billy Budd* ultimately turns on how one views Vere's decision and actions in carrying out his responsibilities in this matter.

ROLE OF MINOR CHARACTERS

Worldly wise, the Dansker is an old sailor who serves as Billy's confidant and tries to warn him about Claggart's evil intent. Billy, however, cannot understand the old man's "pithy guarded cynicism," and what he does understand—the warning that Claggart has ill will against him— he refuses to believe (*Billy Budd* 1379). It is the Dansker who gives Billy the nickname "Baby Budd," and although "in his ascetic way" he likes the young sailor, the "salt seer" will not commit himself and so refuses opportunities to speak up and take a stand for Billy (*Billy Budd* 1378–79). At least one critic claims that "the Dansker's silence lies at the core of our pain felt in reading this work" because through his help Billy might have been able to steer a safe path (Barris 166).

The ship's chaplain is a pious man who comes to talk to Billy during the night before the execution. He is thwarted in his mission of Christian consolation, however, because he finds Billy "wholly without irrational fear" of death. Although Billy is "a barbarian" in his eyes, he senses that his innocence will serve him better than religion on Judgment Day (*Billy Budd* 1423). The narrator observes that "having been made acquainted with the young sailor's essential innocence the worthy man lifted not a finger to avert the doom of such a martyr to martial discipline. So to do would...have been an audacious transgression of the bounds of his function, one as exactly prescribed by military law as that of the boatswain or any other naval officer." Ironically, this "Prince of Peace" serves "the host of the God of War" (1425).

The ship's surgeon pronounces Claggart dead. Some days after Billy's execution, he discusses the event with the purser. The purser questions whether the fact that Billy's body did not twitch in spasms during the hanging might be a sign of the supernatural. As a man of science, however, the surgeon refuses to consider such a possibility. Unable to provide a rational explanation for the body's stillness in the gallows, he walks away from the conversation.

A sailor on the *Rights-of-Man* with Billy, Red Whiskers is the only man on the merchant vessel who initially hates Billy, a response motivated "out of envy, perhaps, of the newcomer" (*Billy Budd* 1356). After Billy strikes him for insultingly giving him "a dig under the ribs," however, this man's hatred turns to love (1357). The shipmaster on the *Rights-of-Man* relays this enigmatic occurrence to Lieutenant Ratcliffe, the boarding officer of the *Bellipotent*, prompting the lieutenant's response, "well, blessed are the peacemakers, especially the fighting peacemakers" (1357). In this way, Melville foreshadows the conflict between Billy and Claggart.

ALLEGORY AND SYMBOLISM

Early scholarship on *Billy Budd* focused on the novella as a Christian allegory. Billy in his innocence often is likened to the Christian figure of Adam before the Fall. Billy is described as "a sort of upright barbarian, much such perhaps as Adam presumably might have been ere the urbane Serpent wriggled himself into his company" (*Billy Budd* 1362). Claggart, from such a perspective, is the satanic figure who tempts Billy to do evil.

Those who favor this reading point to the description of Claggart's corpse, whose touch is "like handling a dead snake," which suggests Satan's assuming the form of a serpent in the Garden of Eden (1405). "With Billy as 'Adam' and Claggart as Satan, we are invited to read the action in terms of sacral history, engendered by the father. It is the habit of those Fathers to lose or sacrifice their children, as God the Father himself does with Christ" (Goddard 103). In fact, Melville specifically compares Vere to Abraham, who was willing to sacrifice his son Isaac at God's command. Further, in addition to his comparison to Isaac, Billy, as an innocent victim, has been interpreted as a Christ figure who suffers and sacrifices his life for the sins of humanity. Significantly, before he strikes Claggart, Billy's face registers "an expression which was a crucifixion to behold" (*Billy Budd* 1404). In particular, the description of Billy's execution suggests clear parallels to Christ on the cross. After Billy blesses his executioner, Vere, who correlates to Pontius Pilate in authorizing the sacrifice of Christ, gives the signal for the execution. As the narrator explains, "At the same moment it chanced that the vapory fleece hanging low in the East was shot through with a soft glory as of the fleece of the Lamb of God seen in mystical vision, and simultaneously therewith, watched by the wedged mass of upturned faces, Billy ascended; and, ascending, took the full rose of the dawn" (*Billy Budd* 1427).

Ultimately, however, the pervasive religious imagery and allusions do not cohere into one consistent allegorical interpretation. "Billy becomes the Adam who does not fall, the Isaac who is not saved, the Christ who does not redeem" (Rathbun 28). Although the defeat of the *Bellipotent* by the *Athée* suggests the end of Christianity, Billy's ascension at death can be read as a positive sign of salvation. Faced with this frustrating, ambiguous impasse, scholars have realized that the full meaning of the text cannot be deduced at the simplistic level of a religious allegory.

In looking beyond the complex web of religious allusions, scholars have interpreted the novel as an allegory of America. Since the events depicted take place in 1797 and Billy is 21 years old at the time, it can be discerned that he—like America—was born in 1776. "Billy's character is not in conflict simply with organized war or the military, but with the inevitable external rule of an industrialized civilization, principally represented in the novel by the king and his military force." America in its founding was a "radical experiment in democratic government based on guaranteeing the rights of man." This "New World established for itself a position of natural moral leadership.... But the America that Melville saw in the late 1880s was no longer like the innocent Handsome Sailor Billy Budd." Just as Billy was killed, "so too was this mythic ideal of moral leadership, innocence, and natural rule being destroyed, if not already destroyed, by the realities of history in the economic and industrial development of the nation and the inevitably concomitant warfare" (Evan Davis 179). Thus Melville suggests through this reading that America's naïve innocence—like Billy's—may by the reason for its downfall.

The *Bellipotent* represents modern society—whether a specifically American or more universally human society—a realm that is governed by law and in which discipline and force are required to maintain order. By contrast, the *Rights-of-Man* represents an older, more idealized or romantic form of society in which individuality still reigns. As its name suggests, the *Athée*, which defeats the *Bellipotent*, represents the godless and war-driven state to which modern society seems headed.

Recent scholarship on *Billy Budd* refuses to read the text as a clear-cut conflict between good and evil, either in religious or secular terms. Billy's history of violence and his failure to report a possible mutiny suggest he is not perfectly innocent or without human flaw. Further, his "vocal defect" is described as the "one thing amiss in him," making Billy "a striking instance that the arch interferer, the envious marplot of Eden, still has more or less to do with every human consignment to this planet of Earth. In every case, one way or another he is sure to slip in his little card, as much as to remind us—I too have a hand here" (*Billy Budd* 1362–63). With these words, Melville suggests that Billy's stutter also represents his human imperfection and susceptibility to evil. In addition, "[h]is stutter is a physical index of the conflict within himself between speech and silence, the self-enforced suppression of a language of protest. The tongue that should cry out against empressment becomes the arm that strikes the agent of injustice" (Martin, *Hero* 108).

The novella incorporates significant sexual symbolism as well. Claggart's ambiguous feelings for Billy incorporate elements of envy, hatred, love, and desire that he is unable to understand and accept. "Claggart is depraved not because of the male-directed nature of his desire, here seen as natural or innocuous, but, rather, because he feels toward his own desires only terror and loathing" (Eve Sedgwick 219). Unable to resolve his conflicting feelings, he exhibits a homosexual-homophobic paranoia in his response to Billy. "Claggart's desire for Billy is not only a desire to hurt Billy, but also a desire to *provoke* Billy, so that *he* (Claggart) can be raped by Billy. His false accusation achieves his purpose by finally provoking Billy to raise his arm." Thus, [w]hen Billy strikes Claggart, he in some ways fulfills Claggart's desire: Claggart dies instantly, at last possessed by that which he sought to possess" (Martin, *Hero* 112). For his part, "Billy's beauty makes him a homosexual icon, not a figure in a realized homosexual relationship.

His blankness is a kind of slate on which others inscribe their desires. Lacking his own identity, he becomes that which others desire. He is a sexual object, made over by the perceiver. But he is also the figure of the homosexual as victim. His death indicates Melville's failure of belief in the possibility of change" (Martin, *Hero* 108).

THEMES

As the names of the ships suggest, one of the major themes in *Billy Budd* is the individual versus society. When Billy is compelled to serve England by participating in its war against France, he loses many of his rights as an individual. In deciding that Billy must be executed for striking and killing Claggart, Vere rules against the individual, despite Billy's compelling personal circumstances and Vere's own conscience. Adhering to his duty to enforce the letter of the law, untempered by human mercy, Vere serves the State by upholding the Articles of War and sacrificing individual innocence to protect the common good. The decision that each reader must make is how to interpret Vere's decision. Is it a necessary but regrettable act that is required for humans to live together in civilization, or is it indefensible because it results in the destruction of innocence and virtue in service to a society that has lost sight of human values?

Melville's purpose is not so much to determine right or wrong but rather to articulate the dilemma that Vere faces in judging innocence and guilt, good and evil, nature and society. As the captain of the *Bellipotent* (the "power of war") rather than the *Rights-of-Man*, Vere acts in concert with his training as a military officer and defender of modern civilized society. In the end, the point is not to judge Vere, but rather to ponder whether his world, the world of the *Bellipotent*, is that much different from our own. In its focus on how law deals with the complexities of human nature in society, *Billy Budd* poses questions that have long preoccupied historians, philosophers, and other thinkers. Billy's death suggests how difficult it is for innocence to survive in the modern world. Neither law nor human nature is perfect, but the governing influence of law is increasingly necessary as society becomes more advanced. In asking whether modern society's conflict with human values is beyond resolution except as played out on board the *Bellipotent*, Melville requires each individual reader to find his or her own answer, just as Vere was forced to find his.

In *Billy Budd*, Melville also incorporates the theme of fathers and sons in ways that go beyond the allegorical reworking of the story of Abraham and Isaac. Although Vere is a bachelor, by age, position, and affection, he stands in a paternal relationship to Billy. Reading the novella without irony, that is without discerning any discrepancy between appearance and reality, several critics claim that in this fictional relationship, Melville was attempting to reconcile his own conflicted relationship with his son Malcolm, who committed suicide in 1867 at the age of 16. "Melville the 'strict parent,' who in childhood had been estranged from his father, understood the psychology of the stern disciplinarian and that of the acquiescent yet threatened son. But out of that understanding, coupled with the enormous guilt and trauma Melville must have felt about the self-destruction of his oldest son, undoubtedly came a great need for justification and reconciliation" (Hays and Rust 332). In making Billy's blow to Claggart an instinctive one that was not motivated by conscious intent, Melville exonerates Malcolm, who shot himself under unclear circumstances, for his suicide. Likewise, in their "closeted interview" after the trial, as well as in Billy's blessing of Vere at the moment of his execution, Melville absolves his own guilt for his son's death (*Billy Budd* 1423). Although the world is still at war and not even the Handsome Sailor can now be ignorant of its facts, Billy-Malcolm and Vere-Melville perhaps find some peace for themselves in acceptance. In *Billy Budd,* thus, Melville can be said to accept "the tragedy implicit in human nature." Additionally, his acceptance of life may now reach "beyond the human lot of suffering" to discover "the mysterious reserves of life which go a long way to mitigate the tragedy that is inseparable from human consciousness" (William Ellery Sedgwick 233). Both Billy and Vere die without rancor or remorse. Furthermore, in Billy's ascension, Melville once again—as he did first in *Clarel*—holds out the possibility of salvation beyond human mortality.

ALTERNATE READING: DECONSTRUCTION

Based largely on the writings of the French philosopher Jacques Derrida, deconstruction, rather than being a formal school or movement of literary criticism, is a strategy for reading, interpreting, and writing about texts. Instead of seeing a text as a "closed entity, equipped with definite meanings," deconstruction sees each text "as irreducibly plural, an endless play of signifiers which can never be finally nailed down to a single centre, essence or meaning" (Eagleton 120). Typically, a deconstructive reading focuses on binary oppositions (e.g., male/female, good/evil, up/down) within a text. In Western thinking, the first term of the opposing pair is traditionally privileged or favored over the other. In deconstructing the pair, one first inverts the terms to show that the second term also may be privileged by the text, and then dissolves the binary altogether by putting the two terms within a nonhierarchical relationship of "difference," or what Derrida calls *différance*. Deconstruction looks for such contradictions within a text to show how the text deconstructs itself. The texts we read and write are always in flux and so subject to changing meanings. As a result, no final statement about a text's "meaning can be made, for each reading is provisional, just one in a series of interpretations that decenter each other in ongoing play" (Dobie 147).

The difficulty in determining the "real" meaning of *Billy Budd*, and whether Melville's intensions are straightforward or ironic, "may reflect an inherent instability, either in Melville's text … or in the nature of the critical enterprise itself" (Sealts Jr., "Innocence" 424). The critic Barbara Johnson has made a well-known deconstructive study of the novella that begins by inverting and ultimately displacing the binary opposition of innocence and guilt that Billy and Claggart seemingly represent. "Billy is sweet, innocent, and harmless, yet he kills. Claggart is evil, perverted, and mendacious, yet he dies a victim." Melville "both invites an allegorical reading and subverts the very terms of its consistency when he writes of the murder: 'Innocence and guilt personified in Claggart and Budd in effect changed places'" (Barbara Johnson 571).

Continuing by noting that the critical debate over *Billy Budd* reiterates an opposition within the novella "between two conceptions of language, or between two types of reading," Johnson observes that Billy, is a "literal reader" who "reads everything at face value, never questioning the meaning of appearances." Thus, when Claggart appears to be nice to Billy, Billy accepts that the master-at-arms *is* being nice to him. By contrast, Claggart, who is himself "a personification of ambiguity and ambivalence" can be termed "an ironic reader" (573). Nevertheless, as a literal reader, Billy still seems capable of editing out what fails to agree with his naïve view of the world, and he is clearly capable of deception as well—as when he fails to report the mutiny he is asked to join. Likewise, Claggart does not *always* discern the difference between appearance and reality. For instance, when a corporal known as "Squeak" makes up stories about what Billy has done, Claggart "never suspected the veracity of these reports" (*Billy Budd* 1386). Thus Claggart also can be naïve when such a perspective fits his agenda and biases. As a result, the binary oppositions between innocence and guilt and between naivety and irony break down within the text. These qualities, which have both positive and negative aspects, are present in both characters, and it is left to Vere to serve as "the 'balance wheel' not only in the clash between good and evil but also in the clash between 'accepting' and 'ironic' interpretations of the story." Ironic readers charge that Vere misuses history "for his own self-preservation or for the preservation of a world safe for aristocracy"; accepting readers view his verdict as "tragic but necessary" (Barbara Johnson 588, 591). Both kinds of readers can find ample evidence within the text to support their view, suggesting the final difficulty of the act of judgment itself. Ultimately, all readers—whether inside or outside of the text—suppress whatever they are unable to reconcile with their own worldview. In this way, both *Billy Budd* and those who read it illustrate the complex and dynamic relations between reading and judging, knowing and acting.

Bibliography

Note: Parenthetical references to Melville's works in the text are to the following editions:

Battle-Pieces and Aspects of the War: Civil War Poems. Ed. Sidney Kaplan. Amherst: University of Massachusetts Press, 1972.
Clarel: A Poem and Pilgrimage in the Holy Land. 2 vols. *The Works of Herman Melville*. Reprint ed. New York: Russell and Russell, 1963.
Herman Melville. Ed. G. Thomas Tanselle (vols. 1, 2) and Harrison Hayford (vol. 3). 3 vols. New York: Library of America, 1982–1985.
  Vol. 1: *Typee, Omoo, Mardi*.
  Vol. 2: *Redburn, White-Jacket, Moby-Dick*.
  Vol. 3: *Pierre, Israel Potter, The Piazza Tales, The Confidence-Man, Uncollected Prose, Billy Budd*
The Letters of Herman Melville. Ed. Merrell R. Davis and William H. Gilman. New Haven: Yale University Press, 1960.

WORKS BY HERMAN MELVILLE

"Fragments from a Writing Desk" (1839)
Typee (1846)
Omoo (1847)
Mardi (1849)
Redburn (1849)
White-Jacket (1850)

"Hawthorne and His Mosses" (1850)
Moby-Dick (1851)
Pierre (1852)
Israel Potter (1855)
The Piazza Tales (1856)
The Confidence-Man (1857)
Battle-Pieces and Aspects of the War (1866)
Clarel (1876)
John Marr and Other Sailors (1888)
Timoleon (1891)

Posthumous Publications

The Apple-Tree Table and Other Sketches by Herman Melville (1922).
The Works of Herman Melville. 16 vols. [*Billy Budd and Other Prose Pieces* is vol. 13.] London: Constable, 1922–24. [Reprinted in 1963 by Russell and Russell.]
The Complete Works of Herman Melville. 7 vols. to date. Chicago and New York: Hendricks House, 1947–.
The Writings of Herman Melville: The Northwestern-Newberry Edition. 13 vols. to date. Evanston: Northwestern University Press, 1968–.

BIOGRAPHIES

Anderson, Charles Roberts. *Melville in the South Seas.* New York: Columbia University Press, 1939.
Arvin, Newton. *Herman Melville.* New York: William Sloane, 1950.
Delbanco, Andrew. *Melville: His World and Work.* New York: Knopf, 2005.
Freeman, John. *Herman Melville.* Macmillan, 1926.
Garner, Stanton. *The Civil War World of Herman Melville.* Lawrence: University of Kansas Press, 1993.
Gilman, William H. *Melville's Early Life and* Redburn. New York: New York University Press, 1951.
Hillway, Tyrus. *Herman Melville.* Rev. ed. Boston: Twayne, 1979.
Howard, Leon. *Herman Melville: A Biography.* Berkeley: University of California Press, 1951.
Leyda, Jay. *The Melville Log: A Documentary Life of Herman Melville, 1819–1891.* 2 vols. New York: Harcourt, Brace, 1951. Rpt. with additions. New York: Gordian, 1969.
Metcalf, Eleanor Melville. *Herman Melville: Cycle and Epicycle.* Cambridge: Harvard University Press, 1953.
Miller, Edwin Haviland. *Melville.* New York: George Braziller, 1975.
Mumford, Lewis. *Herman Melville.* New York: Harcourt, Brace, 1929.

Parker, Hershel. *Herman Melville: A Biography.* 2 vols. Baltimore: Johns Hopkins University Press, 1996, 2002.

Robertson-Lorant, Laurie. *Melville: A Biography.* Amherst: University of Massachusetts Press, 1996.

Rosenberry, Edward H. *Melville.* London: Routledge and Kegan Paul, 1979.

Sealts, Merton M., Jr. *The Early Lives of Melville: Nineteenth-Century Biographical Sketches and their Authors.* Madison: University of Wisconsin Press, 1974.

———. *Melville as Lecturer.* Cambridge: Harvard University Press, 1957.

Stone, Geoffrey. *Melville.* New York: Sheed and Ward, 1949.

Weaver, Raymond M. *Herman Melville: Mariner and Mystic.* New York: George H. Doran, 1921.

CRITICAL STUDIES OF MELVILLE'S WORK

Abrams, Robert E. "*Typee* and *Omoo*: Herman Melville and the Ungraspable Phantom of Identity." *Arizona Quarterly* 31 (1975): 33–50.

Adamson, Joseph. *Melville, Shame, and the Evil Eye: A Psychoanalytic Reading.* Albany: State University of New York Press, 1997.

Anderson, Charles Roberts. "Contemporary American Opinions of *Typee* and *Omoo*." *American Literature* 9.1 (March 1937): 1–25.

Bellis, Peter J. *No Mysteries Out of Ourselves: Identity and Textual Form in the Novels of Herman Melville.* Philadelphia: University of Pennsylvania Press, 1990.

Berthoff, Warner. *The Example of Melville.* 1962. New York: Norton, 1972.

Brodhead, Richard. *Hawthorne, Melville, and the Novel.* Chicago. University of Chicago Press, 1976.

Bryant, John. *A Companion to Melville Studies.* New York: Greenwood, 1986.

———. *Melville and Repose: The Rhetoric of Humor in the American Renaissance.* New York: Oxford University Press, 1993.

———. "The Persistence of Melville: Representative Writer for a Multicultural Age." *Melville's Evermoving Dawn: Centennial Essays.* Ed. John Bryant and Robert Milder. Kent: Kent State University Press, 1997. 3–28.

Davis, Clark. *After the Whale: Melville in the Wake of Moby-Dick.* Tuscaloosa: University of Alabama Press, 1995.

Dillingham, William B. *An Artist in the Rigging: The Early Work of Herman Melville.* Athens: University of Georgia Press, 1972.

Dimock, Wai-chee. *Empire for Liberty: Melville and the Poetics of Individualism.* Princeton: Princeton University Press, 1989.

Dolan, Marc. "The 'Wholeness' of the Whale: Melville, Matthiessen, and the Semiotics of Critical Revisionism." *American Quarterly* 48.3 (Autumn 1992): 27–58.

Dryden, Edgar. *Melville's Thematics of Form: The Great Art of Telling the Truth.* Baltimore: Johns Hopkins University Press, 1968.

Duban, James. *Melville's Major Fiction: Politics, Theology, and the Imagination.* DeKalb: Northern Illinois University Press, 1983.

Franklin, H. Bruce. *The Wake of the Gods: Melville's Mythology*. Stanford: Stanford University Press, 1963.

Fredricks, Nancy. *Melville's Art of Democracy*. Athens: University of Georgia Press, 1995.

Grejda, Edward S. *The Common Continent of Men: Racial Equality in the Writings of Herman Melville*. Port Washington: Kennikat, 1974.

Grenberg, Bruce L. *Some Other World to Find: Quest and Negation in the Works of Herman Melville*. Urbana: University of Illinois Press, 1989.

Gunn, Giles, ed. *A Historical Guide to Herman Melville*. Historical Guides to American Authors. New York: Oxford University Press, 2005.

Hayford, Harrison. *Melville's Prisoners*. Evanston: Northwestern University Press, 2003.

Higgins, Brian, and Hershel Parker, eds. *The Contemporary Reviews*. Cambridge: Cambridge University Press, 1995.

Jehlen, Myra, ed. *Herman Melville: A Collection of Critical Essays*. New Century Views. Englewood Cliffs: Prentice-Hall, 1994.

Karcher, Carolyn L. *Shadow over the Promised Land: Slavery, Race, and Violence in Melville's America*. Baton Rouge: Louisiana State University Press, 1980.

Lee, A. Robert, ed. *Herman Melville: Reassessments*. Critical Studies Series. London: Vision, 1984.

Levine, Robert S., ed. *The Cambridge Companion to Herman Melville*. Cambridge: Cambridge University Press, 1998.

Martin, Robert K. *Hero, Captain, and Stranger: Male Friendship, Social Critique, and Literary Form in the Sea Novels of Herman Melville*. Chapel Hill: University of North Carolina Press, 1987.

Mason, Ronald. *The Spirit above the Dust: A Study of Herman Melville*. 1951. 2nd ed. Mamaroneck: Appel, 1972.

McCarthy, Paul. *"The Twisted Mind": Madness in Herman Melville's Fiction*. Iowa City: University of Iowa Press, 1990.

Miller, James E., Jr. *A Reader's Guide to Herman Melville*. New York: Noonday, 1962.

Muchabac, Jane. *Melville's Humor: A Critical Study*. Hamden: Archon, 1981.

Otter, Samuel. *Melville's Anatomies*. Berkeley: University of California Press, 1999.

Post-Lauria, Sheila. *Correspondent Colorings: Melville in the Marketplace*. Amherst: University of Massachusetts Press, 1996.

Pullin, Faith, ed. *New Perspectives on Melville*. Kent: Kent State University Press, 1978.

Radloff, Bernard. *Cosmopolis and Truth: Melville's Critique of Modernity*. New York: Lang, 1996.

Renker, Elizabeth. *Strike through the Mask: Herman Melville and the Scene of Writing*. Baltimore: Johns Hopkins University Press, 1996.

Rogin, Michael Paul. *Subversive Genealogy: The Politics and Art of Herman Melville*. New York: Knopf, 1983.

Rosenberry, Edward H. *Melville and the Comic Spirit*. 1955. New York: Octagon, 1969.

Samson, John. *White Lies: Melville's Narrative of Facts*. Ithaca: Cornell University Press, 1989.

Sanborn, Geoffrey. *The Sign of the Cannibal: Melville and the Making of a Postcolonial Reader*. Durham: Duke University Press, 1998.

Schueller, Malini Johar. "Colonialism and Melville's South Seas Journeys." *Studies in American Fiction* 22.1 (Spring 1994): 3–18.

Sealts, Merton M., Jr. "'The Flower of Fame': A Centennial Tribute to Herman Melville (1819–1891)." *ESQ* 38.2 (Second Quarter 1992): 89–117.

Sedgwick, William Ellery. *Herman Melville: The Tragedy of Mind*. 1944. New York: Russell and Russell, 1962.

Seelye, John. *Melville: The Ironic Diagram*. Evanston: Northwestern University Press, 1970.

Short, Bryan C. *Cast by Means of Figures: Herman's Melville's Rhetorical Development*. Amherst: University of Massachusetts Press, 1992.

Spark, Clare L. *Hunting Captain Ahab: Psychological Warfare and the Melville Revival*. Kent: Kent State University Press, 2001.

Sten, Christopher. *The Weaver-God: Melville and the Poetics of the Novel*. Kent: Kent State University Press, 1996.

Stern, Milton R. *The Fine Hammered Steel of Herman Melville*. Urbana: University of Illinois Press, 1968.

Thompson, Lawrence. *Melville's Quarrel with God*. Princeton: Princeton University Press, 1952.

TYPEE (1846)

Contemporary Reviews

American Whig Review [New York] 3 (April 1846): 415–24.

Athenæum [London], 956 (February 21, 1846): 189–91; 957 (February 28, 1846): 218–20.

Christian Observatory [Boston] 1 (May 1847): 230–34.

[Duyckinck, Evert A.] New York *Morning News*, March 18, 1846, n. pag.; March 21, 1846, n. pag.

[Hawthorne, Nathaniel]. Salem *Advertiser*, March 25, 1846, n. pag.

Spectator [London] 19 (February 28, 1846): 209–10.

"The Story of Toby; a Sequel to *Typee*." *Athenæum* [London], 988 (October 3, 1846): 1014–15.

Washington *National Intelligencer*, May 27, 1847, n. pag.

Criticism

Herbert, T. Walter, Jr. *Marquesan Encounters: Melville and the Meaning of Civilization*. Cambridge: Harvard University Press, 1980.

Ivison, Douglas. "'I saw everything but could comprehend nothing': Melville's *Typee*, Travel Narrative, and Colonial Discourse." *American Transcendental Quarterly* 16.2 (June 2002): 115–30.

Lee, A. Robert. "'Varnishing the Facts': *Typee* and the Art of Melville's Early Fiction." *Durham University Journal* 72 (1980): 203–209.

Martin, Robert K. "'Enviable Isles': Melville's South Seas." *Modern Language Studies* 12.1 (Winter 1982): 68–76.

Rowe, John Carlos. "Melville's *Typee*: U.S. Imperialism at Home and Abroad." *National Identities and Post-American Narratives*. Ed. Donald Pease. Durham: Duke University Press, 1994. 1849 255–78.

Stern, Milton R., ed. *Critical Essays on Herman Melville's* Typee. Boston: Hall, 1982.

OMOO (1847)

Contemporary Reviews

Athenæum [London] 1015 (April 10, 1845): 382–84.

Bourne, William O. "Missionary Operations in Polynesia." *New Englander* [New Haven] 6 (January 1848): 41–58.

[Duyckinck, Evert A.] *Literary World* [New York] 14 (May 8, 1847): 319–21; 198 (November 16, 1850): 393–94.

London *Times,* September 24, 1847, n. pag.

New York *Evening Mirror,* May 21, 1847, n. pag.

P[eck], G[eorge] W[ashington]. *American Whig Review* [New York] 6 (July 1847): 36–46.

"Protestantism in the Society Islands." *United States Catholic Magazine and Monthly Review* [Baltimore] 7 (January 1848): 1–10.

MARDI (1849)

Contemporary Reviews

Athenæum [London] 1117 (March 24, 1849): 296–98.

Bentley's Miscellany [London] 25 (April 1849): 439–42.

Boston *Post,* April 18, 1849, n. pag.

[Duyckinck, Evert A.] *Literary World* [New York] 115 (April 14, 1849): 333–36; 116 (April 21, 1849): 351–53.

London *Examiner,* March 31, 1849, n. pag.

United States Magazine and Democratic Review [New York] 25 (July 1849): 44–50.

Criticism

Brodhead, Richard H. "*Mardi*: Creating the Creative." *Herman Melville: A Collection of Critical Essays*. Ed. Myra Jehlen. New Century Views. Englewood Cliffs: Prentice-Hall, 1994.

Davis, Merrell R. *Mellville's* Mardi: *A Chartless Voyage*. 1952. N.p.: Archon, 1967.

REDBURN (1849)

Contemporary Reviews

Blackwood's Edinburgh Magazine 66 (November 1849): 567–80.
Boston *Post*, November 20, 1849, n. pag.
[Duyckinck, Evert A.] *Literary World* [New York] 145 (November 10, 1849): 395–97; 146 (November 17, 1849), 418–20.
Literary Gazette [London] 1709 (October 20, 1849): 776–78.
[Ripley], R. [George]. New York *Tribune*, December 1, 1849, n. pag.
Spectator [London] 1113 (October 27, 1849): 1020–21.
[Willis, N. P.] New York *Home Journal*, November 24, 1849, n. pag.

Criticism

Hall, Jonathan L. "'Every Man of Them Almost Was a Volume of Voyages': Writing the Self in Melville's *Redburn*." *American Transcendental Quarterly* 5.4 (December 1991): 259–71.
Press, Roger C. "The Unicorn and the Eagle: The Old World and the New World in Melville's *Redburn*." *Arizona Quarterly* 41.2 (Summer 1985): 169–82.

WHITE-JACKET (1850)

Contemporary Reviews

Athenæum [London] 1162 (February 2, 1850): 123–25.
Boston *Post*, April 10, 1850, n. pag.
[Duyckinck, Evert A.] *Literary World* [New York] 163 (March 16, 1850): 271–72; 164 (March 23, 1850): 297–99.
London *Sun*, January 28, 1850, n. pag.
Southern Literary Messenger [Richmond] 16 (April 1850): 250–52.
Southern Quarterly Review [Charleston, S.C.] 1 (July 1850): 514–20.
[Willis, N. P.] "American Literature." New York *Home Journal*, April 13, 1850, n. pag.

Criticism

Albrecht, Robert C. "White Jacket's Intentional Fall." *Studies in the Novel* 40 (1972): 17–26.
McCarthy, Paul. "Symbolic Elements in *White-Jacket*." *Midwest Quarterly* 7 (1966): 309–25.
Reynolds, Larry J. "Antidemocratic Emphasis in *White-Jacket*." *American Literature* 48.1 (March 1976): 13–28.
Vincent, Howard P. *The Tailoring of Melville's* White-Jacket. Evanston: Northwestern University Press, 1970.

MOBY-DICK (1851)

Contemporary Reviews

Athenæum [London] 1252 (October 25, 1851): 1112–13.

[Butler, William A.] Washington *National Intelligencer,* November 16, 1851, n. pag.

[Duyckinck, Evert A.] *Literary World* [New York] 250 (November 14, 1851): 381–83; 251 (November 22, 1851): 403–4.

[Ripley, George]. *Harper's New Monthly Magazine* [New York] 4 (December 1851): 137.

[————]. New York *Tribune,* November 22, 1851, n. pag.

Spectator [London] 24 (October 25, 1851): 1026–27.

Criticism

Bloom, Harold, ed. *Ahab.* New York: Chelsea House, 1991.

Brodhead, Richard H., ed. *New Essays on* Moby-Dick. Cambridge: Cambridge University Press, 1986.

Chang Young-hee. "'One Seamless Whole': Ishmael's Dual Vision in *Moby-Dick.*" *English Language and Literature* 37.4 (Winter 1991): 939–53.

Cowan, Bainard. *Exiled Waters: Moby-Dick and the Crisis of Allegory.* Baton Rouge: Louisiana State University Press, 1982.

Evans, K. L. *Whale!* Minneapolis: University of Minnesota Press, 2003.

Gilmore, Michael T., ed. *Twentieth Century Interpretations of* Moby-Dick. Englewood Cliffs: Prentice-Hall, 1977.

Hartstein, Arnold M. "Myth and History in *Moby-Dick.*" *American Transcendental Quarterly* 57 (July 1985): 31–43.

Heimert, Alan. "*Moby-Dick* and American Political Symbolism." *American Quarterly* 15.4 (Winter 1963): 498–534.

Herbert, T. Walter, Jr. *Moby-Dick and Calvinism: A World Dismantled.* New Brunswick: Rutgers University Press, 1977.

Lawrence, D. H. "Herman Melville's 'Moby Dick'" *Studies in Classic American Literature.* 1923. New York: Viking, 1961. 145–61.

McSweeney, Kelly. *Moby-Dick: Ishmael's Mighty Book.* Boston: Twayne, 1986.

Olson, Charles. *Call Me Ishmael.* 1947. Baltimore: Johns Hopkins University Press, 1997.

Parker, Hershel, and Harrison Hayford, eds. *Moby-Dick as Doubloon: Essays and Extracts (1851–1970).* New York: Norton, 1970.

Peretz, Eyal. *Literature, Disaster, and the Enigma of Power: A Reading of Moby-Dick.* Stanford: Stanford University Press, 2003.

Sealts, Merton M., Jr. "Whose Book Is *Moby-Dick?*" *Melville's Evermoving Dawn: Centennial Essays.* Ed. John Bryant and Robert Milder. Kent: Kent State University Press, 1997. 58–74.

Spanos, William V., Jr. *The Errant Art of Moby-Dick: The Canon, the Cold War, and the Struggle for American Studies.* Durham: Duke University Press, 1955.

Weiner, Susan. "Melville at the Movies: New Images of *Moby-Dick.*" *Journal of American Culture* 16.2 (Summer 1993): 85–90.

Zoellner, Robert. *The Salt-Sea Mastodon: A Reading of* Moby-Dick. Berkeley: University of California Press, 1973.

PIERRE (1852)

Contemporary Reviews

Athenæum [London] 1308 (November 20, 1852): 1265–66.

[Duyckinck, Evert A.] *Literary World* [New York] 290 (August 21, 1852): 118–20.

[Hazewell, Charles Creighton]. Boston *Daily Times*, August 5, 1852, n. pag.

[Peck, George Washington]. *American Whig Review* [New York] 16 (November 1852): 446–54.

Southern Literary Messenger [Richmond] 18 (September 1852): 574–75.

Criticism

Canaday, Nicholas. "Pierre in the Domestic Circle." *Studies in the Novel* 18.4 (Winter 1986): 395–402.

Creech, James. *Closet Writing/Gay Reading: The Case of Melville's* Pierre. Chicago: University of Chicago Press, 1993.

Gray, Richard. "'All's o'er, and ye know him not': A Reading of *Pierre.*" *Herman Melville: Reassessments.* Ed. A. Robert Lee. Critical Studies Series. London: Vision, 1984. 116–34.

Higgins, Brian, and Hershel Parker, eds. *Critical Essays on Herman Melville's* Pierre; or, The Ambiguities. Boston: Hall, 1983.

Kelley, Wyn. "*Pierre's* Domestic Ambiguities." *The Cambridge Companion to Herman Melville.* Ed. Robert S. Levine. Cambridge: Cambridge University Press, 1998. 91–113.

Lackey, Kris. "The Despotic Victim: Gender and Imagination in *Pierre.*" *American Transcendental Quarterly* 4.1 (March 1990): 67–76.

Moorman, Charles. "Melville's *Pierre* and the Fortunate Fall." *American Literature* 25.1 (March 1953): 13–30.

Silverman, Gillian. "Textual Sentimentalism: Incest and Authorship in Melville's *Pierre.*" *American Literature* 74.1 (June 2002): 345–72.

Strickland, Carol Colclough. "Coherence and Ambivalence in Melville's *Pierre.*" *American Literature* 48.3 (November 1976): 302–11.

CONTEMPORARY REVIEWS OF *THE PIAZZA TALES* (1856)

Godey's Lady's Book [Philadelphia] 53 (September 1856): 277.
New York *Atlas,* May 25, 1856, n. pag.
[Powell, Thomas]. New York *News,* May 26, 1856, n. pag.
[Smith, J.E.A.] Pittsfield [MA] *Berkshire County Eagle,* May 30, 1856, n. pag.;
    August 8, 1856, n. pag.
Southern Literary Messenger [Richmond] 22 (June 1856): 480.
United States Magazine and Democratic Review [New York] 38 (September 1856):
    172.

CRITICISM OF MELVILLE'S SHORT FICTION

Bickley, R. Bruce, Jr. *The Method of Melville's Short Fiction.* Durham: Duke
    University Press, 1975.
Dillingham, William B. *Melville's Short Fiction, 1853–1856.* Athens: University
    of Georgia Press, 1977.
Fisher, Marvin. *Going Under: Melville's Short Fiction and the American 1850's.*
    Baton Rouge: Louisiana State University Press, 1977.
Fogle, Richard Harter. *Melville's Shorter Tales.* Norman: University of Oklahoma
    Press, 1960.
Johnson, Claudia Durst. *Understanding Melville's Short Fiction.* Westport:
    Greenwood, 2005.
Leavis, Q. D. "Melville: The 1853–6 Phase." *New Perspectives on Melville.* Ed.
    Faith Pullin. Kent: Kent State University Press, 1978. 197–228.
Leyda, Jay. Introduction. *The Complete Stories of Herman Melville.* By Herman
    Melville. New York: Random House, 1949. ix–xxxvi.
Newman, Lea Bertani Vozar. *A Reader's Guide to the Short Stories of Herman
    Melville.* Boston: Hall, 1986.
Rodgers, James. "Melville's Short Fiction: Many Voices, Many Modes." *Contemporary Approaches to Narrative.* Tübingen: Gunter Narr, 1984. 39–50.
Sealts, Merton M. "The Publication of Melville's *Piazza Tales.*" *Modern Language
    Notes* 59.1 (January 1944): 56–59.

"The Piazza" (1856)

Avallone, C. Sherman. "Melville's 'Piazza.'" *ESQ* 22 (Fourth Quarter 1976):
    221–33.
Clark, Michael. "Authorial Displacement in Herman Melville's 'The Piazza.'"
    CLA Journal 27.1 (September 1883): 69–80.
DeNuccio, Jerome D. "Melville's 'The Piazza' and the Myth of Male
    Transcendence." *Nebraska English Journal* 38.1 (Fall 1992): 57–70.
Roundy, Nancy. "Fancies, Reflections and Things: The Imagination as Perception
    in 'The Piazza.'" *CLA Journal* 20 (1977): 539–44.
Slouka, Mark Z. "Herman Melville's Journey to 'The Piazza.'" *American
    Transcendental Quarterly* 61 (October 1986): 3–14.

"Bartleby, the Scrivener" (1853)

Garland-Thomson, Rosemarie. "The Cultural Logic of Euthanasia: 'Sad Fancyings' in Herman Melville's 'Bartleby.'" *American Literature* 76.4 (December 2004): 777–806.
Guillen, Matthew. "Melville's Wall Street: It Speaks for Itself." *Journal of the Short Story in English* 36 (Spring 2001): 9–24.
Pribek, Thomas. "An Assumption of Naïveté: The Tone of Melville's Lawyer." *Arizona Quarterly* 41.2 (Summer 1985): 131–42.
Sandberg, T. A. "Toward 'Bartleby, the Scrivener': Negotiating the Maze." *Short Story* 6.1 (Spring 1998): 65–84.
Weinstock, Jeffrey Andrew. "Doing Justice to Bartleby." *American Transcendental Quarterly* 17.1 (March 2003): 23–42.

"Benito Cereno" (1855)

Andrews, David. "'Benito Cereno': No Charity on Earth, Not Even at Sea." *Leviathan: A Journal of Melville Studies* 2.1 (March 2000): 83–103.
Feltenstein, Rosalie. "Melville's 'Benito Cereno.'" *American Literature* 19.3 (November 1947): 245–55.
Nicol, Charles. "The Iconography of Evil and Ideal in 'Benito Cereno.'" *American Transcendental Quarterly* 7 (1970): 25–31.
Vanderhaar, Margaret M. "A Re-Examination of 'Benito Cereno.'" *American Literature* 40.2 (May 1968): 179–91.
Zagarell, Sandra A. "Reenvisioning America: Melville's 'Benito Cereno.'" *ESQ* 30.4 (Fourth Quarter 1984): 245–59.

"The Lightning-Rod Man" (1854)

Baldwin, Marc D. "Herman Melville's 'The Lightning-Rod Man': Discourse of the Deal." *Journal of the Short Story in English* 21 (Autumn 1993): 9–18.
Shusterman, Alan. "Melville's 'The Lightning-Rod Man': A Reading." *Studies in Short Fiction* 9 (1972): 165–74.
Verdier, Douglas L. "Who Is the Lightning-Rod Man?" *Studies in Short Fiction* 18 (1981): 273–79.
Werge, Thomas. "Melville's Satanic Salesman: Scientism and Puritanism in 'The Lightning-Rod Man.'" *Christianity and Literature* 21.4 (1972): 6–12.

"The Encantadas, or Enchanted Isles" (1854)

Beecher, Jonathan. "Variations on a Dystopian Theme: Melville's 'Encantadas.'" *Utopian Studies* 11.2 (2000): 88–95.
Canaday, Nicholas, Jr. "Melville's 'The Encantadas': The Deceptive Enchantment of the Absolute." *Papers on Language and Literature* 10 (1974): 58–69.

Howington, Don S. "Melville's 'The Encantadas': Imagery and Meaning." *Studies in the Literary Imagination* 2.1 (1969): 69–75.

Newbery, Ise. "'The Encantadas': Melville's Inferno." *American Literature* 38.1 (March 1966): 49–68.

Sappenfield, James A. "Beyond the Novel: The Structure of Melville's 'The Encantadas.'" *Lineages of the Novel*. Ed. Bernard Reitz and Eckart Voigts-Virchow. Trier, Germany: Wissenschaftlicher, 2000. 121–31.

"The Bell-Tower" (1855)

Costello, Jacqueline A., and Robert J. Kloss. "The Psychological Depths of Melville's 'The Bell-Tower.'" *ESQ* 19.4 (Fourth Quarter 1973): 254–61.

Fenton, Charles A. "'The Bell-Tower': Melville and Technology." *American Literature* 23.2 (May 1951): 219–32.

Hattenhauer, Darryl. "The Scarlet Cipher: Banadonna's Tower as Number One." *CEA Critic* 53.2 (Winter 1991): 46–53.

Vernon, John. "Melville's 'The Bell-Tower.'" *Studies in Short Fiction* 7 (1970): 264–76.

"I and My Chimney" (1856)

McCullagh, James C. "More Smoke from Melville's Chimney." *American Transcendental Quarterly* 17 (1973): 17–22.

Pearce, Sandra Manoogian. "Secret Closets and Ashes: Melville's 'I and My Chimney.'" *Creative and Critical Approaches to the Short Story*. Ed. Noel Harold Kaylor Jr. Lewiston: Mellen, 1997. 81–95.

Sealts, Merton. "Herman Melville's 'I and My Chimney.'" *American Literature* 13.2 (May 1941): 142–54.

Sowder, William J. "Melville's 'I and My Chimney': A Southern Exposure." *The Mississippi Quarterly* 16 (1963): 128–45.

Woodruff, Stuart C. "Melville and His Chimney." *Publications of the Modern Language Association* 75.3 (June 1960): 283–92.

"The Paradise of Bachelors and the Tartarus of Maids" (1855)

Browne, Ray B. "The Views of Commitment: 'The Paradise of Bachelors' and 'The Tartarus of Maids.'" *American Transcendental Quarterly* 7 (1970): 43–47.

Fisher, Marvin. "Melville's 'Tartarus': The Deflowering of New England." *American Quarterly* 23.1 (Spring 1971): 79–100.

Rowland, Beryl. "Melville's Bachelors and Maids: Interpretation through Symbol and Metaphor." *American Literature* 41.3 (November 1969): 389–405.

Weyler, Karen A. "Melville's 'The Paradise of Bachelors and the Tartarus of Maids': A Dialogue about Experience, Understanding, and Truth." *Studies in Short Fiction* 31.3 (Summer 1994): 461–69.
Wiegman, Robyn. "Melville's Geography of Gender." *American Literary History* 1.4 (Winter 1989): 735–53.

ISRAEL POTTER (1855)

Contemporary Reviews

Albion [New York] 14 (March 17, 1855): 129.
Athenæum [London] 1440 (June 2, 1855): 643.
Boston *Post*, March 15, 1855, n. pag.
Christian Examiner and Religious Miscellany [Boston] 58 (May 1855): 470–71.
Leader [London] 6 (May 5, 1855): 486.
Norton's Literary Gazette and Publishers' Circular [New York] 2 (March 15, 1855): 121.

Criticism

Bach, Bert C. "Melville's *Israel Potter*: A Revelation of its Reputation and Meaning." *Cithara* 7.1 (1967): 39–50.
Browne, Ray B. "Israel Potter: Metamorphosis of Superman." *Frontiers of American Culture*. Conference on American Culture, 1967. West Lafayette: Purdue University, 1968. 88–98.
Bruss, Elizabeth W. "The Game of Literature and Some Literary Games." *New Literary History* 9.1 (Fall 1977): 153–72.
Carlson, Thomas C. "The Twin Parables of Melville's *Israel Potter*." *American Transcendental Quarterly* 41 (1979): 85–92.
Jackson, Kenny. "*Israel Potter*: Melville's 'Fourth of July Story.'" *College Language Association Journal* 6 (1963): 194–204.
Keyssar, Alexander. *Melville's Israel Potter: Reflections on the American Dream.* Cambridge: Harvard University Press, 1969.
Obuchowski, Peter A. "Technique and Meaning in Melville's *Israel Potter*." *CLA Journal* 31.4 (June 1988): 455–71.
Rampersad, Arnold. *Melville's Israel Potter: A Pilgrimage and Progress.* Bowling Green: Bowling Green University Popular Press, 1969.
Reagan, Daniel. "Melville's *Israel Potter* and the Nature of Biography." *American Transcendental Quarterly* 3.3 (September 1989): 257–76.

THE CONFIDENCE-MAN (1857)

Contemporary Reviews

Athenæum [London] 1537 (April 11, 1857): 356.
Illustrated Times [London], 4 (April 25, 1857): 266.

Literary Gazette [London] 2099 (April 11, 1857): 348–49.
New York *Dispatch*, April 5, 1857, n. pag.
New York *Times*, April 11, 1857, n. pag.
Saturday Review [London] 3 (May 23, 1857): 484.

Criticism

Bergmann, Johannes Dietrich. "The Original Confidence Man." *American Quarterly* 21.3 (Autumn 1969): 560–77.

Brodtkorb, Paul, Jr. "*The Confidence-Man:* The Con-Man as Hero." *Studies in the Novel* 1.4 (1969): 421–35.

Buell, Lawrence. "The Last Word on 'The Confidence-Man'?" *Illinois Quarterly* 35.1 (1972): 15–29.

Chase, Richard. "Melville's Confidence Man." *Kenyon Review* 11 (Winter 1949): 122–40.

Cook, Jonathan A. *Satirical Apocalypse: An Anatomy of Melville's* The Confidence-Man. Contributions to the Study of World Literature. Westport: Greenwood, 1996.

Drew, Philip. "Appearance and Reality in Melville's *The Confidence-Man.*" *ELH* 31.4 (December 1964): 418–42.

Dubler, Walter. "Theme and Structure in Melville's *The Confidence-Man.*" *American Literature* 33.3 (November 1961): 307–19.

Gaudino, Rebecca J. Kruger. "The Riddle of *The Confidence-Man.*" *Journal of Narrative Technique* 14.2 (Spring 1984): 124–41.

Hayford, Harrison. "Poe in *The Confidence-Man.*" *Nineteenth-Century Fiction* 14 (December 1959): 207–18.

Kern, Alexander C. "Melville's *The Confidence-Man:* A Structure of Satire." *American Humor.* Ed. O. M. Brack. Scottsdale: Arete, 1977. 27–41.

Lamb, Robert Paul. "The Place of *The Confidence Man* in Melville's Career." *Southern Review* 22.3 (Summer 1986): 489–505.

Matterson, Stephen. "Indian-Hater, Wild Man: Melville's *Confidence-Man.*" *Arizona Quarterly* 52.2 (Summer 1996): 21–35.

Oliver, Egbert S. "Melville's Goneril and Fanny Kemble." *New England Quarterly* 18 (December 1945): 489–500.

———. "Melville's Picture of Emerson and Thoreau in *The Confidence-Man.*" *College English* 8 (November 1946): 61–72.

Parker, Hershel. "The Metaphysics of Indian-hating." *Nineteenth-Century Fiction* 18.2 (September 1963): 165–73.

Roundy, Nancy. "Melville's *The Confidence-Man:* Epistemology and Art." *Ball State University Forum* 21.2 (1980): 3–11.

Sussman, Henry. "The Deconstructor as Politician: Melville's *Confidence-Man.*" *Glyph* 4 (1978): 32–56.

CRITICISM OF MELVILLE'S POETRY

Barrett, Laurence. "The Differences in Melville's Poetry." *Publications of the Modern Language Association* 70.4 (September 1955): 606–23.

Buell, Lawrence. "Melville the Poet." *The Cambridge Companion to Herman Melville*. Ed. Robert S. Levine. Cambridge: Cambridge University Press, 1998. 135–56.

Dryden, Edgar. *Monumental Melville: The Formation of a Literary Career*. Stanford: Stanford University Press, 2004.

Hook, Andrew. "Melville's Poetry." *Herman Melville: Reassessments*. Ed. A. Robert Lee. Critical Studies Series. London: Vision, 1984. 176–98.

Lee, A. Robert. "'Eminently Adapted for Unpopularity'?: Melville's Poetry." *Nineteenth Century American Poetry*. Ed. A. Robert Lee. London: Vision, 1985: 118–45.

Shurr, William H. *The Mystery of Iniquity: Melville as Poet, 1857–1891*. Lexington: University Press of Kentucky, 1972.

Spengemann, William C. "Melville the Poet." *American Literary History* 11.4 (Winter 1999): 569–609.

Stein, William Bysshe. *The Poetry of Melville's Later Years: Time, History, Myth, and Religion*. Albany: State University of New York Press, 1970.

Warren, Robert Penn. "Melville the Poet." *Kenyon Review* 8 (Spring 1946): 208–23. Rpt. in *Melville: A Collection of Critical Essays*. Ed. Richard Chase. Twentieth Century Views. Englewood Cliffs: Prentice-Hall, 1962. 144–55.

BATTLE-PIECES AND ASPECTS OF THE WAR (1866)

Contemporary Reviews

Albion [New York] 44 (September 15, 1866): 441.

[Howells, William Dean.] *Atlantic Monthly* [Boston] 19 (February 1867): 252–53.

"More Poetry of the War." *Nation* [New York] 3 (September 6, 1866): 187–88.

National Quarterly Review [New York] 26 (September 1866): 390–93.

New York *Independent*, January 10, 1867, n. pag.

New York *Times*, August 27, 1866, n. pag.

Round Table [New York] 4 (September 15, 1866): 108–9.

Criticism

Cox, Richard H. "A Careful Disorderliness: The Organization of *Battle-Pieces*." *Battle-Pieces and Aspects of the War: Civil War Poems* by Herman Melville. Amherst: Prometheus, 2001. 295–323.

Dowling, Paul M. "Robert E. Lee and Melville's Politics in *Battle-Pieces and Aspects of the War*." *Melville Society Extracts* 128 (February 2005): 1–2, 18–23.

Hand, Harry E. "'And War Be Done': *Battle-Pieces* and Other Civil War Poetry of Herman Melville." *Journal of Human Relations* 11.3 (Spring 1963): 326–40.

Jalal, Mustafa. "*Battle-Pieces and Aspects of the War:* The Novelist as Poet: A Study in the Dramatic Poetry of Herman Melville." *American Studies International* 39.2 (June 2001): 71–85.

Kimbell, William J. "The Melville of *Battle-Pieces:* A Kindred Spirit." *Midwest Quarterly* 10 (1969): 307–16.

Milder, Robert. "The Reader of/in Melville's *Battle-Pieces.*" *Melville Society Extracts* 72 (February 1988): 12–15.

Sweet, Timothy. "Melville's *Battle-Pieces* as a Trace of War." *Traces of War: Poetry, Photography, and the Crisis of the Union.* Baltimore: Johns Hopkins University Press, 1990. 165–200.

Vendler, Helen. "Melville and the Lyric of History." *Southern Review* 35.3 (Summer 1999): 579–94.

Warren, Rosanna. "Dark Knowledge: Melville's Poems of the Civil War." *Raritan* 19.1 (Summer 1999): 100–21.

Williams, Megan. "'Sounding the Wilderness': Representations of the Heroic in Herman Melville's *Battle-Pieces and Aspects of the War.*" *Texas Studies in Literature and Language* 45.2 (Summer 2003): 141–72.

CLAREL (1876)

Contemporary Reviews

International Review [New York] 4 (January 1877): 107–8.
Lippincott's Magazine [Philadelphia] 18 (September 1876): 391–92.
New York *Times*, July 10, 1876, n. pag.
New York *Tribune*, June 16, 1876. n. pag.
New York *World*, June 26, 1876, n. pag.

Criticism

Goldman, Stan. *Melville's Protest Theism: The Hidden and Silent God in* Clarel. DeKalb: Northern Illinois University Press, 1993.

Kenny, Vincent. *Herman Melville's* Clarel: *A Spiritual Autobiography.* Hamden: Archon, 1973.

Porat, Zephyra. "Towards the Promethean Ledge: Varieties of Sceptic Experience in Melville's *Clarel.*" *Literature and Theology* 8.1 (March 1994): 30–46.

Potter, William. *Melville's* Clarel *and the Intersympathy of Creeds.* Kent: Kent State University Press, 2004.

Short, Bryan. "Form as Vision in Herman Melville's *Clarel.*" *American Literature* 50.4 (January 1979): 553–69.

BILLY BUDD (1924)

Contemporary Review

[Murry, John Middleton.] "Herman Melville's Silence." London *Times Literary Supplement*, July 10, 1924. n. pag.

Criticism

Barris, Sharon. "Melville's Dansker: The Absent Daniel in *Billy Budd*. *The Uses of Adversity: Failure and Accommodation in Reader Response*. Ed. Ellen Spolsky. Lewisburg: Buckness University Press, 1990. 153–73.

Davis, R. Evan. "An Allegory of America in Melville's *Billy Budd*." *Journal of Narrative Technique* 14.3 (Fall 1984): 172–81.

Evans, Lyon, Jr. "'Too Good to Be True': Subverting Christian Hope in *Billy Budd*." *New England Quarterly* 55.3 (September 1982): 323–53.

Franklin, H. Bruce. "From Empire to Empire: *Billy Budd, Sailor*." *Herman Melville: Reassessments*. Ed. A. Robert Lee. Critical Studies Series. London: Vision, 1984. 199–216.

Garrison, Joseph M. "*Billy Budd*: A Reconsideration." *Ball State University Forum* 27.1 (Winter 1986): 30–41.

Goddard, Kevin. "Hanging Utopia: *Billy Budd* and the Death of Sacred History." *Arizona Quarterly* 61.4 (Winter 2005): 101–26.

Hays, Peter L., and Richard Dilworth Rust. "'Something Healing': Fathers and Sons in *Billy Budd*." *Nineteenth-Century Fiction* 34.3 (December 1979): 326–36.

Hunt, Lester H. "*Billy Budd*: Melville's Dilemma." *Philosophy and Literature* 26.2 (October 2002): 273–95.

Johnson, Barbara. "Melville's Fist: The Execution of Billy Budd." *Studies in Romanticism* 18.4 (Winter 1979): 567–99.

Milder, Robert, ed. *Critical Essays on Melville's* Billy Budd, Sailor. Boston: Hall, 1989.

Rathbun, John W. "*Billy Budd* and the Limits of Perception." *Nineteenth-Century Fiction* 20.1 (June 1965): 19–34.

Sealts, Merton M., Jr. "Innocence and Infamy: *Billy Budd, Sailor*." *A Companion to Melville Studies*. Ed. John Bryant. New York: Greenwood, 1986. 407–30.

Sedgwick, Eve Kosofsky. "*Billy Budd*: After the Homosexual." *Epistemology of the Closet*. Berkeley: University of California Press, 1990. 91–130. Rpt. in *Herman Melville: A Collection of Critical Essays*. Ed. Myra Jehlen. New Century Views. Englewood Cliffs: Prentice-Hall, 1994. 217–34.

Vincent, Howard P., ed. *Twentieth Century Interpretations of Billy Budd*. Englewood Cliffs: Prentice-Hall, 1971.

Yanella, Donald, ed. *New Essays on* Billy Budd. Cambridge: Cambridge University Press, 2002.

RELATED PRIMARY SOURCES

Emerson, Ralph Waldo. "The Transcendentalist." 1842. *The Collected Works of Ralph Waldo Emerson*. Ed. Alfred R. Ferguson et al. Vol. 1. Cambridge: Harvard University Press, 1971. 201–16.

Hawthorne, Nathaniel. *The English Notebooks*. Ed. Randall Stewart. New York: Russell and Russell, 1962.

RELATED SECONDARY SOURCES

Baym, Nina. "Melodramas of Beset Manhood: How Theories of American Fiction Exclude Women Authors." *American Quarterly* 33.2 (Summer 1981): 123–39.

———. *Novels, Readers, and Reviewers: Responses to Fiction in Antebellum America*. Ithaca: Cornell University Press, 1984.

Dobie, Ann B. *Theory into Practice: An Introduction to Literary Criticism*. Boston: Thomson-Heinle, 2002.

Eagleton, Terry. *Literary Theory: An Introduction*. 2nd ed. Minneapolis: University of Minnesota Press, 1996.

Jarrell, Randall. *Poetry and the Age*. New York: Knopf, 1955.

Matthiessen, F. O. *American Renaissance: Art and Expression in the Age of Emerson and Whitman*. New York: Oxford University Press, 1941.

Mitchell, Thomas R. "In the Whale's Wake: Melville and *The Blithedale Romance*." *ESQ* 46.1–2 (2000): 51–73.

Moore-Gilbert, Bart, Gareth Stanton, and Willy Maley, eds. *Postcolonial Criticism*. London: Longman, 1997.

WEBSITES ON MELVILLE

Berkshire County Historical Society. *Herman Melville's Arrowhead* http://www.mobydick.org/index.html.

The Melville Society http://people.hofstra.edu/faculty/John_L_Bryant/Melville/.

Olsen-Smith, Steven, ed. *Melville's Marginalia Online*. Boise State University http://www.boisestate.edu/melville/.

Index

Battle-Pieces, 9, 20, 22, 136–37, 151;
 characters, 139–41; plot and structure,
 137–39; relationship to other works
 by Melville, 145, 149; setting, 137–39;
 symbolism, 141–43; themes, 144–45.
 *See also titles of individual poems and
 sections in this collection.*
"Bell-Tower, The," 8, 81, 104; allegory, 102–3; characters, 102; plot,
 101–2; relationship to other works by
 Melville, 101; setting, 101; symbolism,
 102–3; themes, 103–4
Bembo (*Omoo*), 31–32
"Benito Cereno," 8, 81, 90, 104; characters,
 91–92; historical context, 94; plot,
 90–91; point of view, 90; relationship
 to other works by Melville, 105;
 setting, 90–91; symbolism, 92–93;
 themes, 94
Bentley, Richard (British publisher), 65
Bergmann, Johannes Dietrich, 121
Berthoff, Warner, 19
Bickley, Bruce, 104
Bildungsroman, 38
Billy Budd, Sailor, 10, 12, 14, 22, 135,
 153–54; allegory, 160–63; characters,
 158–60; deconstructionist reading,
 164–66; historical context, 155–57;
 narrative form, 157; plot, 154–55;
 point of view, 157–58; relationship
 to other works by Melville, 46, 149;
 setting, 154; symbolism, 160–63;
 themes, 163–64
"Billy in the Darbies" (*Billy Budd*), 153,
 155, 157
"Birth-mark, The" (Hawthorne), 101
Black Guinea (*The Confidence-Man*), 127,
 128–29, 130, 131
Bland (*White-Jacket*), 43, 46
Blithedale Romance, The (Hawthorne), 21
Boccaccio, 113
Bolton, Harry (*Redburn*), 39, 40, 41
Bridge, The (Crane), 22
Brown, John (*Battle-Pieces*), 138, 139, 141,
 142, 143
Bryant, John, 104
Budd, Billy (*Billy Budd*), 16, 154–55, 156,
 157–64, 165

Buell, Lawrence, 76
Bulkington (*Moby-Dick*), 55

Calvinism, 2, 17, 55, 60–61, 96–97
Camus, Albert, 22
Carlisle, Thomas, 76
"Carry Me Back to Old Virginny," 113
Cat's Cradle (Vonnegut Jr.), 22
Celio (*Clarel*), 148
Cereno, Captain Benito ("Benito
 Cereno"), 91–93, 94
Cervantes, 84
Cicero ("Bartleby"), 88
Characterization, 16–17; in "Bartleby,
 the Scrivener," 86–87; in *Battle-Pieces*,
 139–41; in "The Bell-Tower," 102;
 in "Benito Cereno," 91–92; in *Billy
 Budd*, 158–60; in *Clarel*, 147–48; in
 Confidence-Man, 126–27; in "The
 Encantadas," 98–99; in "I and My
 Chimney," 106–7; in *Israel Potter*,
 115–16; in "The Lightning-Rod Man,"
 95–96; in *Mardi*, 35–36; in
 Moby-Dick, 53–57; in *Omoo*,
 31–32; in "The Paradise of Bachelors
 and the Tartarus of Maids," 110–11; in
 "The Piazza," 83; in *Pierre*, 68–71; in
 Redburn, 40; in *Typee*, 27; in
 White-Jacket, 44
Charlemont (*The Confidence-Man*),
 125, 126
Chase, Jack (*White-Jacket*), 43, 44, 46,
 156, 158
Chase, John, 4
Chase, Richard, 122
"Chattanooga" (*Battle-Pieces*), 140
"Chronometricals and Horologicals"
 (*Pierre*), 73–74
Claggart, John (*Billy Budd*), 16, 154, 155,
 158, 159, 160–61, 162, 163, 164, 165
Clarel, 9, 17, 20, 21, 136, 145–46, 153;
 characters, 147–48; plot and structure,
 146–47; relationship to other works
 by Melville, 164; setting, 146–47;
 symbolism and themes, 148–49
Clarel (*Clarel*), 146–49
Claret, Captain (*White-Jacket*), 43, 44
Colbrook, Corporal (*White-Jacket*), 44

About the Author

SHARON TALLEY is an Associate Professor of English at Texas A&M University–Corpus Christi, where she teaches Early American Literature and Cultures. Special research interests include Death and Dying in American Literature, and the American Renaissance.